Purrieties of Language

How We Talk About Cats Online

Edith Podhovnik
Independent Scholar, Graz, Austria

CAMBRIDGE
UNIVERSITY PRESS

CAMBRIDGE
UNIVERSITY PRESS

Shaftesbury Road, Cambridge CB2 8EA, United Kingdom

One Liberty Plaza, 20th Floor, New York, NY 10006, USA

477 Williamstown Road, Port Melbourne, VIC 3207, Australia

314–321, 3rd Floor, Plot 3, Splendor Forum, Jasola District Centre,
New Delhi – 110025, India

103 Penang Road, #05-06/07, Visioncrest Commercial, Singapore 238467

Cambridge University Press is part of Cambridge University Press & Assessment,
a department of the University of Cambridge.

We share the University's mission to contribute to society through the pursuit of
education, learning and research at the highest international levels of excellence.

www.cambridge.org
Information on this title: www.cambridge.org/9781108843492

DOI: 10.1017/9781108918909

First published 2023

Printed in the United Kingdom by TJ Books Ltd, Padstow Cornwall

A catalogue record for this publication is available from the British Library.

Library of Congress Cataloging-in-Publication Data
Names: Podhovnik, Edith, author.
Title: Purrieties of language : how we talk about cats online / Edith Podhovnik.
Description: Cambridge ; New York, NY : Cambridge University Press, 2023. |
    Includes bibliographical references and index.
Identifiers: LCCN 2022048414 (print) | LCCN 2022048415 (ebook) |
    ISBN 9781108843492 (hardback) | ISBN 9781108825634 (paperback) |
    ISBN 9781108918909 (epub)
Subjects: LCSH: Language and the Internet. | Internet users–Language. |
    Online social networks. | Human-animal relationships. | Discourse analysis.
Classification: LCC P120.I6 P63 2023 (print) | LCC P120.I6 (ebook) |
    DDC 636.8001/4–dc23/eng/20221110
LC record available at https://lccn.loc.gov/2022048414
LC ebook record available at https://lccn.loc.gov/2022048415

ISBN 978-1-108-84349-2 Hardback
ISBN 978-1-108-82563-4 Paperback

Purrieties of Language

After conquering the Internet, cats are now taking on linguistics! Since the advent of social media, cats have become a topic central to online communication, and the multitude of cat-related accounts now online has made this a worldwide phenomenon. Through cat-inspired varieties of language we have developed a genre of cat-inspired vocabulary. And on our special social media accounts for our cats we take on their identities as we post, write, talk, and chat – as our feline friends. This innovative book provides linguistic analyses of the cyber "Cativerse," exploring online language variation and explaining key linguistic concepts – all through the lens of cat-related communication. Each chapter explores a different sociolinguistic phenomenon, drawing on fun and engaging examples including memes, hashtags, captions, and "LOLcats" from platforms such as Instagram, Facebook, YouTube, and Twitter. Innovative yet accessible, it is catnip for all 'hoomans' interested in how language is used online.

EDITH PODHOVNIK specializes in regional and online language variation and teaches in a media studies–related degree program in Austria. Proficient in several languages, she has taught in Austria, the UK, the US, and Russia, and is a member of·ISLE and BAAL. She currently has two cats.

Contents

List of Illustrations   *page* vii

List of Tables   x

Acknowledgments   xii

1   The Cativerse   1
   1.1   Cats and Their Roles in This Book   2
   1.2   Cats and Their Digital Spaces   4
   1.3   Cats and Their Roles   11
   1.4   Cats and Their Effect   16

2   The Feline Territory of Language   24
   2.1   Cats and Regions   25
   2.2   Cats and Dictionaries   37
   2.3   Cats and Online Dialectology   45
   2.4   Cats and Phonetics   48

3   Meowlogisms   61
   3.1   Meow in Meowphology   62
   3.2   Meow in Public Spaces   78

4   Da Kittehz   86
   4.1   Kittehz and Semeowtics   87
   4.2   Kittehz Can Haz LOLspeak   92
   4.3   Kittehz and Their Idiolects   101

5   Virtual Furever Homes   107
   5.1   Cats and Pawticipatory Culture   108
   5.2   Cats and Digital Ranges   114
   5.3   Cats and Online Narratives   126
   5.4   Cats and Their Stories   131

6   Multimeowdality   138
   6.1   Caterwauling in Multimeowdal Manner   139
   6.2   Caterwauling with Graphicons   146
   6.3   Caterwauling and CMC   164
   6.4   Caterwauling and Its Emoji   167

7   Meow and More   173
   7.1   The Meow Code   175
   7.2   The Meow World   187
   7.3   The Meow Identity   194

8   Going on Pawtrol   199
   8.1   Pawtrol: Checking Cat-Related Digital Spaces   200
   8.2   Pawtrol: Prepurring for Linguistic Research   210
   8.3   Pawtrol: Getting Purrmission   216

9   Linguistic Scratching Posts   221
   9.1   Scratches in the Right Places   222
   9.2   Scratches in the Cattolog ov Pussonyms   224
   9.3   Scratches in the Cat-Related Cat-egories   238
   9.4   Scratches in Numbers   247

10   #StatsWithCats   253
   10.1   #Meow and Places   254
   10.2   #Meow and Purrestige   263
   10.3   #Meow and Social Network Analysis   270

11   Cattitude and Purrception   281
   11.1   Cats and Data from the Surveys   282
   11.2   Cats and Identity   285
   11.3   Cats and Cattitude   288
   11.4   Cats and Purrception   293
   11.5   Cats and Incidental Material   300
   11.6   Cats and Their Final Words   302

Appendix   Meowscellaneous   305
   A.1   Words for Cats   305
   A.2   Endearments for Cats   306
   A.3   Wordlists   311
   A.4   Codebook   317

References   321
Clawssary   331
Index   340

Illustrations

1.1	Rolf at Warwick University	9
1.2	Pawfficer Donut of Troy PD	10
1.3	Instagram post of Murrli	12
1.4	Tweet by Cheddar	16
1.5	Gilly and Pancake, pugs on the Internet	22
2.1	Female cat in SED	31
2.2	Male cat in SED	32
2.3	Rolo, the tortie with tortitude	44
2.4	Hotspot for 'cats' on Wordmapper	46
2.5	Hotspots for 'meow' on Wordmapper	47
2.6	Chairman Miaow from Lancashire	48
2.7	Cat vowel chart	50
2.8	Turbo's meow in acoustic phonetics	53
2.9	Turbo the cat research purrticipant	54
2.10	Ma'a, Purr Reviewer 1	58
3.1	Welcome, class, to our intro to meowphology	64
3.2	Raven explaining 'to depantherise'	67
3.3	Cat Jeoffrey – For he is of the tribe of tiger	68
3.4	Tweet by Arwyn	69
3.5	Kirky Turkey doing peer remews	71
3.6	Funniness and iconicity of cat-related words	77
3.7	Les chattes de l'histoire	80
3.8	Cat graffiti in Graz, Austria, and Glasgow, UK	81
3.9	Hettie and Tilly	83
4.1	Lilly, the Syntax Cat, says hi	98
4.2	The Syntax Cat	102
4.3	Cheddar poetry	105
5.1	Queen(ie)(cat)	114
5.2	Sheder/she(cat)	115

5.3	Tabby(cat)/tib(cat)	116
5.4	Cat: no specific term	117
5.5	#BCC_Halloween2020	119
5.6	Logo of the black_cat_crew	120
5.7	Mikey and Schiller, supurrvisors	122
5.8	Are cats good? An important study	123
5.9	Catterplot	124
5.10	Prince S	124
5.11	Turbo – the real cat behind CatterPlot	125
5.12	Cat is player of the match	126
5.13	Milbrooks Minnie: appeal for information	129
5.14	Milbrooks Minnie and #LoveWins stories	130
5.15	MauMau, research assistant	135
5.16	Honey, research assistant	136
5.17	Puff Marx, research assistant	137
6.1	Wicht zoombombing an online lecture	142
6.2	Meme created from screenshot	144
6.3	Sample Instagram post	145
6.4	Lemmy and Moritz say hi on Slack	148
6.5	Rolf in Birdland	150
6.6	Mauz grooming in a cardboard box	151
6.7	Cat pawtraits of Gaia and Skylar	152
6.8	Fred and human	153
6.9	Balou, canine research inspiration	154
6.10	Cuteness factor of Milis	155
6.11	Keep calm and meow on	157
6.12	Hosico and the Dolly Parton Challenge	158
6.13	Queen Pinky and her official royal photograph	159
6.14	ASCII cat	160
6.15	ASCII box pawty	161
6.16	Cat laptop sticker	162
6.17	WhatsApp stickers of Daisy	163
7.1	Wicht, Purr Reviewer 2	174
7.2	Domains of language use – flowchart	179
7.3	Horst the Hero on Instagram	181
7.4	Bilingualism with Tippy and Pekoe	183
7.5	Happy Miau-o-ween!	185
7.6	Olly the Cat	186
7.7	Gaston	189
7.8	Using Google Translate	191
7.9	Google Translate Korean	192
7.10	Bilingual Russian–English cat Henry	193

8.1	Lilly on #FluffyFursday	205
8.2	Survey shout-out on Twitter	209
8.3	Noodles being cute #AcademicsWithCats	214
8.4	Vigilant Filou working for ELDAH	218
9.1	Instagram post of Murrli	222
9.2	Her Fluffy Floofiness Ma'a, aka Purr Reviewer 1	234
9.3	ECC barmen waiting for orders	241
9.4	ECC Head Honcho Marmite	242
9.5	Jeebus, Sooty, and Betty are family	243
9.6	Tabbyraptor Wicht, aka Purr Reviewer 2	244
9.7	Leo the ginger ninja	246
9.8	Jackson Galaxy raising awareness for foster kitten	247
9.9	Countries with most cat owners	249
10.1	Relative frequencies for 'cat' and 'cats' (per 10,000 words)	257
10.2	Relative frequencies by place	259
10.3	Likelihood of non-meowlogism/meowlogism on platform (row totals)	261
10.4	Probability of meowlogisms by context (column totals)	263
10.5	Relative frequency by type	266
10.6	Likelihood of meowlogisms/non-meowlogisms in types of cat accounts (row totals)	268
10.7	Probability of meowlogisms by cat account type (column totals)	269
10.8	Frequency of #Caturday tweets	271
10.9	Visualisation of #GladdersYoga	274
10.10	Visualisation of #ECCHappyHour	275
10.11	Locations of #Caturday tweets on Saturday 8 May 2021	277
10.12	#Caturday tweet network of Saturday 5 June 2021	278
11.1	Rocket and Nebula – extended family and good friends	291
11.2	Simba, king of our lives	302

Tables

2.1	Cat-related words in the EDD Online	27
2.2	Cat-related questions in the SED	29
2.3	Cat-related headwords in the SED	30
2.4	Cat-related questions in survey of Neath English	33
2.5	Definition of 'cat' in the Urban Dictionary	39
2.6	Questions of April 2019 survey	40
2.7	Hits for 'puddy-tat'	42
2.8	Feline-centric Concepts	45
2.9	Cat consonant table	52
3.1	Iconicity and percentiles	74
3.2	Humour norms for cat-related words	75
4.1	Ceiling Cat Prayer	96
6.1	Proposal of cat face emoji to Unicode in 2009	168
6.2	Cat-related emoji in Emoji Version 1.0	169
6.3	Cat emoji on different platforms	170
6.4	Cat emoji frequency	170
7.1	Domains of language use – table	180
8.1	Diagram used for sampling	203
8.2	Sampling	204
8.3	#JellyBellyFriday: Output generated by Instaloader	206
9.1	Five most frequently occurring content words	225
9.2	Pivot table for 'Amazing'	226
10.1	Absolute frequencies of words in the Purrieties corpus and its subcorpora (platform)	255
10.2	Relative frequencies (RF) of most frequently used content words on the social media platforms (per 10,000 words)	256
10.3	Absolute and relative frequencies of non-meowlogisms and meowlogisms (platform)	258

10.4	Crosstabs for non-meowlogisms/meowlogisms and social media platforms	260
10.5	Absolute frequencies of words in the Purrieties corpus and subcorpora by type	264
10.6	Absolute and relative frequencies of non-meowlogisms and meowlogisms by type	265
10.7	Crosstabs for non-meowlogisms/meowlogisms and type of Cat Account	267
10.8	Languages identified in #Caturday tweets on 5 June 2021	279
11.1	Indexical fields for [t] and [ʔ] in kitty in Greater Manchester	284
A.1	Words for cats	305
A.2	Endearments for cats	306
A.3	Codebook	317

Acknowledgments

Where to start with my thanks? There are so many two-legged and four-legged helpers who deserve to be mentioned.

As cats apparently rule the world, I would like to thank them first, although I am sure they would prefer treats over a written thank-you note.

An enormous thank you goes to Helen Barton at Cambridge University Press, who was so supportive from the very beginning, encouraging me to go for my idea of writing about cats and linguistics; to Isabel Collins at Cambridge University Press, who always made sure I was on track with copyright permissions and images; and to Katja Politt, Susanne Schötz, Naomi Truan, Clive Upton, Mark Dingemanse, Bodo Winter, and David Adger, who provided me with cat-related language data to use in the book.

Fanks a lot to the many cat account holders who participated in my research and allowed me to use their cats' names and images in the book. The cat-related digital spaces are indeed a very friendly corner of the Internet.

I would also like to thank the anonymous reviewers who gave me such constructive feedback along the way to make the manuscript into a book. The section heading 'PURRther Reading' was one of their suggestions, which I gladly incorporated.

Of course, the book would not have been possible without the unwavering support of Tina and our two purr reviewers Ma'a and Wicht, each contributing in their own way.

I'd like to dedicate this book to Murrli, the cat whose social media presence inspired my research on cat-related digital spaces in the first place and whose purresence brought us joy for so many years. Fank mew, sweetie!

1

The Cativerse

Why do you have a cat account?
(July 2019 Survey Question)
Because cats are so pawesome that they deserve it! And it's fun to imagine
what they would be saying about how they see the world.
(Respondent 62)

When we look at the respondent's answer to the question 'Why
do you have a cat account?', we notice linguistic features to study in
greater detail: the word 'pawesome' and the phrases 'they deserve it'
and 'it's fun to imagine'. Like cats pouncing on their prey, we can
jump on the word formation, on the attitude, on the meaning, on the
spelling, and on many things more. How people communicate about
cats online is really a fascinating treasure trove for linguists and cat
lovers alike.

With their half-in, half-out attitude, it is in cats' nature to carefully
check out new territory. The cat owners among us know that our
cats like to take their time before they go out, often standing on the
threshold half inside and half outside. When they are satisfied that
no danger awaits them, the cats step fully outside and explore their
surroundings.

In this chapter, we follow the cats' approach: we first take only a
few steps to get an overview of the book's structure and then enter
the cativerse, the feline online world, to get to know more about cats'
presence in our real and virtual lives. Social media platforms function
as a so-called third place for us to hang out with and meet other like-
minded people. Cat-related digital spaces are only one type of third
places offered to people out there on the Internet. There is a myriad
of other places and communities.

The relationship of cats and humans goes back a long time and has had ups and downs throughout history. We touch on the roles cats have been given by humans and their effect on culture. We also take into account biological and psychological explanations of the effect cats have on humans. Cats function like people magnets, which is what we discover when we consider cats in popular culture, in the media, and in advertising.

Concepts Used in The Chapter

- cat-related digital spaces
- third places
- history
- ethology
- literature
- popular culture
- popular media

Terms from the Clawssary

ethology Hambspeak LOLspeak meowlogism purrieties

1.1 Cats and Their Role in This Book

With this book, the cativerse has now extended its realm to linguistics because our feline friends perfectly illustrate how we communicate online. The cat-related examples show us what we study as linguists and how we can describe the linguistic features we are interested in. The language varieties, which are called 'purrieties' here because they occur in the cat-related digital spaces, provide us with everything we need for our encounter with the fascinating world of language.

Each chapter covers a different linguistic angle to take in our description of how we talk about cats online. In line with the cats' half-in half-out approach, we find out first what is in store for us and then step deeper into the topic, which is why the concepts used and the words from the clawssary are listed at the beginning of each chapter. At the end of each chapter, we list the resources used for the chapter and suggestions for 'PURRther Reading'.

This chapter – Chapter 1 ('The Cativerse') – sets the scene for the linguistic description of the purrieties we encounter on social media and introduces us to the digital world of cats. We discuss the underlying reasons for feline success, not only on social media but also in the real world. We look at the historical roles of cats in our cultures, at biological and psychological explanations for the effects cats have on us, and at feline presence in popular culture.

In our approach to language and language variation, we look at different linguistic features: pronunciation, vocabulary, word creation, grammar, spelling, and meaning. Chapter 2 ('The Territory Range of Language') shows that we pronounce the word 'cat' in different ways and use a wide range of words for our cats, which is what we can study with dialectology. Chapter 3 ('Meowlogisms') explains what we do when we create new words and goes into the word formation processes we use to give our words a feline spin. We also look at the reasons why we find cat-inspired words funny. Chapter 4 ('Da Kittehz') focusses on meaning and grammar by using the examples of LOLcats and LOLspeak. We analyse the spelling, vocabulary, and grammar of LOLspeak.

Chapter 5 ('Virtual Furever Homes') shows us the background of online community building. We look at how we tell and share our cat stories online. Chapter 6 ('Multimeowdality') describes how we use text, audio, and video on social media. Chapter 7 ('Meow and More') leads us to the relationship of language and society and what the way we use language says about us in terms of our social background. The chapter also illustrates how we use language to construct our identity when we are in the cat-related digital spaces.

Chapter 8 ('Going on Pawtrol') describes how to do linguistic research on the Internet. In particular, it shows us how to select the data and how to work ethically, using cat examples from the social media platforms Facebook, Instagram, Twitter, and YouTube. Chapter 9 ('Linguistic Scratching Posts') looks at how to analyse the data to describe our cat-related language varieties. It presents the variation in vocabulary, word formation, spelling, and meaning we come across in cat-related digital spaces. Chapter 10 ('Stats withCats') gives us some statistical methods to interpret and visualise the differences in how we use cat-inspired words on different platforms and illustrates social networks with big data tools.

Chapter 11 ('Cattitude and Purrception') describes how we can analyse, categorise, and interpret the answers of cat account holders when asked for the reasons why they use purrieties and what they think about how we talk about our cats online.

While *Purrieties of Language* is an introductory book to linguistics, it is not a textbook as such. It is like a case study to show us what happens online in terms of language variation. The idea behind the book is to show that linguistics is fun, especially when cats are involved. So, let's go into the cativerse!

1.2 Cats and Their Digital Spaces

Why do you follow cats on social media?
(July 2019 Survey Question)
It makes me happy to see cats from all over the world & the people who love them!
(Respondent 110)

Grumpy Cat, Nyan Cat, and Pusheen – a real cat, a virtual cat, and a toy cat – are among the most famous online stars, whose well-known memes, videos, photos, and GIFs are enjoyed and shared by many of us on social media. Yet, while other cats are not as famous and do not have the merchandise of the big players, many more inhabit the digital world. Today, millions of cats walk the social media platforms of Facebook, Instagram, Twitter, and YouTube, and they have transformed parts of the digital human universe into a cativerse. With these cat-related digital spaces, we have created an online cat park we can take our cats to, which is something we cannot really do in the real world. No longer decried as crazy, we can now meet others like us, talk about our cats, and share our love of cats openly.

The cativerse comprises the digital spaces offered by technology and extends across all the social media platforms. In their ubiquity, cats – or rather the people posting as cats – are present on Facebook, Instagram, Twitter, Reddit, Pinterest, YouTube, 4chan, LOLcats, Tumblr, WordPress, TikTok, and beyond. Cats feature in personal social media accounts, corporate and official accounts, charities, groups, pages, lists, channels, forums, and more. When we enter the cativerse, we immediately meet cats of all shapes, sizes, colours, and ages. We see cats in people's everyday life, cats looking for homes, cats entertaining people, cats simply being cats. And they are all adorable.

In the cativerse, it is common for people to identify themselves to others as cat lovers more or less straight away, for example, by having a cat-inspired username and profile picture, using cat-inspired language varieties (the purrieties), using cat-inspired hashtags, posting cat pictures and videos, sharing other people's cat photos, posting cat-inspired GIFs and emoji, or other means. The hashtag #CatsOfTwitter immediately categorises a tweet as cat-related, and #TabbyTroop tells others that the post is connected to a tabby cat.

Not only the very famous feline stars but also our 'everyday' cats connect and attract us. As the quote at the beginning of this section illustrates, cat lovers go online to the cativerse to see other cats, to meet other people, to get to know each other, and to have fun.

Moggies and pedigree cats alike have social media accounts, and there are quite a lot of social media–savvy cats in the cativerse. I was surprised by the sheer numbers of cats on Facebook when I opened a Facebook account for my black cat Murrli back in 2012. Just like today, the algorithms of Facebook suggested similar people to follow, and in Murrli's case that meant other cats. Within days of being on Facebook, Murrli had acquired 200 cat friends, all of whom were black like Murrli as it was then a personal quirk of mine to only have black cats as friends. If I had not decided to send friend requests just to black cats, Murrli would have had many more friends on Facebook. To meet fellow black cats, Murrli soon followed the *For the Love of Black Cats (Black Cat Appreciation Page)*, a Facebook page dedicated to the joy of living with black cats and to dispelling the myths about them.

Our online cats have very active social media lives, it seems. While it is clear to us that it is people who talk and interact with each other, we tend to accept the pretence that it is often the cats themselves who post online, who share their photos, who come up with poems, and more. More or less loose networks are formed online where we regularly check our timelines for our online acquaintances and/or visit each other's profiles to exchange news, entertainment, and help.

The interaction in the digital cat spaces is very lively, and cats quickly and easily attract other people posing as their cats. Cats, or rather their owners, have always been very active in posting photos and videos of themselves, describing their daily lives and their adventures, asking for help in health matters, sharing pleas for adoptions, and, sadly, also grieving when cats have passed away.

Since Murrli's joining social media platforms, I have been following and befriending many cat accounts on Instagram, Facebook, and Twitter, like Cheddar on Twitter, who is a young 'Catnadian' (Canadian) cat sharing his adventures, writing poetry with the hashtag #CheddarPoetry and actively promoting other kitties looking for 'fwiends'; or like Henry King Cat, the Siberian cat from Russia with his own accounts on Instagram and Facebook, who communicates in English and Russian and whose photos and videos are taken by 'meowmy'; or Curious Zelda on Twitter, Instagram, and Facebook, who has just published her first book, *The Adventures of a Curious Cat*, about a cat's life with humans, in which she is

explaining in her unique voice how to handle humans, how to communicate with furniture, and most importantly how to live a life curiously. (Curious Zelda)

One of the original reasons for creating a social media account for Murrli was to find out more about the perceived feline dominance of the Internet and then the linguistic features occurring in the cat-related digital spaces. Cat-related digital spaces can be considered so-called third places on the Internet. After the home, which is the first place, and work, which is the second place, people also visit third places, which are neither home nor work. Third places are a sort of shared space for people to visit, to hang out, and to socialise with others, to communicate about a certain common topic, among other things.

In the real world, coffee shops, playgrounds, and social centres function as a third place where regulars and newcomers meet. Checking a cat's social media feed is equal to checking in to see which other cats are there in the virtual world. Social media is a virtual meeting place enabling, people to interact with each other across geographic and linguistic boundaries regardless of whether they know each other in real life. In the book, I refer to the third places for cat lovers on the Internet as cat-related digital spaces. We come back to third places in Chapter 7, in which we look at affinity spaces, virtual communities, and communities of practice.

After some time in the cativerse, this interest acquired the new note of having fun with the social media postings of other cats. It is, of course, the owners who post in the names of their cats, although, in online cat spaces, the cat as the actor and author of the post has been accepted. In cat-related digital spaces, users tacitly agree on the community practice that the cats and not the humans are speaking and writing. The users, of course, know that humans are interacting with humans, but they like to pretend that the cats themselves have social media accounts and talk with each other.

Based on observation of the social media platforms Instagram, Twitter, and Facebook, four types of cats inhabit the cativerse: the for-profit celebrity cats, the for-cause working cats, the individual cats, and cats in collective cat accounts. We do not go into too much detail here because the four types of cats are described in Chapters 5 and 10. To get an idea about what we are dealing with, the list below gives us the basic definitions.

For-profit celebrity cats:
Famous feline stars making money for their owners with their own merchandise
For-cause working cats:
Cats working as community outreach cats for organisations, public institutions and owners who support charitable causes
Individual cats:
Cats sharing their daily lives and adventures on social media platforms
Collective cat accounts:
Social media accounts featuring various cats

The cat-related digital spaces are not restricted to a specific region but extend across geographic and social boundaries. These online spaces differ based on various factors, such as the nature of the social media platform, the way of communicating, the roles given to the cats, the function of the posts, the topics discussed, and the languages used.

A look at the general characteristics gives an introductory insight into the cat connection and into what goes on in the digital spaces. In principle, the appeal of cats is global and goes beyond one language, which explains the multilingual environment of some cat-related digital spaces. Just as real cats are companions for humans all over the world, the social media profiles for cats are a worldwide phenomenon and offer spaces for captions and comments not only in English but in many languages. In Chapter 7, our linguistic exploration of the cativerse takes us to multilingualism.

Users write their posts and comments in English and other languages, use purrieties of English, like catspeak purrieties, meowlogisms, LOLspeak, and Hambspeak, communicate with emoji, GIFs, memes, photos, and videos, and interact by liking and sharing.

On her social media timelines, Murrli made cat friends all over the world and wrote in English, German, and Russian, depending on the followers 'she' was communicating with. I shared photos of Murrli on Instagram and liked and commented on other cats' photos, mainly on Instagram.

As already indicated above, the phrase 'crazy cat person' is no longer derogatory, and people openly showing their love of cats are no longer stigmatised as crazy or strange. It does not come as a big surprise, then, that it is not only private individuals who share their cats' photos in their accounts or even open social media accounts for their cats but that non-profit organisations and public institutions are also now using cats on social media platforms.

Cats are literally working the digital scene as community outreach and PR officers. These working cats range from political cats, ambassador cats, police cats, railway station cats, and fire department cats to café cats and library cats. There are also university cats who work on campus.

Campus cats are a worldwide phenomenon and, like Rolf at Warwick University (Figure 1.1), Campus Cat Augsburg in Germany, and VSU Cat in Russia, have gathered a large follower base, and judging from the comments and photos, students and staff are always happy to see them. Rolf at Warwick University was part of the campus cat exhibition of 2019 in the University Museum of Groningen, the Netherlands, and features in the e-book officially published by Rolf's fellow campus cat Professor Doerak. All these university cats are part of the spaces of academics with cats, the digital spaces we are visiting throughout the book.

Murrli, too, was a working cat. She had been designated Spokescat of the Meow Factor, my research blog, and still features in that function on my presentation slides at research conferences and is referred to as 'supurrvisor' and 'purr reviewer' when it comes to posting on Twitter with the hashtag #AcademicWithCats and checking on the updates by the twitter user Cats of Linguists (@linguisticats).

Unlike Murrli, some working cats are well known and attract the interest of the news media. The official Whitehall cats Larry, Gladstone, and Palmerston regularly feature in the British national press as real cats and as political commentators in the virtual world. Felix and Bolt, the Huddersfield Station Cats, with currently two books written about them, are officially the Senior Pest Controller and the Apprentice. Both cats have featured on British national television.

Figure 1.1 Rolf at Warwick University

The news media love cats, and many cat stories are published. When I did an initial research project on cats in the media, I analysed news stories collected in the one-month period of February 2014. Just to give a scale of the sheer numbers of cat-related news stories, I found 108 English-language news articles on www.news.yahoo.com in that month, and 31 Russian-language articles appeared on just one day on www.news.yandex.ru. The story types typically include unbelievable cats, cruelty to cats, cat companions, feral cats, homeless cats, internet cats, cat heroes, show cats, cats and human health, and cats and business. For the news media, the cat is certainly of value and sometimes even takes centre stage in larger events in current affairs or sports. In the aftermath of the Paris terrorist attacks in

Troy Police Dept. @TroyMI_Police · 18 Mar
Interrogation with Pawfficer Donut #PoliceCat

Donut: How long did you wash your hands?

Human: 20 seconds, I swear!

Donut (as she slowly reveals she has CCTV footage of sink area): Do you want to tell me again how long you washed your hands?

#WashYourHands 🐾 #DontLieToThePaw

TROY POLICE Feline Unit Purrrtect and Serve

♡ 17   ⟲ 64   ♡ 378   ⤳

Figure 1.2 Pawfficer Donut of Troy PD

2015, when Brussels was locked down in the hunt for the terrorists, the news media showed the cat pictures posted on Twitter with the hashtag #BrusselsLockDown. Other news includes cats strolling onto football pitches and tennis courts.

In the United States, the police cat Pawfficer Donut made it into the US news after the 2018 public appeal by Troy Police Department (Troy PD) for more followers on Twitter. Pawfficer Donut (Figure 1.2) is now officially employed as a public outreach cat and a guardian for the community. On the official Facebook and Twitter accounts of Troy PD, Pawfficer Donut keeps in contact with the community and posts updates on school visits and charity events. In the meantime, two other US police cats have appeared on the social media platforms, namely Pawfficer Fuzz and Pawperator Cad, both of whom are on Instagram. The UK, too, has a police cat, namely PC Oscar on Twitter.

Interrogation with Pawfficer Donut #PoliceCat
Donut: How long did you wash your hands?
Human: 20 seconds, I swear!
Donut (as she slowly reveals she has CCTV footage of sink area): Do you want to tell me again how long you washed your hands?
#WashYourHands 🐾 #DontLieToThePaw
(Pawfficer Donut of Troy PD)

In the cat-related digital spaces, users typically talk about a wide range of topics. While social media cats are often associated with fun and entertainment, more serious topics are also addressed. Users discuss cat life, cats and wildlife, pet health, owner health, animal shelters, animal rights, animal abuse, pet behaviour, and ownership. Posts range from picture updates and day-specific images, like 'Tongue Out Tuesday', when images of cats with their tongues out are posted, to calls for help and pleas for adoption for cats looking for a 'forever home'. On social media, users share their emotions, positive and negative, when, for example, cats celebrate their birthdays or adoptaversaries, or when cats are ill or 'have crossed the rainbow bridge'. Users themselves or in the name of their cats offer support, like Grizzly, a black cat on Instagram, who asks his followers for a paw circle:

Please take my paw and let's hold paws for our furiend Herbie who just found out he's battling cancer. Thank you Dandelion for starting the paw chain for little Herbie #holdingpawsforherbie.
(Grizzly Cat)

When Murrli passed away in January 2019, more people than usual reacted to show their compassion, commented on the post (Figure 1.3), shared Murrli's picture, and created Instagram stories for Murrli to express their condolences. Murrli was also featured by the collective cat account @black_cat_crew on Instagram.

1.3 Cats and Their Roles

As we have already seen, cats fulfil various roles in the cativerse and feature in social media updates as entertainers, tricksters, guardians, healers, deities, and heroes in addition to being mousers and companions. As an aside, the portrayals of cats online in the shared images of them take us to semiotics in Chapter 4. Yet these cat roles are not an

Figure 1.3 Instagram post of Murrli

invention of the Internet but can actually be traced back to Ancient Egypt, famous for its cat goddess Bastet and its adoration of cats.

Throughout human history, cats have featured in people's lives as fellow creatures, as companions, as symbols, as metaphors, and as allegories in literature, art, and religion. The image of the cat has varied over time, switching from positive to evil and back again. From having been revered as deities in Ancient Egypt, cats were later vilified in Europe in the Middle Ages. It is only fairly recently – in the last 200 years or so – that cats have regained their positive status. A number of scholarly publications, looked at the cat's place in human culture.

The relationship between cats and religion has not always been favourable for the cat, although in the early beginnings of the human–

cat relationship, the cat was given a god-like status. Almost 4,000 years ago, the cat was a household pet in Egypt and came to be associated with Bastet, the Egyptian goddess of the moon, protector of life, fecundity, maternity, happiness, and pleasure. The connection of the cat to Bastet is well-known among cat lovers.

A perhaps rather unknown fact among cat lovers is that the cat was associated also with Egypt's sun god, Ra. Published in 1949, the *Dictionary of Cat Lovers* describes the Egyptian paintings and papyrus scrolls that refer to the cat as the sun god. The dictionary also features names given to cats by Egyptians: cats' names found on early effigies in Egypt include 'Mau', 'Mai', and 'Maau'. In China too, cats got onomatopoeic names like 'Mao' or 'Miu' at about 300 AD. To show the connection of cats to the gods, which is something some cat accounts can relate to, here are some examples of how cats were seen as Sun God Ra.

This male Cat is Ra himself and he was called Mau
26. Praise be to thee, O Ra, exalted Sekhem, thou art the Great Cat, the avenger of the gods, and the judge of words, and the president of the sovereign chiefs [or, accessors] [sic] and the governor of the holy Circle; thou art indeed the bodies of the Great Cat.
(Aberconway, 1949)

Moving on from Egypt to the long history of cats and people, cats have played positive and negative roles in written cat stories. The cat was positively regarded as a deity and divine creature in the Greek and Norse mythologies. In Greek mythology, the cat was attributed to Artemis as a symbol for life and in Norse mythology came, to accompany the goddess Freya as a symbol for joy and merrymaking. In other religions, like Islam and Buddhism, the cat has always had a positive image as some stories involving Muhammad and Buddha show. In Japan, the cat has always been welcome in temples.

In some cultures, the cat was also given magical and mystical powers, and up to the Middle Ages the cat fulfilled the role of a healer and guardian of the home. Then, the image of the cat, positive up to then, became blurred in the folklores of Europe and the Orient. Black cats, especially, suffered from the image change, since they and their mystical and magical powers were good and evil at the same time. This blur already indicated that dark times for cats lay ahead.

In Christianity, cats slowly became to be seen as evil. From initially being regarded simply as distractions for monks and nuns in monasteries, cats turned into the incarnation of the devil, an evil creature, and the witches' familiar. Seen as examples for bad moral behaviour and as evil and lewd, the cat was connected to the figures of Satan and Judas. As if religion was not enough, folklore did its part to vilify cats too. Cats appeared as monsters who could shape-shift into witches and back, and it was popularly believed that cats could make people fall asleep with their magical tales and songs. Since the cat was an evil satanic creature, it was prosecuted and killed together with the witches. Some of these superstitions remain today. Black cats, having to combat human superstition, are among the last animals to be adopted in shelters, and there are social media campaigns by black cat advocates who try to improve the image of black cats.

Turning now to the more positive times for cats, we should have a look at the nineteenth and twentieth centuries, when cats' reputation – and in turn their lives – improved again. The image changed for the better as cats were becoming popular pets, which was reflected in stories. In fables and fairy tales, cats were portrayed as wise and creative. They were anthropomorphised and given various characteristics ranging from helpful, nocturnal, secretive, mysterious, without respect for the high and mighty, to being half-animal and half-divine, cunning, and wild. Cats could talk and started to appear as characters – even as heroes – in nursery rhymes and in literature. While cats still had the same attributes as they had earlier, these feline skills were now regarded as positive rather than negative. As characters, she-cats were associated with feminine witchcraft, shape-shifting, and mystery, while male cats tended to be tricksters and carnival figures.

Many cat heroes are known today, like Puss in Boots and the Cheshire Cat. One cat deserves a special mention, namely Tomcat Murr created by the German Romantic novelist E. T. A. Hoffmann. Tomcat Murr published his autobiography in the early nineteenth century, using his personal voice after having taught himself to read and write. In addition to Lewis Caroll's Cheshire Cat and Hoffmann's Murr, other authors have come up with cat heroes in their works. Only a few authors are mentioned here, like T. S. Eliot, Edgar Alan Poe, Doris Lessing, Charles Baudelaire, Mikhail Bulgakov, James Joyce, and very recently J. K. Rowling, with various cats featuring in the *Harry Potter* series.

Popular fiction is abundant with cats and cat heroes, and the Cheshire Cat has also appeared as a character in the *Thursday Next* books by Jasper Fforde. There is the *No. 2 Feline Detective Agency* series by Mandy Morton, the *Warrior Cat* books by Erin Hunter, the books by Sophie Kelly, and *Mog the Cat* by Judith Kerr. And there are the modern real-life book stars, like Streetcat Bob, Homer the Blind Wondercat, Dewey the Library Cat, Felix the Huddersfield Station Cat, and most recently Curious Zelda and Robert the Allotment Cat. We will meet some of these cats again later in the book.

Just like on the papyrus scrolls of ancient Egypt, the cat also has its place in art. It appears on both religious and secular paintings throughout the centuries and has fulfilled various positive and negative roles. In religious art, cats were depicted as biblical, evangelical, and saintly and were shown as warrior cats in the holy wars. Cats in arms and war are depicted also in secular paintings as well, and cats feature as examples for proverbs, emblems, popular wisdom, sorcery, and jest.

From the second half of the nineteenth century onwards – at the time when cats gained popularity as pets – paintings and portraits of cats alone appeared, and we can now admire cat pictures painted by famous painters, like Manet, Balthus, Gauguin, Picasso, and Renoir. Artists and authors have been fascinated by cats, and many of them had their own.

As the examples from literature, art and the cat-related digital spaces show, cats still play the roles given to them throughout history. Only the methods and technical possibilities have changed. Cats are still the cultural symbols humans associate them with, and they are given characteristics like comfort, healing, wisdom, puns and wordplay, and magical powers. Cats are still able to talk, to travel between the real world and dreamland, to disappear and reappear, and to provide spiritual guidance and help. The tweet by Cheddar (Figure 1.4) shows us how users portray their cats as comforters, helpers, and healers:

I is cuddlin wif mama. She be lots tired lately. And she gots a lil bit of hurty hed too. I not like dat. So I is takin good care of her. I being xtwa snuggly and cute and kwiet. I gibing her lots of purrs too! I gonna twy to not make trubble until mama all better.
(Cheddar)

Cheddar
@FartyCheddarCat

I is cuddlin wif mama.

She be lots tired lately.

And she gots a lil bit of hurty hed too.

I not like dat.

So I is takin good care of her.

I being xtwa snuggly and cute and kwiet.

I gibing her lots of purrs too!

I gonna twy to not make trubble until mama all better.

Figure 1.4 Tweet by Cheddar

1.4 Cats and Their Effect

I put a spell on you, and now your mine.
(Lilly Cat on Twitter)

Despite cat Lilly's statement in the tweet, it might not be a
magic feline spell that makes us fascinated by cats but some more
natural psychological and biological reasons. As already mentioned
above, cats are working the social media scene as community outreach
officers, entertainers, helpers, and guardians. Research on cats in the
social sciences and on people's psychology provides us with some
clues on the effect of real cats and of cat videos on humans in real
life.

Ethology, the study of human and animal behaviour, has shown
some mechanisms that form the bond between humans and cats. The
cuteness theory and social support theory, developed by ethology, talk

about the effect that infant features or cuteness (or 'kindchenschema') have on us humans. The large eyes, bulging craniums, and retreating chins of infants trigger caring responses in adults, and we tend to feel affection not just for human babies but also for animals with these infant features.

In general, as ethological research shows, we tend to care for young, sick, and wild animals, especially when the animals have the cute baby features. Cats are cuteness personified – or catified – as they indeed seem like infants with their size, their big eyes, their softness, and their meows, which are acoustically in the same frequency as human baby cries. It is all of these features combined that make cats so appealing for us humans.

Yet it is not just their infant features that make cats so popular. Ethology also says that cats are affectionate with their owners, are generally clean, and – if seen from a human perspective – are just like humans, and research conducted on human and cat interaction has found that people like these characteristics in cats.

Ethology has found another reason for the success of cats in the therapeutic effect they have on us. Like other pets, cats improve our mood and well-being if the bond is strong between cat and us. As companion animals, cats can be our 'significant other' and provide an additional source of emotional support for us.

That said, not only real cats but also cat videos have been found to have a therapeutic effect on people. Cat videos have a positive impact on people's moods When we watch videos of funny cats and kittens, our spirits are kept up and negative emotions disappear. Anxiety, annoyance, sadness, and guilt tend to decrease when we watch cat videos. In general, people watch internet videos to enjoy themselves or to avoid work. Despite the perhaps negative connotations of cyberslacking in the workspace when people go online to watch cat videos, people pay more attention to their tasks afterwards as it turns out that internet cat videos actually promote attention and re-energise people. Cat videos, thus, are good for us.

Other research has focussed on the cat videos themselves. What makes people like videos of cats is that, in contrast to dogs, cats do not change their behaviour in front of the camera and seem to be oblivious to the fact that they are being recorded. In 2015, the popularity of cat videos was taken up as a theme in the exhibition *How Cats Took Over the Internet* at the Museum of the Moving Image in New York.

In an interview with me, Jason Eppink, the curator of the exhibition, pointed to seven reasons for the popularity of cat videos, namely the rise of user-generated content, pluralistic ignorance, the existence of a virtual cat park, the bored at work network, and the global appeal of pictures with no language, path dependence, and the happiness factor. Put differently, we now have the technical capability to create our own content, we tend to be in the echo chambers and filter bubbles provided for us by the algorithms, and the existence of the cativerse enables people everywhere to post and consume cat videos (and pictures) with enjoyment and without shame.

Over the years, different types of cat videos have emerged: there are funny cat videos, videos showing cats in their daily routines, and cat video compilations. In general, cat videos tend to portray the ordinary and the familiar in domestic locations, and they are easily relatable as viewers see the characteristics of their own cats in these videos. Cat videos reveal things about cats in general and show the cat as its own species, which is different from humans or other animals. As indomitable free spirits, cats are cute, funny, independent, sociable, aloof, intelligent, and secretive. The most widely known cat videos are perhaps the funny cat videos on YouTube. The format of the video tends to follow the same plot: the scene is typically calm at first, with the cat having an active part, then the calmness is interrupted suddenly and the cat acts in a certain way, the effect of which is usually surprising and funny for the viewers.

Some cat videos become viral and are watched all over the world. For example, the video of Pawfficer Donut being sworn in officially by a judge was posted on Twitter and Facebook, subsequently made it into the news, and ended up in one of the popular nightly shows on US television. Troy PD use the popularity of their police cat to reach the community and regularly post videos of the cat. A video of 7 August 2018, for example, shows the cat trying to catch a computer mouse a police officer is dangling in front of her. The caption reads:

Pawfficer Donut's latest training involves catching a mouse. Pawfficer and officers are working hard each day to serve the community. #PoliceCat
(Troy Police Department – Troy, Michigan, on Facebook)

Cats are relatable for humans in many cultures, and, thus, it is not surprising that we encounter cats all around us in the virtual and real worlds as real cats, as virtual cats, and as images. Cats are present in the business world too, and not just in the online and offline media spaces. The cat's characteristic as a culturally meaningful symbol and the cat effect are an ideal combination for business, which is a fact exploited by advertising.

Catvertising (advertising with cats) sees cats as effective tools for fundraising, marketing, commerce, and audience engagement. All the positive characteristics associated with cats, like their cuteness, the connotation of the cat and the home, and their warmth, create a positive connection between consumer and brand and apparently raise brand awareness. Apart from the pet food producers, other big companies have run adverts featuring cats, including Ikea, Skittles, Walmart, Samsung, Kia, O_2, Bouygues Telecom, Sainsbury's, Novartis, and Procter & Gamble. An advert that has become viral is Cravendale Milk's *Cats with Thumbs*, which plays on the possibility that cats develop opposable thumbs, gang up on humans, and steal their milk. The advert's black cat sharpening its claws with a nail file has turned into a meme and a GIF often shared on social media.

Images of cats are used on many consumer goods, like calendars, stationery, mugs, key rings, bags, and clothes. Cats have been inspiring designers like Dolce & Gabbana with their Bengal cat collection, Karl Lagerfeld with his Choupette collection, Charlotte Olympia with her Kitty collection, or Kate Spade with her Meow bags. Perhaps the best-known fashion icon is Hello Kitty, who is a merchandise phenomenon with items ranging from clothes, accessories, and toys to credit cards, airplanes, and food. Other examples include Pusheen, Nyan Cat, and Grumpy Cat.

Cats usually equal commercial success, which translates to cats making money for their owners. On social media, there are for-profit celebrity cats who, with their immense social media presence, make quite a lot of profit. The term 'petfluencer' is also used for for-profit celebrity cats. The most widely known example of a successful celebrity cat is probably Grumpy Cat, with product endorsements, movie and book deals, and more. Grumpy Cat sadly passed away in 2019. Other celebrity cats include Smoothie the Cat from the Netherlands, Lil Bub from the USA, and Hosico from Russia. Their images adorn a wide range of consumer goods, and celebrity cats make additional money with product endorsements on the social media platforms.

A famous example of a celebrity cat from the UK is Streetcat Bob, who is usually portrayed in his role as a healer and guardian. The stray Bob, who was killed by a car in 2020, helped a homeless man to get his life back on track. This real-life story has created quite an industry around the cat, with a book series, Bob's very own movie, an animated series on YouTube, and more. To be fair, Streetcat Bob also did non-profit work for charities.

The fact that cats are still heroes today has turned them into cash-magnets of popular culture. The term 'popular culture' refers to cultural artefacts or media content produced for mass audiences; cats feature in music, popular fiction, and film and have brought commercial success for creators and companies. Feline popular culture includes Andrew Lloyd Webber's musical *Cats*, Erin Hunter's book series *Warrior Cats*, the animated series *Tom & Jerry*, the cat comics of Garfield, Simon's Cat, and The Oatmeal, Disney's animated movie *Aristocats*, and *Puss in Boots*. DreamWorks' spin-off to the successful *Shrek* series.

In some popular productions, cats contribute to the success of the series and have even become icons. The connection of cats with the *Star Trek* series is well-known, at least for the fans of the series. Yet *Star Trek* is not the only TV series featuring cats. They also show up in *Dr Who*, and outside the science fiction genre, cats have become an essential element in series lore, like in the *James Bond* movie series, which features the arc-hvillain's cat in some of the movies. And when we come back to recent popular TV series, we should not forget cats as recurring song themes, such as 'Smelly Cat' in *Friends* and 'Soft Kitty, Warm Kitty' in The *Big Bang Theory*, which has gone viral on the Internet.

As we have already seen, the cativerse stretches across a wide expanse of the Internet, and while cats seem to rule the Internet, other animals are also very popular on social media. There are dogs, llamas, goats, sheep, cows, hamsters, hedgehogs, and more, and the social media platforms provide places for all animal interests: digital spaces form around these animals too. These animal-related digital spaces are not mutually exclusive as people with animal companions are usually animal lovers. The Dodo exemplifies the animal variety on social media and makes use of the visual impact of animal videos. The Dodo wants to reach as many people as possible with

emotionally and visually compelling, highly shareable animal-related stories and videos ... to make caring about animals a viral cause
(The Dodo)

Cross-species friendships, especially, attract people, and images of cats cuddling with dogs or of cats fostering ducks and such like make for highly shareable social media content. It is not just the big animal players who are successful on the Internet: animal shelters make use of social media channels to raise awareness for animal welfare and to find so-called forever homes for their many cats, dogs, rabbits, horses, and more. Examples in the UK are the RSPCA and Cats Protection doing their animal charity work and animal protection.

As in real life, the biggest rivals for cats on the Internet, in terms of popularity in human eyes, are dogs. In fact, the figures for Instagram show that there are many more postings with the hashtag #dog than with #cat. Like cats, dogs have their own dog-related digital spaces, their own followers, and their own stars. It is not just the 'crazy cat people' but also dog owners who like to show their pets to the world and talk about them. Pugs, for example, also have their own pug-related digital spaces on social media, like Doug the Pug, who has become famous for being dressed up like celebrities and for posing in movie scenes, or the not (yet)-so-famous Gilly and Pancake (Figure 1.5), who have their own social media accounts on Facebook, Instagram, and Twitter.

When we go into pug-related digital spaces, we find that pugs, like cats, have their own variety of language – or 'furiety' – with word creations like 'pugtato chips' and pug-specific hashtags like #PugsTakeDC, #PugChat, and #PugLife. On a dog-related sidenote, research has been done on pupper talk, a language variety in dog-related digital spaces on Reddit.

While people cannot be simply divided into cat people and dog people, (news) media and social media like to play on the dog vs cat angle, as exemplified by Troy PD. In their posts, Troy PD also use dogs from their unit to reach out to the community, and when they do, messages and comments are likely to include some remarks on Pawfficer Donut too. However, despite the quantitative advantage of dogs on the Internet, it is cats who are more likely to go viral and to attract more attention. The reason for that is simple, according to internet lore:

Cats rule, and dogs drool.
(Anonymous)

Figure 1.5 Gilly and Pancake, pugs on the Internet

Sources Used in This Chapter

- Turner (1995, 2000); Turner and Bateson (2014) for the human-cat relationship
- Bradshaw (2014) for cat behaviour
- Sacquin (2010) for cats in art
- Foucart-Walter and Rosenberg (1988) for cats in art
- Bobis (2001) for cats in literature and art
- Nikolajeva (2014) for cats in literature
- Aberconway (1949) for the history of cats
- McCulloch (2019) for third places on the Internet
- Eppink (2015) for cats and the Internet
- Shafer (2012, 2016) for cat videos
- O'Meara (2014) for cat videos
- Gall Myrick (2015) for cat videos
- Braunegger (2016) for cats in popular culture
- Podhovnik (2016) for cats in the news media
- Podhovnik (2018) for cats on Instagram
- Mahler (2020) for language in dog-related digital spaces on Reddit

Examples and Quotes in This Chapter

🐾 Aberconway (1949, pp. 460–461)

🐾 Curious Zelda and Taghioff (2019)

🐾 For the Love of Black Cats (Black Cat Appreciation Page) on Facebook at @BlackCatAppreciationPage

🐾 Cheddar on Twitter at @fartycheddarcat

🐾 Rolf the Warwick University Cat on Twitter at @RolfatWarwick

🐾 Troy Police Department on Twitter at @TroyMI_Police

🐾 www.thedodo.com

Suggestions for PURRther Reading

🐾 McCulloch (2019)

2

The Feline Territory of Language

When a cat is happy she begins to [i.]... PURR
(Survey Question for the Dialectological Study on Neath English)

Real cats are very territorial creatures, and they have wide areas that they possess and defend against other cats. Like cats do with their territories, we also have to mark off the areas of language we are looking at – not to defend our territory against feline intruders but to show exactly what we are dealing with. One way to do so is to take cats to dialectology and show how to illustrate regional language variation with our feline friends.

In dialectology, we study the differences in people's pronunciation, in their vocabulary, and in their grammar (which we leave for Chapter 3) based on the region they come from. Here we discover how the word 'cat' was studied in the traditional dialect studies of English, and we go back to the end of the nineteenth century and work our way up to the end of the twentieth century. Having geographic areas in mind, we find out about the differences in people's pronunciation of the word 'cat' and other cat-related words.

We also turn to dialect dictionaries to look for all the different words we use for our cats. Dialect lexicography deals with the art of dictionary making and is a sub-field of dialectology. We find out how to compile a dictionary of cat-related words ourselves, and in order to do so, we take a look at modern dialect studies, which make use of IT tools.

Stepping away from human language to feline language, we focus on how our cats produce and pronounce sounds. We enter the field of articulatory and acoustic phonetics to describe the language of real cats.

Concepts Discussed in the Chapter

🐾 dialectology
🐾 dialect surveys
🐾 dialect lexicography
🐾 online dialectology
🐾 phonetics
🐾 articulatory phonetics
🐾 acoustic phonetics

Terms from the Clawssary

🐾 accent 🐾 consonants 🐾 cardinal vowel system 🐾 dialect 🐾 dialectology 🐾 F0 (F nought, formant) 🐾 formant 🐾 feature 🐾 fundamental frequency 🐾 glossary 🐾 idiolect 🐾 International Phonetic Alphabet (IPA) 🐾 lexicography 🐾 lexicology 🐾 phonology 🐾 phonetics: acoustic phonetics, articulatory phonetics 🐾 Praat 🐾 sociolect

2.1 Cats and Regions

Now for the animal that goes miaow. What do you call the male?
(Survey of English Dialects)

Just like in everyday life, we only need to look closely enough in linguistics to find cats. In dialectology, cats have turned up in various disguises, as entries in dictionaries, as keywords in dialect surveys, and as examples for regional variation in pronunciation. We only have to discover the cats in dialect studies, like the Survey of English Dialects, to find out about dialectology.

In principle, dialect differences occur because language changes and speech communities expand, and languages change and have changed constantly throughout history. However, language does not change evenly across speech communities, which means that not every new language feature spreads to all the communities or at the same time. Geographical distances and natural barriers make languages change differently, as do cultural, economic, and/or social barriers.

When studying language variation, we have two options open to us: we can either take the diachronic approach or the synchronic view. The diachronic approach looks at how language has been developing over time, while the synchronous approach analyses language at a specific point of time.

Dialectology itself has changed during its history. Dialectology as a scientific study started with becoming aware of dialects, went on to showing prescriptive attitudes towards dialects, and finally has turned into its present state, namely the description and study of dialects. The first stage, the awareness of dialects, can be traced back at least to the Middle Ages to *The Reeve's Tale*, in which Geoffrey Chaucer used Northern English to portray characters. The second stage, the attitude towards dialects, started after the mid-eighteenth century and was characterised by very critical and judgemental comments and by stigmatising certain dialect features.

Modern dialectology as the systematic study of dialects started in the second half of the nineteenth century. Both the *Oxford English Dictionary* (OED) and Joseph Wright's *English Dialect Dictionary* (EDD) were started as systematic studies of the language and dialect in the nineteenth century. At that time, the aim of the OED was to compile a list together with definitions and the etymology of the standard words of English, while the EDD was doing the same thing with dialect words in British English. The EDD was compiled between 1898 and 1905 and comprises 4,700 pages of dialect words. Both dictionaries are available online. The OED is a subscription-based online tool available on https://oed.com/, and the EDD can be accessed as the EDD Online, a project at the University of Innsbruck (Austria), and is free to use at http://eddonline-proj.uibk.ac.at/edd/index.jsp.

A quick search on both the EDD and OED results in cat-related results, like 'boar-cat', 'scattle cat', 'tibcat', 'meowl', and 'miauve' in the EDD Online (Table 2.1). In its entries, the EDD Online gives the type of word, its pronunciation in IPA symbols, its definition, the location where it was recorded, and examples, partly indicated with abbreviations and partly as full text.

The OED provides detailed information on the Old English and Middle English forms and on the etymology of 'cat' and the forms of 'cat' in various languages. Reading the OED entry gives us an idea of how and when the word 'cat' appeared in Europe. The interesting fact is that, despite 'cat' being so widely used, the origin of the word is unknown. Egypt might be a logical source given the cat's history, but there is also evidence of a possible Slavonic or Germanic origin.

Forms: Old English *catte, catt,* Middle English-1600s *catt, catte,* (Middle English-1600s *kat,* 1500s *katte,* Old English- 'cat'.

Etymology: The Middle English and modern 'cat' corresponds at once to Old English 'cat' and Old Northern French 'cat'. The name is common

Table 2.1 *Cat-related words in the EDD Online*

Headword	Entry
boar-cat	*sb.* Ken.[boə'kæt.] A tomcat. Ken. (P.M.); Ken.1 [The males will kill the young ones, if they come at them like as the Bore-cats, TOPSELL *Hist. of Foure-footed Beastes* (1607) iii.]
scattle-cat	*sb.* Sus. Also in form **scaital-cat**. [skæ·tl-kæt.] A thieving, mischievous cat. Cf. **scaddle**, 1. Scattle-cats often won't eat what you give them and like to feed themselves. You can set nothing down nowhere if there is a scattle-cat by,*Lewes Church Mag.* Nos. 48, 49; *Monthly Pkt* (1874) 180.
tibcat	*sb.* Yks. [ti·b-kat] A female cat. Yks. (HALL.), n.Yks. (I.W.), w.Yks.1
meowl	*v.* Sc. Cum. Yks. War. Dev. Also in forms **mahl, meahl** nw.Dev.1; **miol** Sc. (JAM.); **mowl** Cum.; **myawl** e.Yks.1 To mew or cry like a cat. Cf. mewl. Sc. (JAM.) Cum. A black cat 'at nivver leeves her house, but sits mowling, yowlin' aw day, DALBY *Mayroyd* (1888) II. 131. e.Yks.1 War.3 How that cat goes meowiing about; she must have lost her kitten. nw.Dev.1 Hence **Meowling**, *sb.* (1) a crying; (2) obs., the cry of a tiger. (1) e.Yks.1 Stop thy myawlin', cease your crying. War.3 'Stop that meowling' – an admonition to a child to discontinue a peevish cry. (2) Sc. Mioling of tygers, bruzzing of bears, &c.,URQUART *Rabelais* (1653) (JAM.).
miauve	*v.* and *sb.* Sc. Also written myauve Bnff.1 1. v. To mew, as a cat. Bch. (JAM.) 2. sb. The mew of a cat. Bnff.1

European of unknown origin: found in Latin and Greek in 1-4th cent., and in the modern languages generally, as far back as their records go. Byzantine Greek had κάττα (in Cæsarius c350) and later κάττος, as familiar terms = αἴλουρος; modern Greek has γάτα from Italian. Latin had *catta* in Martial a100, and in the Old Latin Bible version ('Itala'), where it renders αἴλουρος. Palladius, ? c350, has *catus*, elsewhere scanned *cātus* (Lewis and Short), and probably in both cases properly *cattus*. From *cattus, catta*, came all the Romanic forms, Italian *gatto*, Spanish *gato*, Portuguese *gato*, Catalan *gat*, Provencal 'cat', Old Northern French 'cat', French *chat*, with corresponding feminines *gatta, gata, cata, cate, chate, chatte*. The Germanic forms recorded are Old English *cat, catt*, Old Norse *kött-r* (< *kattuz*) masculine, genitive *kattar* (Swedish *katt*, Danish *kat*); also Old English *catte* ? feminine, West Germanic **katta* (Middle Low German *katte*, Middle Dutch *katte, kat*, Dutch *kat*, also Swedish *katta*), Old High German *chazzâ* (Middle High German, modern German *katze*) feminine; Old High German had also *chataro*, Middle High German *katero, kater*, modern German and Dutch *kater, he-cat*. The Germanic types of these would be **kattuz* (masculine), **kattôn-* (feminine), **kat(a)zon-* masculine; but as no form of the word is preserved in Gothic, it is not certain that it goes back to the Germanic period. It was at least West Germanic c400-450. It is also in Celtic: Old Irish 'cat' (masculine),

Gaelic 'cat' com., Welsh and Cornish *cath* (feminine), Breton*kaz*, Vannes *kac'h* (masculine). Also in Slavonic, with type *kot*-: Old Slavonic *kot'ka* (feminine), Bulgarian *kotka* Slovene *kot* (masculine), Russian *kot* (masculine), *kotchka, koshka* (feminine), Polish *kot* (*koczur*, masculine), Bohemian *kot* (masculine), *kotka* (feminine), Sorbian *kotka*; also Lithuanian *kate*; Finnish *katti*.
('cat' n., 2021)

In addition to the etymology, the OED puts the words in a historical context and lists the examples. The cat as the 'animal' was recorded in an Old English manuscript as 'catte' dating back to the year 800. The cat has an appearance in Chaucer's *The Canterbury Tales*, and in Shakespeare's *Hamlet*, the cat 'will meaw'. The OED gives an overall timeline for 'cat' from 800 to 1832.

A well-known carnivorous quadruped (Felis domesticus) which has long been domesticated, being kept to destroy mice, and as a house pet.

a800 Corpus Gloss. 863 *Fellus (felis), catte.*
a1000 in T. Wright & R. P. Wülcker *Anglo-Saxon & Old Eng. Vocab.* (1884) I. 120 *Muriceps, uel musio, murilegus*, catt.
c1050 in T. Wright & R. P. Wülcker *Anglo-Saxon & Old Eng. Vocab.* (1884) I. 445 *Muriceps*, cat.
c1225 (?a1200) *Ancrene Riwle* (Cleo. C.vi) (1972) 305 Ne schule ȝe habben nan beast bute cat ane.
c1300 *K. Alis.* 5275 By nighth als a cat hy seeth.
c1386 G. CHAUCER *Wife of Bath's Prol.* 348 Who so wolde senge the cattes skin, Than wol the cat wel dwellen in hire in.
?1527 L. ANDREWE tr. *Noble Lyfe Bestes* sig. giiii The mouse hounter or catte is an onclene beste & a poyson ennemy to all myse.
1556 *Chron. Grey Fr.* (1852) 88 Item..was a katte hongyd on the gallos in Cheppe clothed lyke a preste.
1603 W. SHAKESPEARE *Hamlet* v. i. 289 A Cat will meaw, a Dog will haue a day.
1699 B. E. *New Dict.* Canting Crew at Mouse He watcht me as a Cat does a Mouse.
1752 S. JOHNSON *Rambler* No. 188. 12 Purring like a cat.
1832 A. W. FONBLANQUE *Eng. under Seven Admin.* (1837) II. 272 The ruffians who threw dead dogs and dead cats at the Duke.
('cat' n., 2021)

In the twentieth century, linguists became concerned about the disappearing traditional dialects and started documenting them. This concern is the idea and argumentation behind the Survey of English Dialects (SED), led by Harold Orton and Eugen Dieth and published between 1962 and 1978. For this survey, fieldworkers visited rural locations in England, who used questionnaires to study the dialects of non-mobile older rural males. The questions covered the everyday life of the informants and were asked to elicit information about pronunciation, vocabulary, and grammar.

The book *The Survey of English Dialects: The Dictionary and Grammar (The Dictionary and Grammar)* is a good starting point to find cats in the vast material of the SED because it lists the headwords, the questions, the pronunciation in phonetic transcription, and the various words used by the respondents. We can easily find the cats as they were part of the SED questionnaire. Aiming at recording the respondents' pronunciation as well as grammatical and lexical variation, the questionnaire of the SED contained questions on felines (Table 2.2). The Roman and Arabic numbers after the headwords ('tom-cat', 'tabby-cat', 'kitten') refer to the respective book of the SED questionnaire, to its section, and to the identifying number of the question. For the cat-related headwords, this means that the SED fieldworkers used Questions 8 to 11 in Section 13 of Book III of the SED questionnaire.

The Dictionary and Grammar shows the results for male cat, female cat, kitten, and for having kittens and gives a large amount of data on cats (Table 2.3). There are not just the various transcribed pronunciations in IPA symbols and the localities these pronunciations were found in; there are also the various lexical expressions the respondents used in answer to the fieldworkers' questions. Table 2.3 is a simplified version of the data found in *The Dictionary and Grammar*, giving the headwords, the recorded words, and their pronunciations.

Intended as a guide to the full basic material of the SED, *The Dictionary and Grammar* has broadened the narrow phonetic transcriptions given in the SED itself to offer us an overview of the

Table 2.2 *Cat-related questions in the SED*

Headword	Book	Question
tom-cat	III.13.8	Now for the animal that goes miaow. What do you call the male?
tabby-cat	III.13.9	What do you call the female [cat]?
kitten	III.13.10	When she (i.e. a she-cat) is going to have young ones, you say she is going ...
	III.13.11	What do you call a young cat?

Table 2.3 *Cat-related headwords in the SED*

Headword	Lexical Variation and Pronunciation
tom-cat	cat, dick-cat, heeder, ram-cat, the mazger, toby, tom, tommy-cat
	tœmkat, tœːmkat, tamkat, tɑmkæt, tɑmkat, tɑːmkæt, tɒmkɛt, tɒmkɛət, tɒmkæt, tɒmkjæt, tɒmkjæː?, tɒmkat, tɒmkjat, tɒmka?, tɒmkət, tɔmkæt, tɔmkat, tɔmkjat, tɔːmkɛət, tʌmka?, tʊmkæt, tʊmkat, tʊmkjat, kat, dɪkkat, dɪkka?, dɪkkja?, iːdəˑ, ðə mazgə, tɔbɪ, tɒm, tɔm, tɒmɪkat, ɽamkat
tabby-cat	bess-cat, betty-cat, bitch-cat, chid-cat, chit-cat, ewe, ewe-cat, female cat, jen, jenny-cat, moggy, pussy, queen, queen-cat, queeny, she, she-cat, sheeder, sow-cat, tabby, tib, tibby-cat, tib-cat, tit, titty
	tæbɪkæˑt, tabɪkatʰ, bɛskat, bɛ?ɪkɛət, bɛt?ɪkæt, bɛd?ɪkæt, bɛ?ɪkæt, bɪtʃkat, tʃɪdkæt, tʃɪtkat, jɔː, jɔːkæt, jɔːkat, joːkkat, fiːmɛɫ kat, dʒɪn, dʒɪnɪkat, mɔgɪ, pʊsi, kwiːn, kwiːnz, wɪən, kwiːnkat, kwiːni, ʃəɪʃiːkjæt, 'ʃiːkɪˈat, ʃiːkjat, ʃiːkja?, ʃiːkɛt, ʃɪtẓiːkɛət, ʃiːkæt, ʃiːkat, ʃiːka?, ʃɛɪkjat, ʃɛɪkat, ʃəiːkæː?, ʃəɪkat, ʃiːdə, ʃiːdəˑ, sɛʊkɛt, tabɪ, tɪb, tibɪkæt, tɪbɪkat, tɪbkat, tɪt, tɪdɪ
kitten	after kitting, bound to kittle, going to chat, going have kittens, going to have some kittens, going to have young, going to kitten, going to kitten down, have her kittens, have kitlings, have kittens, have some young ones, in kit, in kitten, in kittle, is going to chat, is going to have her kittens, is going to have kits, is going to have kittens, is going to have some kittens, is going to kindle down, is in kitten, kindle, kit, kit down, kitten down, kittle, pup, she's in kit, to have kittens, to have some kittens, to kit, to kitten, to kittle, kit, kitling, kittling, kitty
	kɪtn, kɪtən, kɪt?n, kɪt?ən, kɪ?n, in kɪ?n, kɪtn, kɪtnz, kɪdn, kɪ?n, kɪ?nz, kɪt?n, kɪtən, kɪtənz, kɪt?ən, kɪtlɪn, kɪtlɪnz, kɪtlən, kɪtlənz

results and to point us to the respective volumes of the SED's full basic material for the detailed phonetic descriptions. In phonetics, a 'broad transcription' is more general, while a 'narrow transcription' is extremely detailed. In Section 2.4, we look at phonetics as a sub-field of linguistics in detail.

Dialect maps visualise the results. Recently, the Tweetolectology project has been making use of the SED data. As part of the project, the data from SED's basic material was digitised and then visualised with the programme QGIS. The result is a display of lexical variation

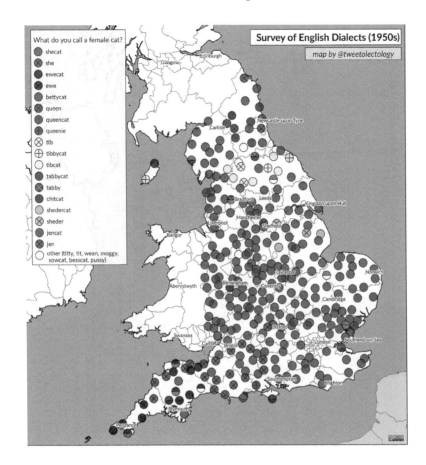

Figure 2.1 Female cat in SED

of female and male cats on a map (Figures 2.1 and 2.2). The circles in various shades on the map indicate the lexical variant of that particular locality.

Like the OED and EDD, the SED gives us a lot of detail on dialect variation for the cat-related words. The SED, however, is not the only big dialect survey conducted in the second half of the twentieth century. For Wales and Welsh English, for example, David Parry, who was a fieldworker for the SED, carried out the Survey of Anglo-Welsh Dialects (SAWD) in a similar fashion from 1968 until 1977.

In its phonetic section, SAWD too includes cat-related keywords. The keywords 'cat' and 'kitten' were asked for in the SAWD

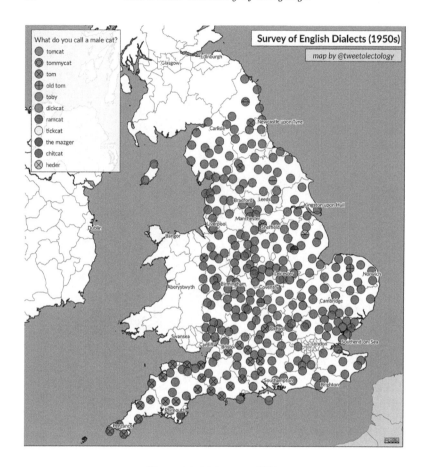

Figure 2.2 Male cat in SED

questionnaire, and, thus, there is a record of the pronunciation of 'cat' and 'kitten' in Wales. Though 'cat' and 'kitten' are not transcribed specifically, and their respective vowels are subsumed under the heading of [a] and [ɪ], it is clear that 'cat' is [kat] and 'kitten' is [kɪtn] in South East Wales. Both keywords have only been specifically named in connection with the pronunciation of the consonant /k/ in word-initial positions in a few of the investigated localities. 'Cat' and 'kitten' have been recorded with initial aspirated k [kʰ] in five localities in Mid Glamorgan, West Glamorgan, and South Glamorgan.

Another smaller dialect survey, carried out in the late 1990s, has looked at accent variation in Wales. Incidentally, it includes

Table 2.4 *Cat-related questions in survey of Neath English*

Number	Question
1	Some people like to keep pets – generally a dog or a ... CAT
2	When a cat is happy she begins to [i.] PURR
3	Birds have feathers but cats have ... FUR
4	What do you call a cat's foot? PAW
	Altogether a cat has four ...PAWS

cat-related keywords. My own research on the phonology of Neath English (South Wales) looks at the keyword 'cat' and additionally asks for 'purr', 'fur', and 'paw/paws'. In the questionnaire, which aimed at recording phonetic data, four questions are cat-related questions (Table 2.4). Following the tradition in dialect surveys, the keywords looked for are in capitals, and the abbreviation '[i.]'means that the fieldworker does an imitation, say, of a cat's purr, to indicate the keyword they are looking for.

Unlike SAWD, which has Middle English as a reference point for the description, my survey uses the system of lexical sets, which was introduced in 1982. The lexical sets, indicated by SMALL CAPS, refer to groups of words with the same pronunciation in a given language variety. The lexical sets TRAP, NURSE, THOUGHT, and KIT are relevant for our cat-related words. The words 'cat', 'purr', and 'paw/paws' belong to the lexical sets TRAP, NURSE, and THOUGHT respectively. If the keyword 'kitten' had been in the questionnaire, it would be part of the lexical set KIT.

When we describe the vowels in the keywords, we refer to the respective lexical set – in the case of Neath English, the TRAP vowel, NURSE vowel, and THOUGHT vowel – give the vowel quality, namely the degree of lip-rounding, tongue height, and length, and then mention any differences we recorded for the lexical set. The terms 'short/long', 'round/unrounded', and 'front/back' refer to the length of the vowel, the rounding of the lips, and the position of the tongue in the mouth.

The keyword 'cat', which belongs to the lexical set TRAP, is described as follows: the TRAP vowel in Neath English 'cat' is generally realised as a short open front vowel [a]. One difference has been recorded: TRAP in 'cat' occurred once as a half-long vowel as [kaˑt]. The keywords 'purr' and 'fur' are part of the lexical set NURSE. In Neath English, the NURSE vowel of 'purr' is the long half-close rounded front vowel [œː]. The keywords 'paw' and 'paws' belong to the lexical set THOUGHT, and in Neath English the THOUGHT vowel is typically the long half-open rounded back vowel [ɔː].

Having dialect surveys available means that we can compare words across time and space. When we look at 'cat' in Neath and in the SED, we can see that the vowel for 'the animal that goes miaow' shows quite some variation in vowel height and vowel length. In the SED, cat is [kæt], [kaˑt], and [kæːt], depending on the locality. The SED records also a diphthongal 'cat' as in [kɛət], and there are occurrences of [kɪ'at] and [kjat]. In Neath, the survey shows [kat] and one occurrence of half-long [kaˑt]. The consonants, too, have some variation in pronunciation: in the SED, the word-final /t/ in 'cat' is realised as [t], aspirated [tʰ], and the glottal stop [ʔ], while in Neath it is mostly [t]. It occurs only once as aspirated [tʰ].

When we include SAWD in our comparison of 'cat', we can see that in South East Wales, the vowel in 'cat' is generally [a], which makes my locality Neath typical for that dialect area of Welsh English. The keyword 'cat' is specifically mentioned in SAWD only once in connection with the consonant /k/, which in 'cat' is [kʰ] in four locations, while in Neath /k/ in 'cat' is always [k]. A comparison of Neath English and SAWD does not yield striking differences in pronunciation, which is hardly surprising in fact, as Neath is situated in South Wales and is close to the localities investigated for SAWD.

We have to be careful with a direct comparison, though, for two reasons. First, language changes with time. The SED and my survey are decades apart, with the SED being from the middle of the twentieth century and my survey on Neath from the end of the twentieth century. Secondly, the keyword asked for is slightly different. The SED asks for 'tom-cat' and 'tabby-cat', but my survey simply asks for 'cat'.

On a concluding note on the relationship of cats with dialectology, there are more dialect surveys than those mentioned here. The OED, EDD, SED, SAWD, and Neath English are just examples in which cats have found their place.

In the excursion into the relationship of cats with dialectology, we have already come across linguistic terms, such as 'dialect', 'accent', 'variation', 'dialectology' , and – although is not a linguistic term – 'cat'. Dictionaries and handbooks, like *The Cambridge Dictionary of Linguistics, A Dictionary of Linguistics and Phonetics*, or *The*

Handbook of Dialectology, give us definitions and explanations of these terms. So let us look at the terms in more detail.

First up is the term 'dialect'. A dialect is shaped by accent, by words, and by grammar. Linguistics defines dialect as a regional or social language variety identified by specific pronunciations, specific words, and grammatical structures. While a regional dialect tells people where a speaker comes from, a social dialect gives clues about their social background. Social varieties of a language are usually referred to as 'sociolects' and are discussed in sociolinguistics.

As we have already seen in Section 2.1, the way people pronounce the word 'cat' gives clues as to where they come from. Not only the pronunciation of cat-related (and other) words, but also the words themselves indicate the speakers' regional background. For example, the word 'moggie' tells us that the speaker is from the UK rather than from the USA.

This definition of dialect already lists the basic parameters to take into consideration when we mark off the linguistic range of cat-inspired language varieties. To approach the language used online in cat-related digital spaces in the way dialectology does, we need to study the variety systematically. As the definition of dialectology also mentions, a particular set of words and grammatical structures can be taken to classify a language variety.

In an analysis, we work our way from individual speakers to dialects and to language itself. We start with the linguistic habits of a single speaker – their idiolect. From a number of idiolects, we derive a dialect and, in one further step, from a number of dialects, we derive a language. The SED and SAWD we have come across in Section 2.1 recorded the idiolects of individual speakers and categorised them into dialect areas of the English language. The dialect surveys gathered data to analyse phonetic and phonological, lexical, and grammatical language variation.

Applied to the cat-related digital spaces, the dialectological method means that we immerse ourselves first in one cat-related digital space to analyse the linguistic habit of one cat account, then look at more cat accounts in the same cat-related digital space to arrive at a dialect of this particular cat-related digital space, and then repeat this process for other cat-related digital spaces to find a 'cat-inspired online language', or 'purriety'.

Our immersion in the cat-related digital space shows us straight-away that we are facing a different situation from the surveys mentioned in Section 2.1. We look at words and grammar but leave out accents. We cannot include pronunciation because the language in cat-related digital spaces is written and not spoken. While the cat account holders have different accents of English (including foreign accents), they share their posts in writing and use specific words and a specific grammar but do not speak, unless, of course, they share videos in which they speak. We could do a survey with the cat account holders, record their answers to the question, 'What do you call the animal that goes miaow?', and, using IPA symbols, transcribe what our respondents say. Such a survey, however, does not really answer our question on what language varieties are specific to cat-related digital spaces.

Yet, on a sidenote in a perhaps not very linguistic approach, we could regard the language purrieties of the cat-related digital spaces as a feline accent of English. In my online survey on the attitudes towards cat-inspired online language (see also Chapter 11), respondents have said that a purriety refers to 'how the cats would say it'. Let us go with this thought – unscientific as it is, since cats do not speak our language(s) – and regard the use of a purriety simply as an indication of Cat English, like Welsh English or RP. The accent would then indicate that the speaker is a cat. In the cat-related digital spaces, the word 'perfect' tends to be spelled 'purrfect' in the cat's voice. In real life, cats do indeed purr and might – if they were able to speak – pronounce 'perfect' as 'purrfect' in their feline accent. Yet, the real cat vocalisations are different as we see in Section 2.4, which describes the sounds cats can produce.

As we have already seen, dialectology looks at people's regional language variation. While cat-related digital spaces may not be regions in the traditional sense, they are not purely social regions either. The cat-related digital spaces extend beyond geographical borders and social backgrounds as people from all over the world and from various societal spheres meet online and communicate with each other.

On Instagram, I was very active with the cat account of Murrli, and she followed and was followed by other cat accounts. Among Murrli's friends were cats from the UK, the USA, Australia, Canada, Germany, France, Finland, Italy, the Netherlands, and many more countries. The common ground was neither a region nor a social background but the common love of cats, which found its expression in a specific type of language. In Murrli's case, the cat-related digital space is characterised by the use of meowlogisms and very specific hashtags.

2.2 Cats and Dictionaries

While a description of the feline territory of language cannot really discuss accent, it can, however, discuss lexical variation. As we have already seen in Table 2.3 and visualised in Tweetolectology's Figures 2.1 and 2.2, the SED has recorded a variety of words for the headwords 'tom-cat', 'tabby-cat', and 'kitten' in England. The male cat is referred to by the respondents as 'tom-cat', 'cat', 'dik-cat', 'heeder', 'ram-cat', 'the mazger', 'toby', 'tom', and 'tommy-cat'. The female cat is 'bess-cat', 'betty-cat', 'bitch-cat', 'chid-cat', 'chit-cat', 'ewe', 'ewe-cat', 'female cat', 'jen', 'jenny-cat', 'moggy', 'pussy', 'queen', 'queen-cat', 'queeny', 'she', 'she-cat', 'sheeder', 'sow-cat', 'tabby', 'tib', 'tibby-cat', 'lib-cat', and 'titty'. There is also quite a variety for 'giving birth to kittens' and 'kittens' themselves: 'to kit', 'to kittle down', 'to kindle', 'to have kittens', 'to have young', 'to chat', as well as 'kits', 'kitting', 'kittling', 'kittens', and 'young'.

To come up with a similar list of word variations and to compile a glossary or even a dictionary for the cat-related digital spaces, we can turn to dialect lexicography which, as the process of making a dialect dictionary, can tell us what to do. The aim of a dialect dictionary is usually either to have a reference work for practical or symbolic reasons or to keep a record of dialect words for the future. Thus, a dictionary or glossary of cat-inspired language varieties would have a practical use for people new to the cat-related digital spaces; it would also be a symbolic statement in giving the purrieties the status of a written language, and it would provide a written record for the future.

Regardless of what our aim is, we ideally focus on two questions when we plan our dictionary of words in cat-related digital spaces: What does a word used in cat-related digital spaces mean? How is a specific meaning expressed in these spaces? Additionally, we need to define whether we want to create a dictionary or a glossary. There is a difference between the two: a dictionary comprises the vocabulary of a language and organises the words in a systematic way. A glossary, on the other hand, is a list of words from, say, a text and is arranged in alphabetical order.

For cat-related words, there are both dictionary and glossary entries. As we have seen, the word 'cat' has, of course, already found its way into the more traditional dictionaries, like the EDD and OED. While undoubtedly useful and interesting, these dictionaries do not give us the specific meaning of 'cat' in the cat-related digital spaces. On the Internet, a source to turn to when we look for modern slang is the Urban Dictionary, which lists the current use and meaning of a word and gives us some insight into the meaning of 'cat' on the Internet.

The Urban Dictionary is a crowd-sourced database where people can leave their entries, which are then upvoted or downvoted with thumbs-up and thumbs-down. The orthography and grammar of the users submitting their definitions are left unchanged. At the time of writing, there were 484 entries for 'cats' in the Urban Dictionary. The entry called 'the top-ranked definition' is

Cats – Ninjas in fur suits with knives hidden in their paws (18 January, 2012) (Urban Dictionary)

The other entries are ranked down from 2 to entry 484, though not all of these entries refer to the feline; they are also used for people, as in 'a person, usually male and generally considered or thought to be cool'. The majority of definitions, however, do refer to the feline. In Entries 2 to 6 (Table 2.5), the image of the cat as a ninja is widened to an epic, fluffy, furry creature that will dominate the human race in the near future.

The Urban Dictionary gives us an inclination of how cats are seen on the Internet in general. The cat-related digital spaces are more cat-specific and, in order to create a dictionary or glossary of purrieties, we are using the approach of dialect lexicography. In our dictionary-making process, we need to follow certain steps. First, we should base our work on fieldwork; second, we should provide a written account of an oral variety; and third, we should account for geographical or social parameters.

The data on cat-related digital spaces in this book has been collected in online fieldwork with surveys and data scraping of posts in cat-related digital spaces, and differences between the digital spaces are taken into consideration. In preparation for the later chapters

Table 2.5 *Definition of 'cat' in the Urban Dictionary*

Entry	Definition
2	an epic creature that will shoot fire at you if you get near it. you can usually find one outside or near/in a house. its main abilities are to chomp and scratch but they can also pounce, shoot lasers out of their eyes, be cute, jump as high as they want, and fly. do not fight one unless you are equipped with extreme power armor and heavy assault cannons. its also better to bring multiple friends. dont say i didnt warn you when you get vaporized from being fooled by its cuteness. (20 February 2013)
3	A small, usually furry creature. It chooses when it will send or receive affection. They will either love you or completely despise you, there is no in-between. Will most likely control the human race in 50 years. (24 July 2014)
4	Cats are medium sized, fluffy felines. Cats love to play and cuddle, but don't be fooled by their cuteness; they have razor sharp claws that can slash out your eyes. But they're still very cute. (19 October 2011)
5	the most cuddly gifts from god. (24 January 2020)
6	A quite pleasant furry creature that vaguely resembles a meatloaf. Cats are the most intellectually superior creature on Earth. They are particularly adept at training human beings to do their bidding, and spend 18 hours a day on average apparently sleeping. What they are really doing is coming up with ways to take over the Earth while still retaining humans to make that yummy cat food for them. If cats had opposable thumbs, they, not us, would be the dominant force on this planet. (29 July 2007)

(Chapters 9–11), two of the three steps were taken, namely collecting the data in fieldwork (described in detail in Chapter 8) and accounting for virtual and social parameters (described in detail in Chapters 9–11). Our as-yet hypothetical dictionary of purrieties is different from other dialect dictionaries because there is no oral element, only a written variety of language in cat-related digital spaces.

Our next decision in making a dictionary of cat-related words is to decide whether to provide a dictionary based on concepts or a dictionary in alphabetical order. Then, we need to think if we want to provide descriptions of meanings, parts of speech, example sentences, etymology, or collocations.

While still undecided whether to compile a dictionary based on concepts or on entries from A to Z, I asked cat account holders in a

Table 2.6 *Questions of April 2019 survey*

Number	Question
1	Which words do you use when you talk about a 'cat' (Please write down as many words as you like)
2	Which words for *cats* do you like best? (Please write down as many as you like)
3	Which endearments do you use when you talk to a cat? (In case you talk to cats) (Please write down as many words as you like)
4	Which country do you live in? (Please write down or leave blank).

small survey in April 2019 how they refer to 'cat' in a neutral way and which endearments they use when they talk to their cats. The aim of the survey was to collect as many words as possible from cat account holders on Twitter, Instagram, and Facebook. Following the SED's and SAWD's tradition, the survey questions for the cat account holders were formulated along the lines of 'What do you call ...?' (Table 2.6).

In the April 2019 survey, 89 cat account holders shared cat words and endearments not just in English but also in German, French, Turkish, Russian, Danish, Dutch, and Slovenian. In this chapter, we consider only the English-language responses and keep the responses in other languages for Chapter 7, in which we discuss multilingualism.

Quite similar to the SED and SAWD, the responses are listed together with the locality where they have been recorded, without mentioning the frequency of a particular response. In terms of a dialect dictionary, the two lists from A to Z resulting from the survey are considered entries for the concepts 'words when talking about cats' and 'endearments for cats'. For the concept of 'words when talking about cats', there are 36 entries from 11 countries, and, for the concept of 'endearments for cats', there are 143 entries, also from 11 countries. The full list of words together with the localities is in the Appendix (Table A.1). When we want to talk about cats, we can choose among quite a variety of words.

baby, Bloody Cat!, bub, cat, catloaf, catpuss, catso, chonk, chonkster, Fat Cat, feline, fleabag, furry, in charge cat, kit, kitteh, kitter, kitten, kittie, kitty, kittycat, meower, mog, moggy, panfur, panther, pootchycat, puppy, puddycat, puss, pusscat, pusslet, pussycat, station cat, tattie, tat
(April 2019 survey responses for 'words when talking about cats')

The list of endearments for cats contains almost four times as many entries as long as the list of words for cats. The abundance of endearments indicates the positive emotion the account holders have for their cats. Cats are regarded as 'baby', 'cute', 'fluffy', 'furry', 'little', 'old', 'pretty', and 'sweet'. Some words like 'idiot', 'gremlin', 'goblin', 'Little Asshole', and 'moron' are not considered swearwords in connection with the cats. The full list of endearments is given in the Appendix (Table A.2).

angel baby, asshole, baby, baby boy, babycat, baby girl, beautiful, beauty, best, big boy, boy, bub, bubba, bubba baloo, cat, Cat the boss, catcakes, cat-cat, catkin, catlet, catpuss, catsy, chap, children, chubby, criminal, cute little murderer, cute stuff, cutie, darling, dear, doofus, dork, fat one, fatty-puss, feline overlord, floof, floofer, fluff, fluff nugget, fluffball, fluffpants, fluffycat, fluffynoo, furball, furry friend, furry thing, furrypurry, fuzzy, fuzzy tracksuit man, goblin, good bean, gremlin, handsome, honey bunches of oats, housebear, hunny bunny, idiot, jerk, kitcat, kitten, kitter, kittentail, kittie, Kitty, kittycat, kittypuss, lil guy, Little Asshole, Little Fuzz, little love, little monster, little mouse, little one, little shit, little tat, little thing, love, lovebird, lovely, Mamma's, m'dear, meat bag, meowcat, mittenpaw, mittentail, moglet, moggins, monster/monstie, moo, moron, mucker, my babies, my Dark Angel, my Prince of Darkness, my princess, my huntress, nasty beast, nerd, old bean, old man, old stick, perfect baby, pretty kitty, pretty lady, princess, puddy, puddy-tat, punkin', purball, puss, pusscat, pusskin, pusslet, puss puss, pussum, pussycat, sausage, scooter, shit butt, silly, smushie, snuggles, snuggle bug, squeaky, squishy, stanky man, stinkerooni, strange horse, sweet, sweet boy, sweet kitty, sweet thing, sweetheart, sweetie, sweetpea, sweetie-pie, sweetpuss, tattie-puss, The Kid(s)
(April 2019 survey responses for 'endearments for cats')

The respondents using words for cats and endearments for cats in English lived in 11 different countries:

Australia, Austria, Canada, France, Germany, Ireland, Montenegro, Netherlands, Turkey, United Kingdom, United States
(April 2019 survey localities)

To show how to use the data of this survey, let us look at two entries, 'catcakes' and 'puddy-tat'. In the survey, 'catcakes' occurred only in the United Kingdom, and 'puddy-tat' was recorded only in Germany. With regard to the localities, however, we cannot generalise the words to the whole of the population of a country. We cannot say, for example, that the entry 'catcakes' is only used in the United Kingdom or that everyone in Germany knows 'puddy-tat'. We cannot say either what the most frequently used expression is in a locality. The survey

Table 2.7 *Hits for 'puddy-tat'*

Entry	Website	Concordance Line
1	appliancesonline.com.au	killers (see right). True, there will be some hard-to-reach places the **puddy-tat** wont be able to get to. And although some say just the scent of
2	simplepickup.com	, but after realizing how chump-like that sound I'll just stop being such a **puddy-tat**. # J Dizzle # So I was dating this girl, who, due
3	pianoadventures.com	Contents: The Boogie Woogie March Fiddler on the Roof I Taut I Taw a **Puddy-Tat** Matchmaker (from Fiddler on the Roof) Once Upon a December (from Anastasia
4	petslady.com	typo there. The cat is named Pwditat. That is the Welsh spelling of **puddy-tat**, as in I tawt I taw a... She is a pretty
5	siliconchip.com.au	. Its average noise level is -127dBm. # Do you have a miscreant **puddy-tat** that likes to jump on kitchen benches (or worse)? It can
6	ohhla.com	ain't doin the trick, drop fucks make me sick cos this po' **puddy-tat** needs a cat nip And that motherfucker representin you, I think he resents you
7	alicublog.blogspot.com	of course, the p-word, father, the bad p-word, worse than **puddy-tat** – you know the one I mean! Let's go back to

just indicates that the person using 'puddy-tat' lives in Germany. We need further research before we can provide more information on the word's usage. That research includes looking for the word in dictionaries and in language corpora, which are large compilations of various texts.

When we search for 'puddy-tat' in the corpus iWeb, which comprises 14 billion words in 22 million webpages, we get seven hits (see Table 2.7), and going to the sources directly, we see that 'puddy-tat' has been used in Australia and the USA and that, interestingly, 'puddy-tat' is part of the lyrics of Coolio's song 'Mama, I'm in Love with A Gangsta' (Hit 6). As for 'catcakes', it appears only once in the iWeb corpus and refers to a recipe. In other words, there is not enough evidence to draw any conclusions for either 'puddy-tat' or 'catcakes'.

While the words in Tables A.1 and A.2 in the Appendix are lists in alphabetical order for two cat-related concepts, *The Comprehensive Unabridged Meowrihamb Blepster's Dictionary of Hambspeak (2019 edition)* provides an A to Z guide to the special words used in the Facebook community *This Cat is Chonky*. In there, we find the entries 'hamb', 'cloud', 'void', and 'tortie':

hamb (n): cat
cloud (n): white cat
void (n): black cat, also: hauspanther, soot sprite
tortie (n): a tortoiseshell cat (black, brown, and amber fur patterns)
tortitude (n): the state of being a tortie with attitude/charisma
(*The Comprehensive Unabridged Meowrihamb Blepster's Dictionary of Hambspeak* – 2019 edition)

Really strictly speaking, *The Dictionary of Hambspeak* is a glossary, but this is not the place for hairsplitting – or fursplitting. It is available online, and some words mentioned are used not only in that Facebook group but also in other cat-related digital spaces. The cat Rolo, the tortie with tortitude (Figure 2.3), is just as likely to show up on Facebook as on Instagram and Twitter.

In another survey conducted in 2018, I collected posts, captions, and comments from a black-cat digital space on Instagram, and using the words gathered in the survey, we can add to our dictionary using concepts. The dictionary shows which concepts are important and how the cat account holders talk about the various concepts. These concepts are feline-centric and include 'cat', 'food', 'people', 'days', and 'hashtags'. Table 2.8 gives a basic overview of the most important concepts for cats and cat-related digital spaces and of the main questions to be addressed.

As was the case with the many words for 'cat' and the endearments, the cat account holders use quite a variety of words and spellings. Chapters 3 and 4 discuss the parts of the words (morphology) and spellings making up the purrieties, and Chapter 9 provides the entries of our dictionary. In this place, only a few examples are given to illustrate the wide variety of vocabulary and spellings used in the cat-related digital spaces.

The language of cat-related digital spaces is written, which is why the cat-related dialect variation comes across in spelling and not in

Figure 2.3 Rolo, the tortie with tortitude

speech. The word 'perfect' is a good example to show the variation in spelling. The feline accent in 'perfect' is made visible in writing with the cat sound 'purr' and, perhaps (purrhaps) depending on the cat's purring intensity, appears as 'purrfect', 'purrrfect', 'pur-fect', 'PURRFECT', and even 'purrrrfect'. Also, the word 'friend', which is used to refer to cats and to humans alike, is written in different ways, as 'friends', 'furends', 'furiends', 'furrends', and 'furriends'.

As for lexical variety, we can look at how cats refer to their human owners. Cats tend to call their owners 'parents', 'pawrents', 'mom', 'mum', 'meowmy', 'humom', 'hoomum', 'humeowmy', 'hudad', 'hoodad', 'my human', 'humans', 'hoomans', 'human servant', 'two-legged servants', and 'staff', and there is also the occasional 'grand-meowmy' or 'grandpaw'. We discuss the mechanisms at work in these words (the meowlogisms) in Chapter 3.

Table 2.8 *Feline-centric concepts*

Concept	Question To Be Answered
animals (other than cats)	Which other animals are there in cat-related digital spaces?
cat	Which names are cats given by their owners?
days	What does a cat do on the various days of the week?
food	How does the cat refer to food and drink?
hashtags	Which hashtags are typically used in the cat-related digital spaces?
feline idioms	Which typical idiomatic phrases are used in the cat-related digital spaces?
people in the life of a cat	How do cats refer to their owners, their human family, and other people?
punctuation	Which punctuation marks and emoji are used in the cat-related digital spaces?
roles of a cat given by the human	Which roles do cats play online?
sounds of a cat	Which sounds do cats make online?

2.3 Cats and Online Dialectology

The Internet has already been used as a resource for dialectological studies, which have combined big data and dialectology. For example, the use of 'y'all' and 'yinz' for 'you guys' on Twitter has been linked to regions in the USA, and geocoded Twitter posts have been taken to identify regional variation in English in the USA and the UK. Not really incidentally, as we are dealing with online spaces, the data includes 'cat', 'kitten', 'kitty', 'puss', and 'meow', and, for the USA, dialect maps have been created.

Additionally, data collected on Twitter between 2013 and 2015 forms the basis of the app *WordMapper*. *WordMapper* is a free online tool available on https://isogloss.shinyapps.io/isogloss/, with which the interested public can create frequency maps and hotspot maps for the 10,000 most common words in American English. On the maps, the colour intensity indicates where in the USA the various words are most often used and where the hotspots are. Testing hotspots is a technique in spacial analysis to find geographic trends. The additional information at the bottom of the map refers to statistical methods and gives more insight into the values of the map (Figure 2.4).

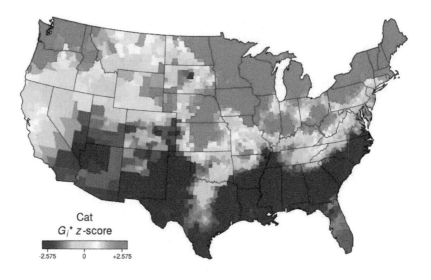

Figure 2.4 Hotspots for 'cats' on Wordmapper

WordMapper provides maps for 'cat' and 'kitten' as well as for 'kitty', 'puss', and 'meow'. A look at the context in which these words were used would clarify whether or not the word in question refers to the actual felines. Another version of *WordMapper* (Quartz version) maps almost 100,000 words that occur at least 500 times in the corpus and is available on https://qz.com/862325/the-great-american-word-mapper/. The map for 'meow' (Figure 2.5) has been taken from the Quartz version.

In addition to regional variation in internet data, there is also virtual variation as far as words in various cat-related digital spaces are concerned. The language used by the account @black_cat_crew and its followers on Instagram is different from the language of the members of the Facebook group *This Cat is Chonky.*

From a feline 'purrspective', it really does seem as if the cats of the two spaces have different accents of English and that the differences are dialectal. The members of the respective cat-related digital spaces communicate in that feline variety of English that is normally used in the respective digital space. The members and followers of the @black_cat_crew use meowlogisms and words related to black cats, while members of *This Cat is Chonky* use Hambspeak. The statement 'My (tom)cat Archer is a male semi-obese black cat, while his sister

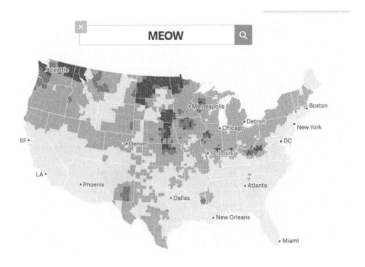

Figure 2.5 Hotspots for 'meow' on Wordmapper

is a tiny, skinny black cat. They are not fat fluffy cats, but their little paws are adorable' is rendered differently by the cat account holders in their respective digital spaces.

Hambspeak:
My boi Archer is a semi-chonk void hamb, while his sister is a smol void slonk. They're not thicc super-floofs, but their lil peets are adorbs.

Meowlogisms:
My boy Archie is a semi-big mini-panfur, while his sisfur is a skinny small mini-panfur. They're not fat fluffy floofs but their little paws are pawdorable.

Catspeak:
Wells, if Archer bees a tabby, himz cood bees a flabby tabby, n hims sisfur cood bees an itty bitty kitty. Meow twy to fink if anudder one Dr. Edith. Fink... Fink.... Fink.... 🐱💜

The original example, taken from an internet article about Hambspeak, has been put to the members of the cat-related digital spaces to be 'translated' to the respective variety. The version using meowlogisms, done by me, has been approved by the black cat community, and the catspeak version is the variation provided by Queen Pinky, a cat with her own account on Twitter. Although Queen Pinky has changed the black cat to a tabby cat in her suggestion, the three

Figure 2.6 Chairman Miaow from Lancashire

versions show the differences in vocabulary ('void' – 'panfur'), grammar ('his' – 'hims', 'is' – 'bees'), and spelling ('boi' – 'boy').

The tweet by Chairman Miaow, who won the #CatNamesWorld-Cup in May 2020, sums up the relationship of cats with accents and dialects perfectly: the sound cats in Lancashire make is 'miaow' (Figure 2.6) and not 'meow'.

Chairman Miaow thanks 🐾 @Number10Cat for the brilliant #CatNames-WorldCup idea, and everyone who voted in the competition- over23k in the final alone. Both cats came from Lancashire where cats Miaow 🐈 🌱 (Chairman Miaow)

2.4 Cats and Phonetics

Meow, meow, meow, meow
Tastes so good, cats ask for it by name.
(Meow Mix advertising slogan)

In truth, cats would ask for the Meow Mix with [miau]. The cat sound 'meow' consists of the bilabial voiced nasal consonant [m] plus the vowels [i], [a], and [u]. Combining phonetics, which usually studies the language of humans, with cat vocalisations may seem a bit of a stretch in a book on linguistics, but only at first glance. When we look more closely, we see that cats and humans produce sounds in a similar way. The vocal tracts of humans and cats are essentially the same, just differing in size and shape. Therefore, we can analyse the speech sounds in a similar way in phonetics. Using the phonetic symbols of the IPA, we can describe the purrs, trills, growls, hisses, meows, and shrieks of cats. The sub-fields of acoustic phonetics and articulatory phonetics tell us how cats use their voices and how they produce the sounds as part of the – literal – feline range of language.

Articulatory phonetics is the branch of phonetics that looks at how the sounds are produced by the speech organs. Like humans, cats have vocal organs, vocal cords, a hard and a soft palate, a tongue, teeth, and lips, which means the cat sounds can be described in phonetic terms and phonetic symbols we humans can relate to, such as the IPA symbols.

The abbreviation IPA stands for both the International Phonetics Association and International Phonetic Alphabet. The alphabet is the most widely used system to transcribe languages with phonetic notation. By using IPA transcriptions and other phonetic expressions, we can list the vowels and consonants cats produce, and a table of the feline vowel and consonant inventory is possible, just like for a human language. On a scientific note, though, the vowels and consonants are often similar to, but not exactly like, human consonants.

Phonetics uses two main categories to define speech sounds, namely vowels and consonants. Vowels are produced when the airstream flows smoothly over the upper surface of the tongue and are classified based on the so-called cardinal vowels. Phoneticians and dialectologists use the cardinal vowel system to show where the vowels of the language variety they study are articulated. The cardinal vowels are not real vowels of a particular language but have been defined arbitrarily as the standard set, and phoneticians and dialectologists learn how the cardinal vowels are pronounced and what their articulatory features are.

The vowels are classified according to the degree of openness of the mouth, the position of the tongue, and the degree of lip rounding. In the vowel chart (the more common name for the vowel quadrilateral), the cardinal vowels are placed on the exact points of the open, half-open, half-close, and closed mouth and the tongue position as front, central, or back. The vowel quadrilateral represents the mouth cavity.

The vowel chart of cat sounds

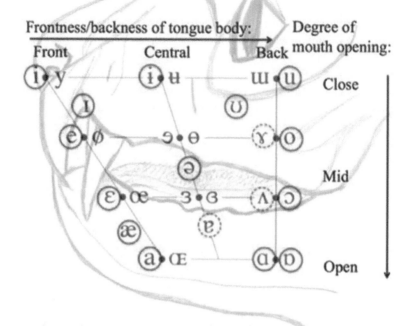

Figure 2.7 Cat vowel chart

Just like the vowel chart in the cross-section of a human head, the catified vowel chart has been placed in the cross-section of a feline head (Figure 2.7).

As we can see in the cat vowel chart (Figure 2.7), the feline vocalisation comprises 14 vowels, namely front [i], [ɪ], [e], [ɛ], [æ], and [a], then central [ɨ], [ə], and back [u], [ʊ], [o], [ɔ], [ɑ], and [ɒ]. These vowels have been recorded and occur in the various cat vocalisations. Interestingly, cats are able to produce rounded back vowels [o] or [u], although cats do not visibly protrude and round their lips as we humans do for the rounded back vowels. That said, cats open their mouth – or jaws – more for the vowel [a] and close their jaws more for the vowel [i] than humans can. The three vowels surrounded by dashed circles in the chart are theoretically possible for cats to produce but have not yet been recorded.

Consonants are the second category used by phoneticians to describe human sounds and are formed by modifying the airstream in the larynx, throat, or mouth. The airflow is either completely blocked or restricted, and audible friction is produced. Consonants are usually described in terms of place of articulation and manner of articulation. The IPA offers a table and symbols for transcribing the consonants, with columns to indicate the place and the rows to show the manner of articulation. Just like for the vowels, there is a catified version of the consonant table (Table 2.9).

As we can see in Table 2.9, cats produce 16 consonants, namely [b], [m], [f], [t], [r], [ɹ], [ʃ], [ş], [ç], [j], [k], [g], [ŋ], [ʀ], [ʔ], and [h]. Theoretically cats should also be able to pronounce [p], [d], [l], [w], [ɦ], and [ɥ]. The IPA do not include the sounds [w], [ɦ], and [ɥ] in their main consonant table, which is why they are not included in the table here either.

The place of articulation refers to the place in the mouth where the airstream is blocked or constricted by lips, teeth, tongue, palate, throat, or vocal cords. Cats are able to use their lips for bilabial [m] and to hold the tip of the tongue just behind their upper teeth for the alveolar [t], [r], and [ɹ]; the tongue a bit further back than the alveolar for [ʃ]; the tongue – sometimes curled back -between the alveolar ridge and the hard palate for retroflex [ş]; the tongue towards the hard palate for palatal [ç] and [j]; the tongue against the soft palate (velum) for [k], [g], and [ŋ]; and the tongue against the uvula for uvular [ʀ], as well as using the vocal folds for glottal [ʔ], and [h].

The manner of articulation refers to the type of constriction of the airflow. There are plosive, fricative, approximant, nasal, trill, and lateral consonants depending on how the articulators – lips, tongue, teeth, palate, and throat – interrupt and modify the airflow. The constrictions range from a complete block and sudden audible release, narrowing, which makes the airflow turbulent, to vibrating and to the air escaping through the nose. Cats can pronounce the plosives [t], [k], [g], and [ʔ], the fricative consonants [ʃ], [ş], [ç], and [h]. the trills [r] and [ʀ], the nasals [m] and [ŋ], and the approximants [ɹ] and [j]. In theory, cats are also able to produce the lateral consonant [l].

Articulatory cat phonetics divides the vocalisations into ten main types based on the cat's mouth position: two with a closed mouth, four with an opening-closing mouth, and four with an open tense

Table 2.9 *Cat consonant table*

	bilabial	labiodental	alveolar	postalveolar	retroflex	palatal	velar	uvular	glottal
Plosive	b, (p)		t, (d)				k, g		ʔ
Nasal	m						ŋ		
Trill			r					ʀ	
Fricative		f		ʃ	ʂ	ç			h
Approximant			ɹ			j			
Lateral			l (?)						

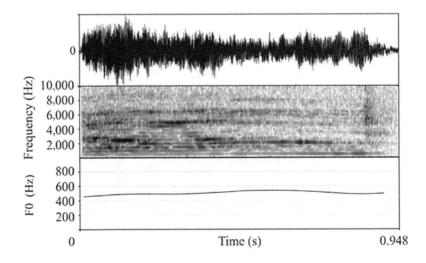

Figure 2.8 Turbo's meow in acoustic phonetics

mouth, namely purr, trill, meow, trill-meow, howl, the mating call, growl, hiss and spit, snarl, chirp, and chatter.

Acoustic phonetics deals with physical properties of sound and is based on the principles of acoustics. In their vocalisations, cats and humans produce sound in a similar way, and cat sounds share acoustic properties, like timbre and pitch, with human sounds. Therefore, we can measure cat sounds with the same phonetic instruments. One such phonetic instrument is the computer programme Praat, a freeware programme used by many linguists doing phonetics. The output of Praat for cats is similar to what we get for human sounds: waveform (top), spectogram (middle), and F0 (formant) contour (bottom). The example in Figure 2.8 is the visualisation of the meow sound of Turbo, a cat research purrticipant (Figure 2.9).

meow
(Turbo, a cat research purrticipant)

Cat phonetics has found that the cats' vocal repertoire is large and highly varied. Cats have learned how to get the attention of humans and are also able to recognise the voice of their human owners and their own names. Like humans, cats adapt their voice depending on whether their vocalisation is intended for humans or for other cats.

Figure 2.9 Turbo the cat research purrticipant

The cats use a higher voice in their human-directed vocalisations and have a wider pitch range when their vocalisations are directed to other cats. One such cat-directed vocalisation is the chirrup:

[mr̃ :h]: chirrup, bright and high-pitched, rising intonation, used during friendly approach and greeting

With this phonetic information about cat vocalisations, we can now compile a first version of a dictionary of feline language. Based on what research has found out so far, we divide the vocalisations into three main concepts: friendly and affiliative, agonistic, and prey-directed. The entries include phonetic transcriptions of the vocalisations, the meaning, and the context. In other words, our dictionary of cat vocalisations provides phonetic, semantic, and pragmatic information.

Concept 1: Friendly and Affiliative Vocalisations
meow, trill, trill-meow, purr
(Friendly Cat)

When cats are friendly, they vocalise meow, trill, trill-meow, and purr as signals. The meow and trill have several sub-types.

The meow is the eponymous cat sound. Cats produce meows with an opening-closing mouth, often starting with a bilabial consonant [m] or [w], continuing with one or more vowels, and closing their mouth again, occasionally adding an additional consonant, like [w]. Meows are voiced and usually loud and generally have a rising-falling tone, although they can also be pronounced with level, rising, falling, and falling-rising tones. Cats meow to get human attention, and their meows can be assertive, plaintive, friendly, bold, welcoming, complaining, and sad, which can be seen (or heard) in the different vowel qualities and varying pitch patterns.

The meow has four sub-types, namely the mew, the squeak, the moan, and the meow (or miaow), each with a different vowel quality. The mew is high-pitched with vowels like [i], [ɪ], or [e], as in [mi], [wi], and [mɪu]. The mew is associated with kittens wanting their mother's attention and adult cats in need of help. The squeak is high-pitched with a hoarse voice quality and somewhat nasal. It has an [ɛ] or [æ] vowel, as in [wæ], [mɛ], and diphthongal [ɛʊ]. Cats squeak when they want to cuddle, to play, or to get a treat.

The moan has vowels like [o], [u], and [ʊ] as in [moʊ] and [wuæu]. Cats moan when they are sad, discontent, frustrated, and demanding. It is the sound cats produce when they have been put in the cat carrier to be taken to the vet. The meow (or miaow) consists of a combination of vowels like [iaʊ] as in [miau], [ɛau], and [wɑːʊ]. Cats meow (miaow) to get their human's attention because they want food or to be let in or out the door.

Next up is the (feline) trill. To not confuse the trill of the cat with the category of trill consonants, which refers to the manner of articulation, the word 'feline' is put in brackets before the word 'trill'. The (feline) trill is a soft, short, and nasal sound, sometimes with a harsh voice quality. The (feline) trill has three sub-types, namely the chirrup, the grunt, and the murmur, which differ in their pitch.

Chirrups tend to be high-pitched and bright with a rising pitch, whereas grunts and murmurs are lower and darker with a level or falling pitch. The chirrup is pronounced [mr̃ːh] or [mːr̃ːt]. Cats usually chirrup when they approach in a friendly manner, greet, or would like some food or play. The grunt is dark, harsh, and low-pitched with a level or falling pitch. The grunt is pronounced [br̃ː]. Grunts signal greetings as well as friendly confirmations when the cats get something they like. The murmur – also called coo – sounds like a soft [m]. Unlike the chirrup and grunt, the murmur does not use a trill consonant. The murmur, too, serves as a greeting. Then there is the trill-meow (or murmur-meow), which is a combination of a (feline) trill and meow. The trill-meow has a very distinctive melody, starting with a low pitch in the (feline) trill or murmur, rising between the (feline) trill and meow, and ending with a considerably higher pitch in the meow. It is pronounced [mrhiauw], [mhrŋ-au], and [whrːau]. With trill-meows cats signal in a friendly way that they want something, like food or to be let out. The rising pitch seems to be an effective trigger for human attention

Finally, we come to the purr. Cats purr on their out-breath as well as on their in-breath – or on an alternating (pulmonic) egressive and ingressive airstream, in the proper phonetic terms. The purr's fundamental frequency is very low, which is why we hear every pulse of the purr and not a single tone. Cats pronounce the purr as [↑hːr̃ -↓hːr̃ - ↑hːr̃ -↓hːr̃] ad infinitum seemingly. The arrows [↑] and [↓] represent the egressive and ingressive airstream, respectively. The meaning of the purr depends on the context and the mental state of the cat, and it probably means something along the lines of the cat saying 'I don't pose a threat' or 'Keep doing what you are doing' as cats purr in very different situations, like when they are content, hungry, stressed, in pain, giving birth, or dying.

Concept 2: Agonistic Vocalisations
howl (yowl), growl, howl-growl, snarl, hiss and spit
(Cat in a cat fight, literally)

Agonistic cats howl (yowl), growl, howl-growl, snarl, hiss, and spit. The main purpose of agonistic vocalisations is for the cat to say 'Keep your distance, (fr)enemy!'. There is a relation between distance and type of agonistic vocalisation. Across longer distances, cats howl, growl, and howl-growl at each other; the closer our cats come to each other, they more likely they are to hiss and spit, and when they are finally in physical reach, they would snarl, scream, and let out pain shrieks.

The howl is also called yowl, moan, or anger wail. Howls tend to be quite long, and there are real cat duets of two opposing cats often lasting 30 minutes and more. When cats howl, they gradually open their mouth wider and then close it again and produce a vowel-like sound, usually two or more vowels or semi-vowels, such as [ɪ],[i], and [j], and repeated diphthongs, like [aʊ], [ɛʊ], [ɑʊ], [ɔɪ], and [ɑɔ]. Howls sound like [awɔɪɛʊ:], [jɪɛɑʊw], [ɔ:ɪɔɪɔɪɔɪɔɪɔ:ʊ], and [ɪ:aʊaʊaʊauawawaw]. The intonation of howls rises and falls slowly, and there is a wave-like rising–falling intensity. Cats howl in highly annoying situations – without physically fighting – and often combine it with the growl. The howl is intended to be threatening or defensive.

The growl is low-pitched, fairly weak, guttural, and long. When our cats growl, they hold their mouth slightly open in the same position, sometimes showing their teeth. Their voice sometimes creaky, cats produce deep trill consonants like [gʀ:], [ʀ:], and [ɹ:]. Sometimes cats start their growl with [m]. Growling means danger and is used to scare off an enemy.

The howl-growl is, as the name implies, a combination of a howl and a growl, where one turns into the other. The cat either starts with a howl and changes into the growl or starts with the growl, which then turns into the howl. The howl is vowel-like with a high rising-falling melody, while the growl is stable and low-pitched.

The snarl is also called scream, cry, or pain shriek and is a short loud sound, usually with a harsh voice. The snarls include vowels like [a] and [æ] as in [æ:o], while the pain shrieks are slightly different with short intense vowels like [æ], [ɛ], or [i]. Cats snarl when they are about to fight or are already fighting. The meaning of the snarl is not so clear-cut because some cats use the cry or shriek to signal pain, being in heat, or that they have caught prey.

In their hissing and spitting, cats hold their mouth tensely open, exposing their teeth and producing a fricative consonant. Hissing cats sound like [h:], [ç:], [ʃ:], [fi:], and [s̩:], and spitting cats produce more intense fricatives or even affricates like [tʃ:], [kh:], and [kʃ:]. Cats hiss voluntarily to warn or scare off another cat and involuntarily when they are surprised by an opponent.

Concept 3: Prey-Directed Vocalisations
chirp, chatter
'Here, mousey, mousey, mousey' by the Hunting Cat

Cats chirp and chatter when they see prey they cannot quite yet reach. Research says that chirping and chattering is a hunting instinct, and cats imitate the calls of birds and insects, on the one hand, and, on the other hand, vocalise their frustration at not being able to get to the prey.

Figure 2.10 Ma'a, Purr Reviewer 1

The chirp has three sub-types, namely the typical chirp, the tweet, and the tweedle. They differ in their pronunciation. For the typical chirp, cats produce a glottal stop [ʔ] followed by the vowels [ə] or [ɛ], often in a repeated sequence, like [ʔə], [ḵ ḵ ḵ ḵ ḵ ḵ], and [ʔɛʔɛʔɛʔɛʔɛ...]. Cats imitate the call of a bird or rodent with a chirp. Tweets are longer than chirps, and cats use an approximant like [w] instead of the glottal stop. The vowels differ, too. Tweets sound like [wi] or [ɦɛu]. In their tweedles, cats extend either the typical chirp or the tweet and modulate their voice. There is a clear tremor or quaver in their voice, and there is quite a variation in pitch and intensity. A tweedle is pronounced like [ʔəɛəɥə] and [waɛəɥə].

Chatter is also called teeth chattering. Cats produce a quick clicking sequence like [ḵ ḵ ḵ ḵ ḵ ḵ ḵ] or [ʔ ʔ ʔ ʔ], or even a voiced variation like [g d g d g d g d]. Cats probably use the chatter to practise their killing bite.

On a personal note, the name of my cat *Ma'a*, known as *Purr Reviewer 1* (Figure 2.10) in the digital spaces of academics with cats, comes from her habit of vocalising [mɑʔɑ]. She did that a lot as a youngster to announce herself when she entered a room. She is a very vocal cat, and my first impression of her was phonetic with her repeated [ç:] [ç:] [ç:] (hisses) and [gʀ:] [gʀ:] [gʀ:] (growls) to scare me off at our first meeting in the shelter, in which she obviously did not succeed.

Sources Used in This Chapter

🐾 Boberg et al. (2018a, 2018b) for dialectology

🐾 Hickey (2018) for dialectology

🐾 Penhallurick (2018) for dialectology

🐾 Van Keymeulen (2018) for dialect dictionaries

🐾 Wells (1982) for lexical sets

🐾 Markus (2019) for EDD

🐾 Parry (1977) for SAWD

🐾 Upton et al. (1994) for SED

🐾 Podhovnik (2008) for Neath English

🐾 Eisenstein (2018) for regional dialects on social media

🐾 Grieve (2013), Grieve et al. (2017) for regional dialects on social media

🐾 Davies (2013, 2018) for the iWeb corpus

🐾 Tweetolectology (2021) on the Tweetolectogy project

🐾 QGIS (2021) on the QGIS programme

🐾 Boersma and Wennink (2021) for Praat

🐾 Bradshaw (2014) for cat sounds

🐾 Turner (1995), Turner and Bateson (2014) for cat sounds

🐾 Schötz (2016), Schötz et al. (2016) for Meowsic project

🐾 Schötz (2018, 2019, 2020), Schötz et al. (2019) for cat phonetics

🐾 Brown and Miller (2013) for linguistic terms in the glossary

🐾 Crystal (2008) for linguistic terms in the glossary

Examples and Quotes in This Chapter

🐾 EDD Online: http://eddonline-proj.uibk.ac.at/edd/index.jsp

🐾 'cat' (2021) for the Urban Dictionary entry of 'cat'

🐾 'cat' n. (2021) for the OED dictionary entry of 'cat'

🐾 Kooser (2019) for the Hambspeak sentence

🐾 @_chrysalism_ (2019) for *The Comprehensive Unabridged Meow-rihamb Blepster's Dictionary of Hambspeak*

🐾 WordMapper (Quartz): https://qz.com/862325/the-great-american-word-mapper/ for the the hotspots *meow*

🐾 WordMapper: https://isogloss.shinyapps.io/isogloss/ for the Hotspots 'cat'

🐾 Tweetolectology (2021) for the SED maps

🐾 Schötz (2020, p. 340) for the cat vowel chart

🐾 Schötz (2018, p. 155) and Schötz (2020, p. 343) for the cat consonant table

🐾 Schötz (2020, p. 326) for Figure 2.8

🐾 Schötz (2018, 2020) for the IPA transcriptions of the cat vocalisations

Susanne Schötz has kindly allowed the use of all examples and figures.

Suggestions for PURRther Reading

🐾 Penhallurick (2018)

🐾 Schötz (2018)

3

Meowlogisms

Looking for cat names/puns based around historical figures.
(User on Twitter)

When the call for cat names for historical figures went out on Twitter at the end of April 2020, many people liked, commented, and shared that tweet. The user started with 'Winston Purrchill' and ended up with an amazing array of names ranging from 'Ruth Bader Ginspurr' and 'Furrdinand Meowgellan' to 'Mousey Tongue'. At about the same time, starting in March 2020, the #CatNamesWorldCup took place, run by Larry the Cat (@Number10Cat). In groups just like in the FIFA World Cup, 64 cat names were fighting for followers' votes in several rounds, and among the contestants were 'Freddy Purcury', 'William Shakespurr', 'Cleocatra', 'Jean-Clawed Van Damme', 'Jeremy Clawbyn', 'Jacob Fleas-Mogg', 'Elvis Purresley', 'Cat Damon', and 'Will Feral'. We know from Chapter 2 that Chairman Miaow was the winner.

Studying this list of cat names and puns, we notice a process typical for cat-related digital spaces, namely the formation of meowlogisms. These cat-inspired words 'purrfectly' illustrate with which chunks and mechanisms we create words. Here we are following the cats' lead into morphology to study the chunks (morphemes and lexemes) and word formation processes.

Then we turn to sound symbolism when we look at the words like 'purr' or 'hiss', which resemble the sound they describe. We continue onwards to find out why we find certain words funny in our discussion of the concepts of funniness and iconicity.

Cats and cat-inspired words are not limited to the digital places; we can see them in our surroundings, too. Signs, graffiti, advertising, and T-shirts, can display our relationship with cats. We discover that meowlogisms are a feature of the linguistic landscapes around us.

Concepts Discussed in the Chapter

🐾 morphology
🐾 word formation processes
🐾 semantics
🐾 sound symbolism
🐾 funniness
🐾 iconicity
🐾 humour
🐾 linguistic landscapes

Terms from the Clawssary

🐾 acronyms 🐾 affix 🐾 blending 🐾 clipping 🐾 code-mixing 🐾 compounding 🐾 conversion 🐾 iconic sign 🐾 iconicity 🐾 ideophone 🐾 lexeme 🐾 linguistic landscape 🐾 meowpheme 🐾 morph 🐾 morpheme 🐾 morphology 🐾 neologism 🐾 onomatopoeia 🐾 phonestheme 🐾 prefix 🐾 prosody 🐾 reduplication 🐾 sound symbolism 🐾 suffix

3.1 Meow in Meowphology

#Caturday

Even if we do not actively follow cats on social media, we will have come across the word 'Caturday'. The word for the cat-dedicated Saturday is very well known outside the cat-related digital spaces, too. Originally, 'Caturday' appeared on the platform 4chan on a very specific board (the /b/ board, which is used for random images) to identify cat photos posted on a Saturday. Soon, sharing funny cat images on a Saturday became a community practice among 4chan users, and the hashtag #Caturday to categorise the cat images developed. The rest is history, as the saying goes. Now #Caturday is very common in the many posts on various cat-related digital spaces and beyond. On a sidenote, we look at #Caturday with big data tools in Chapter 10.

'Caturday' is just one example of a meowlogism. The term – 'meowlogism' was originally invented as a word play on 'neologism', which is the term used to refer to a word newly introduced to a language either by borrowing or by inventing. In 2016, I wrote the blog post *Meow's the Word* on cat-inspired words I had found online – like 'mission pawsible', 'meowntain', 'meowtini' (Martini), 'furriends', 'pawsome', 'magificent meowdels', 'meowmy' (mummy), 'pawtrait', 'meowjestic', and 'meow' (now) – and called them 'meowlogisms' and 'meow-words'. Now, the term 'meowlogism' has found its way into the *Cambridge Encyclopedia of the English Language*:

And cat neologisms ('meowlogisms') such as purrfect are found across the media.
(Crystal, 2018)

Strictly speaking, meowlogisms are not really new words but feline-sounding varieties of already existing words. By altering the spelling of an existing word or by substituting a part of the word with cat-specific words, the word is given a feline angle. With the change of the letter 's' to the letter 'c', the syllable 'Sat' of 'Saturday' has been turned into 'cat' to form the feline 'Caturday'. The purrification or catification of words can be studied and described as a process in linguistics, namely as a process in morphology.

The study of morphology looks at the structure of words. In morphology, we divide words into small parts and talk about morphemes as the smallest chunks into which we can divide a word. Morphemes can be lexical and grammatical, which means that the small chunk either means something or fulfils a grammatical function. When we look at the word 'furiends' for example, we can identify two chunks, namely the lexical morpheme 'furiend', which carries the meaning of a person attached to another by feelings of affection or personal regard, and the grammatical chunk 's', which denotes the plural. The morpheme carrying lexical meaning is also called a lexeme.

In the case of meowlogisms, we are dealing with one more morphological chunk, the meowpheme. The lexemes (the chunks with the meaning) have an additional part, which catifies, or purrifies, the lexeme. The word 'furiend' has been made a meowlogism by inserting the meowpheme 'fur' to the lexeme 'friend'.

Strictly speaking, 'meowpheme' as a term does not exist in linguistics. That said, it does illustrate the morphological processes behind the formation of meowlogisms rather well: meowphemes carry the cat-related meaning in a lexeme and make a word feline. The term 'meowpheme' was suggested on Twitter in a discussion on linguistics

Katja Politt
@lingucat   ...

Welcome, class, to our intro to meowphology.

[ALT]

cc @Meow_Factor

Figure 3.1 Welcome, class, to our intro to meowphology

and cats. As we will see in Chapter 5, there are affinity spaces around
academics and their cats. The cat Gin in Figure 3.1, welcoming her
class to an introduction to meowphology, is shown in the typical role
of the cat helping out in teaching.

Just like meowphology and meowpheme (meowlogisms based on
morphology and morpheme), other linguistic terms can become
meowlogisms, too:

furneme and purrneme (phoneme)
purrfect and impurrfect tense
impli-cat-ure
purrliteness (politeness)
epurrstemic modality (epistemic modality)

Meownimalist Purrgram replacing the older framework of Transfurmational Grammar (Minimalist Program replacing the older framework of Transformational Grammar)
(#CatsInLinguistics #AcademicsWithCats)

The most common meowphemes are 'cat', 'meow', 'purr', 'fur', 'paw', 'hiss', and 'claw'. With these meowphemes, various words are catified, like 'cattitude', 'necromeowncer', 'purrfect', 'furiends', 'hisstory', 'pawsome', and 'clawsome'. Other meowphemes include 'puss', 'mew' (as a spelling variety of 'meow'), 'litter', 'kitten', 'mrow', 'panther', 'tiger', and, of course, 'mouse'. Any cat-related word can become a meowpheme as long as a connection to the cat is recognisable. The many answers to the call for historical figures mentioned at the beginning of this chapter show the various meowphemes in action:

Aaron Purr, Adele Purry, Alexander Pusskin, Andrew Catson, Anne Meowlyn, Anne of Clawves, Anne Purrleyn, Archduke Fur-dinand, Ben Eat a Mouse-Alini, Bill Purray, Bobcat Marley, Boudiccat, Cardinal Richelmew, Cat herine the great, Cat Stevens, Catavaggio, Caterine the Great, Catherine Meoward, Catherine of Purragon, Catherine Purr, Catimir Purrtin, Catlitter the Hun, Catnip Hepburn, Catnipsy Russel, Catpurrnicus, Cats Domino, Chairman Meow, Chairman Miaow, Charles Lickens, Charles Meowrice de Taileyrand-Périgord, Christofur Clawumbos, Clawed Debussy, Clawed Monet, Claws von Bulow, Cleocatra, Cleopawtra (and Meowc Antony), Copernicat, Copernipuss, Copurrnicus, David Ben-Purrion, David Meowie, Don Kitty-Ote, E.P. Tomcat, Edgar Alan Paw, Eleanor Purrsivelt, Elizabeth Cat-y-Stanton, Elizabeth the Purrst, Elizapet Purren, EmFeline Pankhurst, Emily Lickinson, Emmanuel Le Roy Litterbox, Emperor Catligula, Enrico Furr-me, Eric Hobspawm, Eva Purron, Evita Purrrrone, Feline of Purrgell, Fidel Catstro, Field Marshal Mikhail Catuzov, François Litterrand, Franklin Purrsevelt, Franz Furdinand, Furnand Brrrreoowdel, Furrdinand Magellan, Furrdinand Meowgellan, Fuzz Aldrin, General Blackcat Purrshing, General Eisenmeower, General Purrman, Genghis Kat, Genghis Khat, George Bernard Paw, George Meowshington, Grace O'Meowlley, Guido Paws, Guy Pawkes, Hampurrabi, Hilary Rodham Kitten, Hisstopher Columbus, Ian Meowsby, Isaac Mewton, James Meowdison, Jane Pawsten, Jane Seymeowr, John Belshaw, John Catams, John F Kittendy, Jonathan Edpurrds, JP Meowgan, JRR Tailkin, Konrad Adenmeower, Leo Catstoy, Lord Kittenchener, Lord Kitty-chener, Luke Skywhisker, Macatma Ghandi, Marcus Pawrelius, Margaret Catcher the Iron Kitty, Margaret Scratcher, Margcat Thatchfur, Marie Purrie, Marie Puuuurie, Martin van Purren, Meow Zedong, Meowcalm X, Meowdicea, Meowiweather Lewis, Meowlexander the Great, Meowpatra, Meowpoleon, Meowses, Meowsollini, Meowtezuma, Mewdicca, Mewgaret Patches, Mewhamad Ali, Michel Foucat, Moggy Queen of Scots, Mother Theresa of Calcatta, Mousegret Catcher, Mousey Tongue, Mrowsputin, Napoleon Bonapurr, Napoleon Bonepaws, Napurrleon, Nathaniel Pawthorne, Nebucatnezzer, Neville Chamberlion, Neville Litterpan, Ni-Cat-a Krushev, Oedipuss, Pablo Piclawso, Pantherny and Cleocatra, Pawblo Picasso, Pawgustus, Pawl Pot, Pawsimodo, Pope John Paw II, Princess Mewgret, Purrack Opawma, Purrcahontas, Purrerre Trudeau, Purrgood Marshal, Purrham Lincoln, Purrnest Hemmingway, Purrnie Clawnders, Purrnie Sanders, Purrris Hilton, Purrseidon, Purrsephone, Purrseus, Queen Cattoria, Queen Elizapurrs, Raspurrtin, Richard the Purred, Rosa Luxempurrg, Ruth Bader Ginspurr, Ruth Catter Ginspurr, Ruthapurrd B. Hayes, Salomeow Alexanpurra, Sir Isaac Mewton, Sparcatus, Tabby Roosevelt, The Great Catsby, Theodore Pussyvelt, Theopaw Roosevelt, Tutancatmun, Whisker the Conqueror, William Meowart Tafft, William S. Purroughs, William Shakespaw, William Shakespurr, Winston Purrchill, and Wolfgang Amadeus Meowzart.

By including the meowphemes in the names, the users have created new words by following certain linguistic processes. In English and many other languages, there are some general ways of forming new words, namely the processes of prefixation, suffixation, conversion, and compounding. In prefixation, a so-called affix is added at the beginning of the base word, so adding the affix 'mini' to 'panther' or 'panfur' makes 'mini-panther' or 'mini-panfur'. Suffixation is the same process just at the opposite end of the word, with the affix coming at the end of the base word, such as '-ise (-ize)', as in 'to pantherise', which is 'panther' and 'ise'. The third general process is conversion, which means that one word class is turned to another without a change in form, like the noun 'cat' becoming a verb in 'to cat', and finally there is compounding, which is the process of putting two base forms together, as in 'paw' and 'circle' becoming 'pawcircle'.

The word 'pantherise' is a verb that can be used by black cat owners. The black cat Raven on Instagram (Figure 3.2) gives us an explanation of it in her post, having created the words with prefixation with the affix 'de-' in 'depantherise' and additional suffixation with '-isation' for the noun 'depantherisation'. As Raven is from the US, she uses the US spelling with '-ize' and '-ization' in her post.

Mom was a bit under the weather this weekend so I got to have a lot of couch cuddling time. But when I get in her lap, she always becomes incapacitated and can't do anything. This has become such a problem that she has coined the term #pantherized to explain it: "Can you bring me a glass of water? I can't get it myself because I am being pantherized." "Can you put the laundry in the dryer, or do I have to depantherize myself to do it?" "I'll make dinner as soon as I am done with the depantherization process."
(Raven on Instagram)

ravenvonmaven • Abonniert　···

rainbow bridge. We are being
#Naughty　　　we hope you join
us.

Mom was a bit under the weather this
weekend so I got to have a lot of
couch cuddling time. But when I get in
her lap, she always becomes
incapacitated and can't do anything.
This has become such a problem that
she has coined the term #pantherized
to explain it: "Can you bring me a glass
of water? I can't get it myself because I
am being pantherized." "Can you put
the laundry in the dryer, or do I have to
depantherize myself to do it?" "I'll
make dinner as soon as I am done with
the depantherization process." •

Gefällt　　　　　und
weiteren Personen

Figure 3.2 Raven explaining 'to depantherise'

Here, another process has taken place, though not a morphological process but a meaning-related one. The words 'panther' and 'panfur' have undergone a semantic change from its dictionary meaning of 'a black leopard (=a wild cat) or a cougar' to 'black house cat'. Often the word 'mini' is added to the beginning of the word to make clear that we are dealing with a cat – 'a mini-panther' or 'mini-panfur' – and not a real panther.

Apart from the 'mini-panfurs', there are also 'mini-tigers', like Cat Jeoffry (Figure 3.3), and 'mini-lions' in the cat-related digital spaces. To the cat owners among us, this view of moggies as big cats is probably not surprising as the cats themselves tend to project that image to us, their human servants. The allusion to the 'tribe of the tiger' was recognised and immortalised in the poem 'Jubilate Agno' by Christopher Smart in the eighteenth century.

In addition to prefixation, suffixation, conversion, and compounding, there are more word formation processes: reduplication, clipping, acronyms, and blending. All these processes are found in cat-related digital spaces. There is reduplication as in 'itty-bitty kitty', which is a type of compound where the two elements are the same or slightly different. Another word-forming process is clipping as in 'nip' short for 'catnip'. Clipping refers to an informal shortening of a word, New words can also be formed as acronyms, as in 'bcc' for

Figure 3.3 Cat Jeoffrey – For he is of the tribe of tiger

'@black_cat_crew' or '#tot' for '#TongueOutTuesday', simply by taking the first letters of the words making up the name. A special kind of acronym, a fake acronym, has been created from the word 'vet' (a clipping of 'veterinarian'), which some cat account holders change to the acronym 'V.E.T.' so as not to scare the cat by mentioning the real thing. And there is blending, like 'pantheriffic' or 'Caturday'. Blending describes the process of merging two words into each other, such as blending 'panther' and 'terrific' and 'cat' and 'Saturday' to get to 'pantheriffic' and 'Caturday'.

In the cat-related digital cat spaces, these word formation processes regularly occur in quite a condensed space. For example, the cat Arwyn uses both blending and clipping in a single post when she talks about 'chillaxing', a blend of 'chilling' and 'relaxing', in her 'shroom', which is a clipping of 'mushroom' (Figure 3.4). There is one

Moxxi is burb watching from her tower. I am #chillaxing in my 'shroom. #catsoftwitter #cat #lazy

Figure 3.4 Tweet by Arwyn

more feature in Arwyn's post, namely 'burb watching', which is 'bird watching'. While birds also play a role in the lives of cats, 'burb' is not really a meowlogism but a feature of Arwyn's cat-inspired idiolect (for cat-inspired idiolect, see Chapter 4).

Moxxi is burb watching from her tower. I am #chillaxing in my 'shroom.
#CatsOfTwitter #cat #lazy
(Arwyn)

Meowlogisms make the English language sound more cat-like and create the feeling of the cats speaking with their very own feline accents. In general, people use meowphemes for those parts of the words that are similar in spelling and/or pronunciation.

Strong similarities in orthography and phonetics lend themselves to easily becoming meowlogisms. The very well-known meowlogism 'purrfect' is a case in point. 'Perfect' and 'purrfect' are pronounced the same. The spelling differs in two letters only and both words have the NURSE vowel and the same consonants. The word pair 'sister' and 'sisfur' is more similar in pronunciation than in spelling. While the consonants /t/ and /f/ differ, the unstressed vowel in the second syllable is the same, namely the unstressed vowel as in lettER.

On the other hand, 'parents' and 'pawrents' have different vowels and seem closer in spelling with only one additional 'w'. 'Parents' has the TRAP vowel, while 'pawrents' belongs to the lexical set of THOUGHT. Some meowlogisms are similar in both spelling and pronunciation, such as 'claw enforcement' and 'law enforcement'. 'Claw' and 'law' both belong to the lexical set THOUGHT and differ in one letter only. While similarity in spelling and/or pronunciation governs the choice of meowpheme, a specific meowpheme can also bring across a different feline aspect, as the example of 'claw' and 'paw' in Pawfficer Donut's job in 'claw enforcement' as well as in 'paw enforcement' shows. The explanation of the two existing forms is as follows:

Paw Enforcement protects the community. Claw Enforcement lays down the law on bad guys.
(User on Twitter)

Some meowlogisms have been created with more freedom, like 'Mousey Tongue' (the example given in the introduction to this chapter), which refers to the historic person Mao Zedong, the Chinese leader. Although a similarity in spelling and pronunciation exists, some imagination is needed to understand the meowlogism. In the examples, the Chinese leader has also been referred to as 'Meow Zedong', 'Chairman Miaow', and 'Chairman Meow'.

Yet, not just for the name of Mao Zedong but also for some other meowlogisms, spelling variants exist. The reason for the spelling variation is the fact that the meowphemes 'purr', 'fur', and 'meow' may be written in different ways. The case of 'meow' is straightforward; the cat's meowing sound is listed as 'mew', 'miaow', and 'meow' in the dictionaries, which explains the spelling variation in the meowlogisms. By the way, there are slight differences between 'mew', 'miaow', and 'meow', as the result of a quick search on question and answer forum Quora shows:

Question: What is the difference between these words: "mew", "meow" and "miaow"? If none, which variant is prefered?
Depends on were [sic] you live and the exact cat expression you want to evoke. "Meow" is the standard US spelling of the bog-standard adult cat noise. "Mew" usually suggests a quieter sound, especially the noise kittens make. "Miaow" is not the go-to US spelling, but it common elsewhere.
(Quora.com)

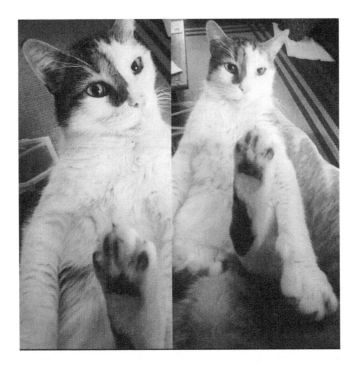

Figure 3.5 Kirky Turkey doing peer remews

The other two meowphemes, 'purr' and 'fur', are recorded in the dictionaries only with exactly this spelling. Yet, in meowlogisms, 'purr' and 'fur' is spelled differently, and meowlogisms of 'perfect' and 'friend' display a varying number of the letter 'r' – probably reflecting the intensity of a cat's purr: 'purfect', 'purrfect', 'purrrfect', 'purrrrfect' as well as 'furiends' and 'furriends'.

In general, there is no limit to people's creativity in coming up with meowlogisms in the cat-related digital spaces. The formation of new words is an ongoing process, and I regularly come across new meowlogisms. Examples of such 'first occurrences' are the word 'tiny necromeowncer', which I saw on Twitter for the first time at the end of June 2020 referring to a tiny black cat scaring off a big dog, and 'peer remews' (Figure 3.5), which was used by Kirky Turkey's owner, an academic. Up until April 2020, I had recorded only 'purr review(s)' for the peer reviewing process in academic publishing.

Meowlogisms are not limited to the English language but also occur in other languages. In French, 'Caturday' is used alongside

its equivalent 'chamedi' (a blend of 'chat' and 'samedi'), and there
is 'Chatmone de Beauvoir' for Simone de Beauvoir. In Spanish,
the meowlogism 'advogato' has been used for a former stray cat
that has made an 'advocato's' (a lawyer's) office his new home and
'gatitectura' for the special architecture of a cat's cardboard box, and
in German, a 'Mittwoch' (Wednesday) might be a 'Miezwoch' ('Mieze'
is another word for 'Katze'). The meowlogisms I have observed in
other languages are formed with the respective words for 'cat'.

In sound, languages have onomatopoeic words such as English miaow, a verb
imitating the noise produced by cats
(*The Cambridge Dictionary of Linguistics*)

The question to address now is why meowlogisms are so popular
in cat-related digital spaces and beyond. As we have seen in Section
3.1, the meowphemes in the meowlogisms carry the meaning of 'cat',
and people really do enjoy playing with words. Additionally, the
meowphemes 'purr', 'meow', and 'hiss' imitate the real sounds of a cat,
which makes the pretence of having a feline accent more believable.
When we take a look at what linguistic research has found out, we
find that research on iconicity – or sound symbolism – and humour
provides some answers. After all, 'purr', 'meow', and 'hiss' are onomatopoeic, and meowlogisms are fun. Chapter 11 shows us, though,
that some people think the meowlogisms are not funny but silly.

In language research, there is the understanding that individual
sounds (the phonemes) do not have a meaning and that the relationship between words and meaning is arbitrary, which means that
sounds and meaning do not have a – let's call it – logical original
connection. This claim of arbitrariness, however, is not entirely true as
there is increasing evidence in research that spoken words (phonemes
and clusters of phonemes) can in fact be iconic, or put differently,
that the words do sound like what they mean. Linguistic research
has shown a balance of arbitrariness and iconicity in the spoken
vocabulary of languages. Thus, the likelihood that the meaning of a
word has developed with or without a connection of form and meaning
may be equal.

The terms 'iconic' and 'iconicity' refer to the resemblance between
word form and meaning, and the research on the English language
has shown that iconicity is considered highest in onomatopoeic words,
in verbs, and in words related to the five senses. Among these words

from the sensory domain, verbs referring to sound and touch are more iconic than those referring to sight, taste, and smell.

Languages also have so-called ideophones in their vocabularies, like the ideophones 'sara-sara' for smooth surfaces and 'zara-zara' for rough surfaces in Japanese. These ideophones have the highest iconicity rating and indeed sound like what they mean. The ideophones have characteristic properties in grammar and pronunciation, and we experience a vivid, sensory-motor imagery when we pronounce ideophones like 'sniff', 'snout', and 'sneeze'. The phoneme cluster of initial /sn/ is said to refer to meanings related to the nose and the final /ɪf/ to the noise of breath or liquor. Phoneme clusters related to a particular meaning are also called phonesthemes. A word of warning needs to be inserted here: there is also a statistical regularity between phoneme clusters and meaning that has nothing to do with ideophones.

In *The Cambridge Dictionary of English*, the verb *meow* has been included as the example of an onomatopoeic word, and while only some onomatopoeic words are ideophones, they can be considered ideophone-like. If we say that there are also ideophones in English, which is a statement some researchers may find contentious, we could see the meowphemes 'meow', 'hiss', and 'purr' as English ideophones. The words are from the sensory domain as 'meow' and 'hiss' relate to sound and 'purr' is connected to both sound and touch.

There is nothing canine or feline sounding about the words DOG and CAT. These words are arbitrary. If you did not know English, you would not be able to guess the meanings of the words.
(Winter et al., 2017)

To test the iconicity of words, a study conducted in 2017 asked almost 1,600 people to judge the iconicity of 2,409 English words. The quote above is from the introductory text of this study. The participants rated the words based on a scale from −5 ('words that sound like the opposite of what they mean') to +5 ('words that sound like what they mean'). Perhaps not surprisingly, the word 'hissing' is among the three top-rated words, with a rating of 4.46. In the study, several statistical tests were used to make the results reliable, to account for phoneme combinations unrelated to sound symbolism, and to show the connection between iconicity and the senses. The data is available on the Internet and includes the following cat-related

Table 3.1 *Iconicity and percentiles*

Word	Iconicity	Percentile
hissing	4.46	100
hiss	4.15	100
purring	3.75	99
purr	3.54	98
meow	3.5	98
fluffy	3.5	98
meowing	3.5	98
fluff	3.21	97
furry	2.1	86
cat	0.54	41
kitten	0.1	24

words: 'cat', 'kitten', 'purr', 'purring', 'hiss', 'hissing', 'furry', 'fluff', 'fluffy', 'meow', and 'meowing'. Their rating is given in Table 3.1.

Apart from the words 'cat' and 'kitten', the meowphemes are rated as rather iconic, with iconicity ratings of 3.5 and above. Percentile, a term used in statistics, refers to the percentage of items with a lower rating. In our case, the percentile refers to all the words sounding less like what they mean than, say, 'hissing', and we can see that all words – or 100% of the words – show less iconicity. Phrased differently, no other word shows more resemblance between sound and meaning than 'hiss' and 'hissing'. The meowphemes occurring in the data of the study have a high iconicity score as the words 'hiss', 'purr', and 'meow' are related to sound and 'fluff', 'fluffy', and 'furry' to touch. So, while the word 'cat' may not be feline-sounding and is, thus, arbitrary, the words for the sounds a cat produces and sense-related words connected to cats are iconic.

Another study looks at humour and at the connection between humour and language. In 2018, two psychologists asked people to provide humour words on a crowd-sourcing platform. Almost 5,000 words were collected and rated on a scale from 1 ('humourless – not funny at all') to 5 ('humorous – most funny') by 821 participants. The outcome of this study is so-called humour ratings for the collected words, which should help to shed more light on why people appreciate different kinds of humour. Humour has actually been studied for a long time, and many theories about humour have been developed.

Table 3.2 *Humour norms for cat-related words*

Word	Mean	Male	Female	Young	Old
fluff	3.72	3.73	3.71	3.48	4.08
mew	3.44	3.6	3.21	3.47	3.41
puss	3.3	3.31	3.29	3.54	3.12
tomcat	2.81	2.62	2.95	3.14	2.56
purr	2.8	2.31	3.36	2.56	3.17
fur	2.71	2.64	2.76	2.74	2.67
paw	2.385	2.142	2.56	2.47	2.23
claw	2.09	1.89	2.29	2.21	2

Whatever the theory, humour – like cats – has a positive impact on our well-being and health.

In this study, too, various statistical tests have been used to interpret the data, and overall results indicate that more words are considered humourless than funny and that there are gender and age differences in the perception of which words are funny. The dataset is available for download, and it, too, includes some meowphemes, namely 'claw', 'fluff', 'fur', 'mew', 'paw', 'purr', 'puss', and 'tomcat'. Table 3.2 shows the values.

In the dataset of the study, we see not just the overall ratings for the cat-related words ('mean') but also how male and female participants ('male/female') as well as young and old participants ('young/old') have rated the words. Generally, the cat-related words are considered humorous, with 'fluff' leading the humour rating, followed by 'me[o]w', with 'claw' in final position. We can also see a variation in the various categories, 'male/female' and 'young/old'. With all these figures, however, we need to be careful not to draw conclusions too soon as we need some proficiency in statistical methods to see whether the differences are 'statistically meaningful'. In any case, the word 'fluff' would deserve further research as there is a change in funniness and humour based on age.

Humour and fun are indeed research-worthy subjects. In 2019, other psychologists extended the 2018 study on almost 5,000 English words and found a method to rate and predict the funniness of previously unrated words. Their method has been used on a corpus of three billion words. The outcome includes the following. First, words which are not so common and have an unorthodox spelling and/or pronunciation are considered funnier. Second, the more words violate people's expectations, the more they are perceived as funny. Psychology refers to this as the incongruity theory of humour. Third, there are specific semantic attributes of words considered funny. Only partly consistent with the superiority theory, which sees denigration as the basis of humour, the specific attributes of meaning include more than scorn, namely insult, sex, party, animal, bodily function, and expletive.

The model to rate funniness and humour is based on ten predictors. The dataset, for which the model calculates the figures, also contains cat-related words 'catkins', 'catnap', 'catnip', 'cats', 'claws', 'fluff', 'fluffy', 'furry', 'hiss', 'kitten', 'kittens', 'meow', 'paws', 'purr', 'purring', 'pussycat', 'pussycats', and 'tomcat'. A table with the figures for these words would require too much explanation of the model, which is why we are not going into the figures, although the data is available.

This study from 2018 is relevant because meowlogisms show the characteristics of funniness, namely unorthodox spelling and pronunciation, violation of people's expectations, and specific semantic attributes: the spelling of meowlogisms is non-standard, violating the writing norms people expect, and meowlogisms carry the meaning of cat.

In January 2020, a study was published that combines humour and iconicity – the two concepts we have been looking at so far – and says that words sounding like what they mean (ideophones) are fun to say. Ideophones often have elements of play in pronunciation and spelling and are used for dramatisation and entertainment. The study goes further and says that the words perceived as funny stand out from other words because they have specific phonotactic patterns and structures deviating from other words. In linguistics, these specific patterns and structures are called 'structural markedness'.

This structural markedness in language is like a signalling beacon that draws attention to the word itself and thus makes it playful, poetic, and performative for the language users. It is like a signal that says 'this is play'. It is not only the meaning of the word itself but also its particular pronunciation and/or form that make it funny. The study is based on a large dataset to show that playfulness and iconicity are connected. Simply put, highly iconic words are highly funny, and words not considered iconic are seen as not so funny. For us,

Iconicity and funniness (n = 70200)

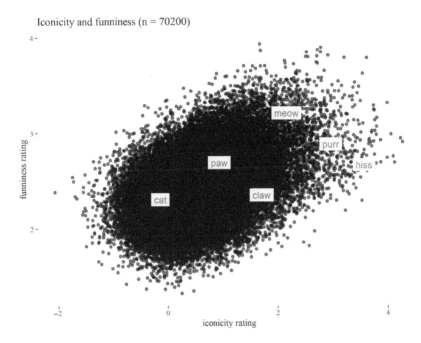

Figure 3.6 Funniness and iconicity of cat-related words

words with expressive prosody (pitch, loudness, tempo, and rhythm of speech) and playful morphology are both iconic and playful. Once more, a word of caution is needed: not all funny words are iconic, and not all iconic words are funny.

This 2020 study also included some cat-related words: 'cat', 'claw', 'paw', 'meow', 'hiss', and 'purr'. A so-called scatterplot (Figure 3.6) shows how these words are rated in comparison with all the other words in the study. Each of the 70,200 words (indicated by the 'n' in the figure) has been plotted as a point in the coordinate system, with the x-axis showing the iconicity rating and the y-axis the funniness rating. While 'cat' is not particularly high in either rating, we can see that 'paw' and 'claw' are rated higher and that 'meow', 'purr', and 'hiss' are furthest up in the rating. As has already been mentioned in the other studies, 'hiss' is one of the most iconic words rated, and 'meow' and 'purr' are considered the funniest of the meowphemes.

Although the studies have included a number of meowphemes, the actual meowlogisms have not found their way into the data yet. When we apply the various criteria mentioned in the studies, we can conclude that the meowlogisms are structurally marked and, thus, signal 'Attention! This is play' to people. Meowlogisms have an unorthodox spelling, and people used to 'normal' words will be alerted to the different spelling, to the meowphemes in the word formation, and to a different pronunciation of the meowlogisms. If we were to pronounce the meowlogisms, we would find them playful and iconic as we are pretending to imitate the cats' accents.

3.2 Meow in Public Spaces

I am feline good right meow.
(Writing on a mug)

Like cats, meowlogisms are everywhere if we care to look, regardless of whether we use meowlogisms ourselves or not. On social media, sponsored posts keep popping up that advertise products with meowlogisms on them, like the mug in the example above. In the media, too, meowlogisms are used when a cat story hits the news. Memes and linguistic forms spill over from the virtual world into the real, or rather offline, world, and when I am wearing T-shirts with 'Meowee Catmas' or with 'Quit stressing meowt' on them, people can see the meowlogisms as I am carrying a language variety displayed on my T-shirts into the public space.

The research into linguistic landscapes studies the visual representations of language in public spaces, like road signs, advertising boards, street names, place names, shop signs, public signs on government buildings, and more. All these signs form the linguistic landscapes in a specific territory. Linguistic landscapes research is a part of sociolinguistics as it describes how the signs and visual representations reflect the role of language in society or societies. Research is done in urban regions as well as in rural areas to show the linguistic diversity and multilingual contexts of society. Linguistic landscapes record change in language and society.

Various factors play a role in the creation of linguistic landscapes, and there are ethnic, political, ideological, commercial, and economic factors that interact with each other. Signs may reflect language policies in place. The official language policies regulate the signs of an official nature, but the non-official signs, like commercial and private signs, are usually not affected. Linguistic landscapes research differentiates between 'top-down signs' (official, dominant) and 'bottom-up signs' (non-official, individual).

In linguistic landscapes, minority languages may become visible on official top-down signs. While it has been argued that signs make minority languages visible, give status to the languages, and express vitality and actual linguistic behaviour, research has also pointed out that putting minority languages on signs only has an economic value (e.g. for tourism), and reduces them to tokens of leisure and consumerism.

Unless cats have their own political agenda to rule the world, which is a thought not entirely uncommon in the cat-related digital spaces, meowlogisms are usually not ethnic, political, or ideological. The work by Parisian artist Laure Lamaison photographed on a street in Paris, France, is an exception as the cats in the drawings 'Les chattes de l'histoire' (The Female Cats of History, Figure 3.7) are the feminist icons Simone de Beauvoir, Agnès Varda, and Assa Traorè, whose names have been made into meowlogisms in French as 'Chat-mone de Beauvoir', 'Agnes Var-chat', and 'As-chat Traorè'. The caption on Instagram by @therealhappycatlady says

Met the cat version of Simone de Beauvoir, Agnès Varda & Assa Traoré when taking a stroll in Paris! 🐾(Fuck off to the douchebag who tried to remove Assa Traoré 😼 Taken aback by the fact that feminist icons are now calmly accepted while antiracism is still widely contested in France) (@therealhappycatlady)

Among the ubiquitous cats in the public sphere, meowlogisms with a political and ideological meaning are very rare. Commercial and economic factors, however, have had an influence on the use of meowlogisms in the public space. Perhaps it is more correct to say that business has made talking about pets – and especially cats – as companion animals acceptable in society, which is reflected in the use of cat images and meowlogisms on consumer products. The concept of the crazy cat lady is no longer derogatory, as we have seen in Chapter 1, and some memes have crossed over from the virtual world into the real world, like cats seeing themselves as tigers. In that sense, the display of cats and meowlogisms in the public space does show a societal change and does have a kind of ideological background. A side note is needed here as well: this societal change is not limited to cats but also includes other animals.

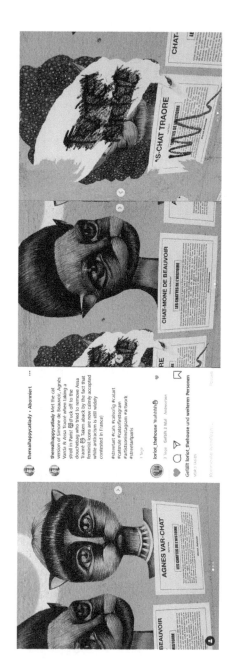

Figure 3.7 Les chattes de l'histoire

Figure 3.8 Cat graffiti in Graz, Austria, and Glasgow, UK

Another issue in linguistic landscapes refers to the physical placement of signage and the mode of signage. In other words, where a
sign is placed and how the sign has been made tells us something
about its meaning, its relevance, its function, and its relationship to
society. Graffiti and tattoos are found in different places and have
different meanings from, say, shop signs or road signs. That said, the
meaning of the graffiti in Figure 3.8 is not so clear apart from the
fact that graffiti can be words or illustrations. The graffiti on the left
reading 'Katze' (cat) is in Graz, Austria, and the mural showing cats
is located in Glasgow, UK.

The presence of an English saying in the German-speaking environment in Austria signifies how far English has spread as the language of
globalisation. The sentence 'Home is where my Miezekatze is', written
on a placemat bought in Austria, is a mix of English and German. The
German word 'Miezekatze' (cat) has been inserted into the English
sentence. Regardless of whether the local population is proficient in
English or not, the English saying 'Home is where my heart is' is
known in Austria, and the writing on the placemat makes sense to
the population.

In addition to indicating the status of English, the writing on the
placemat also points to another linguistic process, namely language
mixing. Also called code-mixing, this can happen when people are
bilingual or multilingual, and it is often reflected in the signage in a
community. Code-mixing often occurs in linguistic landscapes, and,

like the placemat, signs use two or more languages. The code-mixing may result in borrowings of words, pronunciation, spelling, and grammar on the signs. When code-mixing, people can be highly creative in their linguistic landscapes. Chapter 7 talks about multilingualism and code-mixing in greater detail.

The linguistic landscape for cat-related signs and meowlogisms is dominated by economic and commercial factors. In other words, they are classified as bottom-up and informal signs. T-shirts, jumpers, mugs, and more are used to display very frequent meowlogisms, like 'feline good right meow', 'Meowy Catmas', or 'purrfect'. In my newsfeeds on Instagram, Facebook, and Twitter, I often see adverts for such goods as the algorithms have me characterised as somebody who would buy cat-related goods.

Meowlogisms also occur in more official channels, like literature and the news media, which might give them a more approved status. Claiming that meowlogisms have, thus, also become top-down signs may be too far-fetched, but the fact remains that meowlogisms have passed some sort of editing test and have received a stamp of approval.

In popular fiction, books apparently written by cats have been published. One example of a feline author is the cat Curious Zelda, who has published a handbook for cats. Zelda, who is named as the main author of the book, uses a number of meowlogisms to describe her life as a cat and to advise other cats on how to manage their humans to get the best treatment. In Zelda's own words:

I'm purrmanently startled
Consistently I'm shook!
Unearth a spooky mewniverse
Inside my quirky book!
(Tweet by CuriousZelda on 25 January 2020)

Meowlogisms also underline the feline purrspective of the settings and plots in the book series *The No. 2 Feline Detective Agency* by Mandy Morton. Meowphemes like 'paws' and 'tabby' feature quite prominently in the book titles *The Death of Downton Tabby* and *The Ghost of Christmas Paws* as word plays on the TV series *Downton Abbey* and the character in Charles Dickens *A Christmas Carol*. In *The Cat and the Pendulum*, the detective duo Hetty Bagshot and Tilly Jenkins (Figure 3.9) are faced with a 'claw-biting case'. In the books themselves, there are 'Tabby Road Studios', 'feline interest stories' in the news, a character named 'Alfred Hitchcat', and 'tabby

Figure 3.9 Hettie and Tilly

chic'. Feline linguistic landscapes are created on T-shirts with the writing 'Littertray' on them and with addresses like 'Sheba Gardens', 'Whisker Terrace', 'Much-Purring-on-the-Rug', and 'Pontymog'. We come back to the feline purrspective and human perspective in Chapter 9.

The news media, too, makes use of meowlogisms in their stories. Not only tabloids but also quality media include the occasional 'purrfect', 'cattitude', and 'paw prints' in the headlines, photo captions, and body of the text when the article is on a cat. In my study on meowlogisms in which I analysed 79 news stories, I found that all the news sources I analysed, namely the BBC, *Daily Mail*, *The Sun*, and *The Guardian*, give their articles a feline spin with meowlogisms. The most common meowphemes in the media are 'cat', 'meow', 'purr', and 'paw'.

Meowlogisms are quite common in positive cat-related news. Searching for the keyword 'cat', we will come across meowlogisms in the news, like 'cat-astrophe', 'fur real', 'hiss-tory', 'cat burglars', or 'purrsonalities'. While the number of meowphemes in the news is smaller than in the cat-related digital spaces, creativity and meowlogisms have their place in the news media, too.

Purrfect.

Sources Used in This Chapter

- Dingemanse et al. (2020), Dingemanse and Thompson (2020) for iconicity and humour
- Winter et al. (2017) for iconicity and humour
- Engelthaler and Hills (2018) for language and humour
- Westbury and Hollis (2019) for language and humour
- Crystal (2010, 2018) for morphology
- Holmes and Wilson (2017) for linguistic landscapes
- Van Mensel et al. (2016) for linguistic landscapes
- Galtung and Ruge (1965) for news values
- Brubaker (2008) for LOLcats and media
- Podhovnik (2016) for cats in the media
- Schötz (2018) for the real language of cats
- Mahler (2020) for language in dog-related digital spaces
- Crystal (2008) for linguistic terms in the glossary
- Brown and Miller (2013) for linguistic terms in the glossary

Examples and Quotes Used in This Chapter

- Winter et al. (2017, p. 437) for quote on cats and dogs
- Winter (2016) for dataset
- Engelthaler (2017) for dataset
- Larry Number 10 (2020): #CatNamesWorldCup
- Claw enforcement and paw enforcement: example provided by Loren Sztajer on Twitter
- Brown and Miller (2013, p. 217) for quote on miaow
- Crystal (2018, p. 459) for 'meowlogism'
- Katja Politt in a tweet for 'tiny necromeowncer' https://twitter.com/lingucat/status/1274983829770469381?s=20&t=8aJPynV8NoRTZa-FcK38AA
- Question on Quora: www.quora.com/What-is-the-difference-between-these-words-mew-meow-and-miaow-If-none-which-variant-is-prefered
- Mark Dingemanse, personal communication for scatterplot
- Laure Lamaison has kindly permitted the use of her artwork in the book. The photographs published on Instagram were taken by @therealhappycatlady.

- Curious Zelda: https://twitter.com/CuriousZelda/status/12211244 86541561857?s=20
- Mandy Morton: *The No2 Feline Detective Agency.*

Suggestions for PURRther Reading

- Crystal (2010, 2018)
- Holmes and Wilson (2017)
- Podhovnik (2018)

4

Da Kittehz

kitteh
Online usage of the word "kitty" or "cat". Found most often in the context of lolspeak, or in the anthropomorphism of cats in pictures and other media.
OMG I wanna pet teh kitteh!
by kittehz 9 September 2007
('kitteh', 2007)

When we google 'cats on the Internet', the first hits among the search results offer us LOLcats. Although the cativerse comprises a lot more than funny cat memes, the LOLcat is still regarded by some as the typical cat of the Internet. The phrase 'cats on the Internet' (or 'kitteh' as the Urban Dictionary says) evokes the famous memes of Grumpy Cat, Ceiling Cat, the Cheezburger Cat, and Nyan Cat. Together with the LOLcat, sites like Wikipedia mention LOLspeak, which is the language associated with LOLcats.

For this chapter, therefore, the LOLcat is the perfect subject to study more closely. We first look at the visual side of the LOLcat meme and find out what differentiates a cat meme from snapshots of everyday life. In order to do so, we find out more about semiotics, which is the study of signs. Then we describe LOLspeak, with its typical spelling, vocabulary. and grammar. With the help of a 'kitteh', namely Lilly the Syntax Cat, we go into the syntax of LOLspeak and look at examples of grammatical language variation.

Yet, as we have seen in Chapter 1, the presence of cats on the Internet has gone far beyond the LOLcat universe, and there is more to online cat life than the LOLcat meme and LOLspeak. In this chapter, we discover that LOLspeak is only one online language variety among others and that individual cat account holders and various online groups have developed their own ways of talking about their cats online.

Concepts Discussed in the Chapter

🐾 semiotics
🐾 special internet language variety (SILV)
🐾 ludlings
🐾 pidgins
🐾 morphology
🐾 syntax
🐾 idiolects

Terms from the Clawssary

🐾 creole 🐾 ludling 🐾 morphology 🐾 pidgin 🐾 pidginisation
🐾 semantics 🐾 semiotics 🐾 sign 🐾 substrate and superstrate
🐾 substratum 🐾 suffix 🐾 syntax

4.1 Kittehz and Semeowtics

For internet cats, English uses the words 'kitteh' and 'LOLcat'. In other languages, too, people have found specific expressions to refer to the ubiquity of cats and cat memes on the Internet. The German language, for example, calls cats on the Internet 'Cat Content' or 'Katzencontent', and in Russian people say 'котэ' (kote), which means 'cats' or 'kitties'. Why cats and the Internet are so interconnected is the topic of Chapter 5, in which we look at cats in participatory culture, so we are not going into that now.

Maybe because the topic of cats and LOLcats is judged as too cutesy and not serious enough, only a handful of scientific publications on LOLcats are available for us to draw on in our own research. Some of these publications study the syntax of LOLspeak, which we will be looking at in Section 4.2. The other available studies discuss LOLcats and their relation to semiotics, which is the theory of linguistic and non-linguistic signs. For memes, which consist of text (the linguistic signs) and images (the non-linguistic signs), semiotics gives us insights into online cat photo sharing.

Online cat photo sharing goes back to the beginning of the new millennium. As early as 2000, the posting of cat photos became a common activity in the English-speaking world in email messages and on so-called memetic hubs, like 4chan. Some of these early birds – or rather cats – were active for a long time. The blog *My Cat Hates You*, for example, posted cat pictures until 2016, and *The Infinite Cat Project* (www.infinitecat.com), which features cats looking at other cats looking at other cats ad infinitum, is still ongoing. The first cat, Frankie, was posted in 2004, and the latest cat is Oliver, 'watching Shelly watching Knucklehead watching...', who joined the infinity queue as cat #1856. Cat photos, which have to fulfil certain criteria to be added to the so-called infinity queue, were still accepted for the project in 2020.

Then came the time of the LOLcat. The term 'LOLcat' is made up of the Internet acronym 'lol' ('laughing out loud') and 'cat' and refers to image macros, which are user-generated images composed of a photo and a superimposed text.

lolcat
A photo of a cat doing a seemingly-innocuous thing, with large text superimposed. Sort of an offshoot of the orly owl. Also called cat macros
"I made you a cookie but I eated it", "ceiling cat is watching you masturbate", and "I see what you did there" are good examples of lolcats.
by Yet Another Josh Cohen, 9 February 2007
('LOLcat', 2007)

While the history of the term 'image macro' is obscure, it could have originated in the forum called *Something Awful*, where it was used to describe photos with captions. Very quickly, LOLcats took off on 4chan and YouTube, launched in 2006, and became mainstream on the website *I Can Haz Cheezburger?* in 2007. This still-active website, also referred to as ICHC, made LOLcats viral.

Published in 2012, the entry for 'cats' on the website https://Know YourMeme.com calls cats

culturally influential and relevant on some of the largest media-sharing communities and publishing networks such as YouTube, Tumblr, Reddit and Cheezburger.
(KnowYourMeme.com, 2007)

Although the popularity of some social media channels has changed and new social media has come into our lives, the statement is still true. Cats, and not just LOLcats, are still influential on social media.

Semiotics sees the LOLcat macros as similar to news images with their captions and silent movies with their intertitles. Both captions and intertitles help us in our interpretation of the image and create a semiotic relationship between text and visual content.

The view of the semiotic relationship between text and image is based on the theory of Roland Barthes, a French theorist, who said that it is the text that attaches the meaning to the visual image and that we as the readers or viewers create the meaning based on the text. The practice of captioning a photograph is common in the news media, and we are used to the photo captions telling us what we are seeing in the photograph. The same principle applies to the LOLcat image macros. The caption in the LOLcat macro suggests to us how we are supposed to interpret the cat.

While one reason for the LOLcats' popularity is that creating and sharing LOLcat images is easy, their success lies more in the use of the superimposed text. Just like in silent movies, the captions on LOLcat macros function either as dialogues or as explanations. Accordingly, the captions are called dialogic and expository. In silent movies, dialogic intertitles refer to the utterance of a character on screen, and expository text indicates the voice of an omniscient narrator.

For LOLcats, the same stylistic conventions and points of view are used: on an image, the text is either said by the cat, which means the caption is like the part of a dialogue, or the LOLcat's creator makes a statement about the intended meaning of the picture, which makes the caption act as an explanation. The choice of caption, whether a dialogue or explanation, impacts on the choice of language: dialogic captions are written in LOLspeak, and expository captions are more likely to be in standard English. Choosing LOLspeak in the caption means that it is the cat talking, while standard English indicates the LOLcat's creator. The relationship of language and identity is a field of sociolinguistics, and we go into the connection of purrieties to cat identity in more detail in Chapter 7,

In addition to the text style, there is also the visual component of the captions that is seen as typical for LOLcats: the original typeface for LOLcats on 4chan was a white Impact typeface with a thin black line, a style that was carried over to other LOLcat spheres. Despite technical advances, the captions are still written as text and have not been substituted by soundbites on the digital images of LOLcats. Silent movies with their intertitles have disappeared, but the LOLcats have not been swept away by new technologies. They are still there for us to analyse.

In semiotic terms, cats represent cultural units in the online world. By looking at how kittehz are portrayed in online communication, we can study the online world. There used to be a division of the online world into the Internet and the Social Web. The Internet was located at the periphery and the Social Web in the centre of the Web. Both these spheres had their own ways of creating meaning, of using text, and of leading their online lifestyles. The cat had a special place in all this because cat images featured in both spheres but were used differently.

On the Internet, cat images were posted as memes to make the Web more playful again. In general, memes represented the characteristics of the Internet, its anonymity, playfulness, humour, and parody. The memes were a typical product and, at the same time, a key element of the Internet. The memes are essentially anonymous as their creators are unknown; they are playful, are being repeated, and occur in many varieties. Some historic and very famous memes include *I Can Has Cheezeburger?*, *If it fits I sits*, *Business Cat*, and *Chemistry Cat*.

An example of humorous trolling with cats is the hashtag #GattiniSuSalvini in Italy in 2015, when activists posted cat macros on a politician's Facebook page. The *Progetto Kitten* (kitten project) created kitten macros by using photographs of Matteo Salvini, the leader of the right-wing party *Lega Nord* in Italy, and shared the kitten macros to Salvini's Facebook page to protest against Salvini's politics. In semiotic terms, this is a 'reductio ad cattum' because all the actions are thus reduced to a cat on the Internet.

The cat images shared in the Social Web were reflections of people's daily lives. In the Social Web, users tended to see their online lives as extensions of their real lives. While humour did undoubtedly exist, the Social Web was more about reflecting the seriousness of everyday life, and people took shared content seriously.

Memes have now become mainstream. Grumpy Cat, whose real name is Tardar Sauce and who died in 2019, is perhaps the LOLcat meme par excellence. Tardar Sauce's photos posted on Reddit in 2012 became an instant hit because her apparently scowling and frowning expression were ideal for meme creation, and she has actually become a meme icon. The term 'meme icon' means that one and the same image has been used with various captions, and there are other cat memes referring to Grumpy Cat memes.

An online survey of 2019 claims that cat owners take seven photos of their cats each day. Whether the results of this survey – conducted by a marketing agency for a cat litter producer – are true or not is beside the point here. The important thing to take away is the fact that we do take photos of our cats and do share them online.

For many of us, cats are persons with their own thoughts, their own emotions, and their own individuality. When we share our cat images in our cat accounts, we socially construct our cats as persons. Sociologists say that the concept of person hood is not a pre-existing category but a social construct, which means that we can give and indeed often award animals the status of a person. In our online cat accounts, we show our cats as family members, talk about feline caretaking, share our cats' biographies, and engage in mourning rituals. For us, our cats are persons with the same familial and social functions as humans.

The anthropomorphic character of cats makes them ideal for memes and, combined with feline idiosyncrasies and clichés, there is no limit to human creativity when it comes to cat memes. As the example of LOLcats shows, cats can easily be anthropomorphised because people often perceive the cats' faces as blanks just waiting to be filled in. Regarded as simple repositories of meaning, cats, like other animals, can be made to mean anything and everything.

When we look at images, we experience anthropomorphism in two forms, namely weak and strong. Very broadly speaking, image macros and mass-produced commercial photographs evoke weak anthropomorphism, and so-called vernacular photography, which essentially refers to snapshots of everyday life, produces strong anthropomorphism in us.

Weak anthropomorphism in cat photographs means that, for us, the cats have the human ability to think but nothing more. We only see the humorous side and, by doing so, may actually deny the cats any humanness or even the status of a living being. To express what they have to say in image macros like LOLcats, the cats do not need any other human traits apart from the the ability to think. While the creators of LOLcat images might not intentionally wish to ridicule the animal in the image, the animals themselves serve only as instruments for humour, which attaches an element of human arrogance to the whole endeavour.

When we experience strong anthropomorphism, however, we feel that the cat indeed possesses the human characteristics and abilities shown in the image, and we see them as persons. Vernacular cat photos present our daily life with cats. An analysis of Reddit images shows that most cat images are vernacular photos and that for their owners, the cats are persons. Cats are intelligent, have a language, are able to imagine a future, can solve problems, and can choose alternatives. Judging from the owners' beliefs, cats are also able to share meaning and adopt the roles of other cats when it comes to initiating play, for example. Cats can act intentionally and meaningfully, and through the photographs we share, we award them the status of a feline person.

4.2 Kittehz Can Haz LOLspeak

lolspeak
An extremely complicated language that is often mistaken for textspeak. It is mainly used for Kitteh pictures, but people don't realize that there's a huge organization running lolspeak. There is even a bible translation project going on where they will translate the entire bible into lolspeak. Ceiling Cat is the god behind this language. It's not as easy as you think, trust me.
lolspeak iz difehcualt too lern, an yu noe itt.
(lolspeak is difficult to learn and you know it)
('LOLspeak', 2010)

The definition of LOLspeak in the Urban Dictionary gives us a vague idea of what LOLspeak is: it is used for kitteh pictures, it is complicated, there is a Bible translation project, and there is Ceiling Cat. But there is more to know about LOLspeak, and if we want to base our observations of linguistic practices in cat-related digital spaces on a systematic analysis of LOLspeak, we need to look at existing research.

Despite the immense popularity of LOLcats, LOLspeak has made only a very light impact on linguistics and the social sciences. Searching the scientific databases ScienceDirect, EBSCO, SpringerLink, Emerald Insight, and Google Scholar in July 2020 only yielded a handful of results for the keywords 'LOLcat' and 'LOLspeak'. There are only a few 'hoomans what studiez teh kittehs', but those who did look at the 'kittehs' include actual LOLspeak in the titles of their publications, like 'Cats Can Has Grammar', 'wants moar', 'Srsly Phenomenal', 'I Can Haz Language Play', 'ZOMG! DIS IZ A NEW LANGUAGE!', and 'Who run the world?'.

Apart from illustrating examples, LOLspeak is used also in headings and sub-headings in two of these publications. The LOLspeak subheadings 'I R IN UR HISTORIEZ' (I am in your histories) and 'k thx bai' (OK, thanks, bye) appear in a research paper called 'wants moar'. In the linguistic study 'I Can Haz Language Play', the authors use LOLspeak practices in the sub-headings, and we find 'oh hai!' ('Introduction'), 'how teh LOLkittehs was maded?' ('The origins of LOLspeak and LOLcats'), 'what teh kittehs sedz?' ('So what is LOLspeak?'), 'hoomans what studiez teh kittehs' ('Work on LOLcats'), 'grammarz, how we makez it' ('A "sketch grammar" of LOLspeak'), 'kthxbai! Srsly' ('Conclusion'), and 'teh readinz' ('References').

For completeness sake as far as research is concerned, research on LOLspeak has been included in the book chapter 'Grammar and Electronic Communication', in the *Encyclopedia of the English Language* and in the book *Because Internet*. There has been the occasional unpublished student thesis dealing with LOLspeak. To base our own observations of kitteh language on the existing findings, a summary of the studies is necessary.

The first question to answer is how we can classify our kitteh varieties. Several suggestions have been made, including ludling, pidgin, and play language. It turns out that a definition of LOLspeak is not that easy because it draws on linguistic strategies found in all these types of language. LOLspeak uses features of leet speak, text speak, language acquisition, pidgins, and play language. We can describe LOLspeak as a special internet language variety (SILV).

The use of capitalisation and exclamation marks as well as numbers and symbols to replace letters, such as 'L0Lsp33k' (LOLspeak), is typical of leet speak with its background in gaming. Rebus-like substitutions, such as '4 (for)' and 'R (are)', come from text speak, which has been used in text messaging. The over- and under-application of plurals and regular verb forms, as in 'eated' for 'ate', mimic first or second language learners. Pidginisation and play language manipulation of a linguistic system are also present in LOLspeak.

The language used in LOLspeak is far too complex to be seen as an as-yet incorrectly acquired English. While LOLspeak seems full of mistakes that children or learners of English would make as they acquire the language, LOLspeak cannot be explained in its entirety as acquisition errors.

This caused early LOLspeak researchers to refer to LOLspeak as 'kittehpidgin', but LOLspeak does not fulfil all the necessary characteristics to classify it as a pidgin. The superstrate–substrate language contact situation of pidgins is missing. For LOLspeak, we only have the superstrate, namely English, but there is no indigenous kitty language to mingle with it. While LOLspeak uses English as the source language for the bulk of LOLspeak vocabulary and employs the reduction and simplification strategies usually ascribed to pidgins, we do not have a historical cat language that has imposed its phonological, grammatical, or lexical features on English. Additionally, the users writing in LOLspeak have a very good command of English, which also points to the fact that LOLspeak is not a pidgin.

As for the suggested notion of play language, LOLspeak involves playing with language, but it is not a play language. A play language like Pig Latin, a schoolchildren's antilanguage that disguises words by inserting syllables after the initial consonant cluster, for example, has a small set of rules. LOLspeak, however, has more than just a small set of rules and involves manipulation on every linguistic level.

In the *Encyclopedia of the English Language*, LOLspeak is classified as one of the internet ludlings. The term 'ludling' refers to new and playful manipulations of language. In principle, all ludlings use the same methods: users invent new vocabulary and manipulate the rules of standard English spelling and grammar. Some of the linguistic strategies used in ludlings are the same as for pidgins and creoles, in child language acquisition, and in foreign language acquisition. Internet ludlings are, of course, not a domain related to felines only. To be fair to dogs and other animals, dogs have their own internet variety, namely 'Doggo', 'Doge', and 'pupper talk', and there is also 'snek', the internet ludling for snakes.

Oh hai thare So you want to speak lolcat? It isn't very easy and you may end up with some kitty scratches in the end.
(LOLCatBible, 2008)

We may not want to speak LOLspeak ourselves, but we want to find out which linguistic features LOLspeak uses. The positive side effect of LOLspeak's continued existence is that we can do a more or less comprehensive linguistic description. What is more, there is the LOLcat Bible project, which was initiated on a crowdsourced wiki-based website and which aimed to provide a LOLspeak version of

the Bible. Though the website www.lolcatbible.com (2008–2018) is
now archived, it can still be accessed via www.web.archive.org, and a
printed version of the LOLcat Bible is available to buy. The Library
of Congress calls the LOLcat Bible

one of the largest bodies of text documenting the use of the vernacular
[LOLspeak]
(Library of Congress)

As such, the LOLcat Bible is often taken as a resource for linguistic
analyses because it offers longer stretches of text and its language has
been checked by the many people who participated in the project. For
example, the study *I Can Haz Language Play* uses the initial verses of
Genesis in the LOLcat Bible to describe the typical features of LOL-
speak and to offer us 'grammarz, how we makes it' in a subchapter.

Oh hai. In teh beginnin Ceiling Cat maded teh skiez An da Urfs, but he did
not eated dem
(In the beginning God created the heavens and the earth, but he did not eat
them)
(www.lolcatbible.com)

We can do a similar analysis and give a brief overview of LOLspeak
features. As an example of a LOLspeak text in the LOLcat Bible, we
take the LOLcat translation of The Lord's Prayer, which has become
the Ceiling Cat Prayer in the LOLcat Bible (Table 4.1).

The study *ZOMG! DIS IZ A NEW LANGUAGE!* is based on captions and comments of image macros on www.icanhazcheezburger.com
(ICHC), like the comment 'Izz lolspeek. Lolspeek izz allaways opshu-
nal tho' (It's Lolspeak. Lolspeak is always optional, though). Both
studies stress that they are not based on a statistical analysis but
rather on a qualitative exploration to find out which linguistic features
actually exist in LOLspeak.

What we need to keep in mind is that, unlike natural languages,
LOLspeak does not really have robust group-validated norms and
tendencies and seems more like an emergent language. In other words,
the features described here are not yet used consistently throughout
the language, and sometimes there are several possibilities to express
one and the same thing in LOLspeak. For example, standard English
'the' is both 'teh' and 'da' in LOLspeak.

LOLspeak has its own orthography, vocabulary, and syntax, and
this is how we will describe it: we will have a look at the sound system

Table 4.1 *Ceiling Cat Prayer*

Ceiling Cat Prayer	Translation
Dis is found in teh Book of Matthew 6 an in teh Book of Luke 11, srsly. Dis beez teh Ceiling Cat Prayer.	This is found in the Book of Matthew 6 and in the Book of Luke 11, seriously. This is the Ceiling Cat Prayer.
Our Ceiling Cat, whu haz cheezeburger, yu be spechul	Our Ceiling Cat, who has cheeseburger, you are special.
Yu ordered cheezburgerz,	You ordered cheeseburgers.
Wut yu want, yu gets, srsly.	What you want, you get, seriously.
On the ceiling and on teh flor.	On the ceiling and on the floor.
Giv us dis day our dalee cheezburger.	Give us this day our daily cheeseburger.
And furgiv us for makin yu a cookie, but eateding it.	And forgive us for making you a cookie but eating it.
And we furgiv kittehs who steal our bukkits.	And we forgive kitties who steal our biscuits.
An do not let us leed into teh showa, but deliver us from teh wawter.	And do not let us lead into the shower but deliver us from the water.
Ceiling Cat pwns all. He pwns teh ceiling and teh floor and walls too.	Ceiling Cat owns all. He owns the ceiling and the floor and walls too.
Forevur and evuhr. Amen.	Forever and ever. Amen.

of LOLspeak and how the sounds are represented in writing, at the words, and at the structure – all with the help of Lilly, the Syntax Cat.

Da Spellin

Like the meowlogisms in Chapter 3, LOLspeak is essentially a written language to represent the voice of the cats, who should come across as over-excitable beings with erratic personalities and as young children. In its spelling, LOLspeak uses abbreviations such as vowel omissions ('srsly' for 'seriously'), phonetically influenced spelling ('z' to show the voiced [z] in 'haz cheezburgerz', 'a' in 'showa' indicating [ə] in 'shower', 'd' for [ð] as in 'dis' and 'da' for 'this' and 'the', the unvoiced equivalent 'f' for [θ] as in 'Urfs' for 'Earth'), omission of word-final consonants ('makin' indicating final [n] rather than [ŋ] in 'making'), and other common spellings ('yu' for 'you', 'fur' for 'for', 'aw' for long [ɔː] as in 'wawter' for 'water'). We also find misspellings originally associated with fast typing, like 'teh' for 'the' and 'pwn' for 'own'. Rebus-like substitutions, such as '4' instead of 'for' and 'ur' instead of 'your', are also common in LOLspeak. Additionally, capitalisation and all-caps words can also be considered a standard feature of LOLspeak.

Da Kitteh Wordz

From a feline purrspective, it seems only logical that a feline language variety would use words from the feline world. LOLspeak accordingly includes words and concepts from the cat world. Additionally, it comprises words originating in the ICHC world, which is essentially a kitteh domain. The 'cheezburgerz', 'invisible' items, and 'kittehz' are repeatedly found in the ICHC universe and the words 'pOwn' (own) and 'kthxbai' (OK, thanks, bye) come from leet speak and other gaming communities.

The cat owners among us are probably familiar with the typical associations of cats with certain concepts. The stereotypical cats see us as servants and think they deserve the best possible treatment and luxurious comforts. Cats are very fond of food, special treats, and other goodies. It does not come as a surprise, then, that in the LOLcat Bible, we find 'can openers', 'cookies', 'tuna', 'cheeseburgers', and 'biscuits'. As most cats hate getting wet, 'water' and 'showers' are taken to exemplify the evils of the world. The Ceiling Cat Prayer gives us 'An do not let us leed into teh showa, but deliver us from teh wawter' instead of 'And do not lead us into temptation but deliver us from evil' of the Lord's Prayer.

With concepts taken from ICHC, Bible-specific items have been changed to reflect the LOLcat world. The Bible's 'blessings' and 'bread' have been made into the ubiquitous '(dalee) cheezburgerz', God has become 'Ceiling Cat', Jesus is now 'Happy Cat', and there is also Satan, who has been turned into 'Basement Cat'. Accordingly, we find 'ceiling' and 'floor' in the Ceiling Cat Prayer instead of 'heaven' and 'earth' in the Lord's Prayer.

Da Grammarz

Lilly – that's the most famous cat in syntax,
(Comment by a linguist when Lilly zoombombed an online meeting with David Adger)

Before we go into the specifics of LOLspeak structures (morphology and syntax), let's introduce the cat Lilly (Figure 4.1). Labelled in a tweet as 'Syntacian Cat', Lilly is the cat of David Adger, professor of

Figure 4.1 Lilly, the Syntax Cat, says hi

linguistics, who used many examples with Lilly in his book to explain
how human language works. The scenario of Lilly having caught a
mouse in the garden, for example, is taken to show how questions
are formed in English. By the way, Lilly does not only catch mice in
the book but also frogs, and she apparently scratches furniture and

people. On a semiotic sidenote, Lilly is not a LOLcat. Lilly is a cat in the digital space of #AcademicsWithCats.

Words and parts of words are the basic units of language with which sentences are formed. We have already come across morphology in Chapter 3, where the meaning-related side of morphology (the processes with which new lexemes are formed) is covered. In this chapter, though, we apply morphology to syntax. LOLspeak structures involve several categories that can be described morphologically: plural, verb forms, word order, questions, and negations. Being a syntax cat, Lilly is predestined for syntax-related features of LOLspeak and therefore takes her proper place in our LOLspeak examples.

In LOLspeak, the plural is generally formed by adding the plural morpheme '-z' to the word. Thus, 'kitteh' becomes 'kittehz' and 'cheezburger' becomes 'cheezburgerz'.

LOLspeak example:
Lilly iz a kitteh. Lilly and Cheddar iz kittehz.
(Lilly is a cat. Lilly and Cheddar are cats).

The plural suffix '-z' is not consistently used, though, as we can see in the Ceiling Cat Prayer, which also has the plural suffix '-s' as in 'bukkits'. The explanation for 's' ([s]), which is the voiceless counterpart of '-z' ([z]), may be phonetic: the [t] in 'bukkits' is a voiceless stop, and that has perhaps influenced the plural morpheme and made it voiceless too. More likely, though, the reason is much simpler: '-s' could be an interference from standard English. We should also note that the linguistic study we are basing our analysis on, 'I can haz language play', uses the plural suffix '-s' in 'kittehs'.

In the verses of the LOLcat Bible version of Genesis, both plural forms '-z' and '-s' occur. Interestingly, the plural form '-z' (and '-s') is also taken for nouns which are generally singular in standard English. Standard English 'water', 'stuff', and 'food' are 'waterz' (waters), 'stuffs', and 'foodz' in LOLspeak.

LOLspeak example:
Lilly wantz teh foodz but hatez da waterz.
(Lilly wants the food but hates the water)

The examples have already shown that LOLspeak verb forms, too, differ from standard English. Just like for the plural form, the suffix '-z' is generally used for standard English '-s' to indicate the third person singular in LOLspeak. Standard English 'wants' and 'hates' are 'wantz' and 'hatez' in LOLspeak. The suffix '-z' is also used in combination with the first person 'ai' (I) and second person 'yu' (you), as in 'ai iz' and 'yu iz'. To complicate matters a bit, the form 'be' is also possible with 'you' as in 'yu be spechul' (you are special) in the Ceiling Cat Prayer, and there is the occurrence of 'beez' for standard English 'is' in 'Dis beez teh Ceiling Cat Prayer'. However, there is also the form 'is' as the auxiliary form of 'to be' in LOLspeak, as in 'Dis is found in teh Book of Matthew 6'. The auxiliary form 'are' can also occur as 'be', such as in 'And we furgiv kittehs who be steelin our bukkits'.

Expressing the past tense in LOLspeak is quite simple in comparison with the forms of 'to be' at first glance. All verbs, including the verbs that are irregular in standard English, take the '-ed' suffix. We find 'ordered' in the Ceiling Cat Prayer as well as 'eated', 'sayed', and 'doed' in the LOLspeak version of Genesis. Occasionally, double marking of the past tense occurs, like 'maded', 'haded', 'sawed', 'gotted', 'knockeded', and 'wented'.

LOLspeak example:
Lilly wented outside and sawed da mouse.
(Lilly went outside and saw the mouse).

Verbs may also be reduplicated to indicate either intensity or a repetitive action. We may come across forms like 'licklicklick' (to lick) and 'lublublubs' (to love). By the way, the word reduplication is not limited to verbs but is also extended to nouns, adjectives, and adverbs. In the ICHC universe, there are occurrences of 'fastfastfast' (fast) and 'daze of sleepsleepsleep' (days of sleep).

On the level of the clause, LOLspeak makes use of so-called phrasal templates or catchphrases. In the phrasal templates, all words apart from one or two placeholders or slots – signified typically as 'X' and 'Y' – are always the same, and people insert their own element into the slot. The most famous template is probably 'I can haz X', which comes from the meme *I can haz cheezburger* and has subsequently spread from the website www.icanhazcheezburger.com. In Genesis, this phrasal template occurs quite frequently, like 'i can haz lite', 'i can has lightz', and 'i can has MOAR living stuff'. Other well-known templates are the phrases 'do not want X' and 'X haz not/did not eated Y'.

LOLspeak example: Lilly can haz foodz, but Lilly do not want foodz. Lilly haz not eated foodz.
(Lilly can have food, but Lilly does not want food, Lilly has not eaten the food.)

When it comes to asking questions, there is usually no subject–auxiliary inversion. In standard English, we exchange the position of subject and auxiliary verb, and we change 'Lilly can have food' to 'Can Lilly have food?' by swapping the subject ('Lilly') with the auxiliary ('can'). In LOLspeak, however, there is no change in the word order, and we only need to insert a question mark to indicate that we are asking a question. The word order of 'Lilly can haz foodz' (Lilly can have food) remains 'Lilly can haz foodz?'. The only difference is the question mark.

The features so far have given some insight into LOLspeak. A convention in research is to include a suggestion for further research, and we are doing the same here: A more comprehensive description of LOLspeak would benefit from something like a corpus-based approach and other statistical analyses. Once this is available, we will be able to give a more complete overview of LOLspeak and additionally dive into the more abstract system of LOLspeak as a language system. We might also be able then to draw a so-called syntax tree to show the structures and grammatical hierarchies of LOLspeak, and we could create a meme especially for and with Lilly – as the Syntax Cat (Figure 4.2).

4.3 Kittehz and Their Idiolects

Not all online cats are LOLcats, and not all cat images posted on social media are image macros. On the contrary, many people share photos of their own cats to essentially give insight into their daily life with cats. These are the types of photos labelled as 'vernacular', mentioned in Section 4.1. There are dedicated social media accounts for cats, and there the cats may use a form of cat language. And these cat languages do not always fall into the categories of either LOLspeak or meowlogisms but are something else. The language used by cats may be based on the idiosyncrasies of a particular person or a particular digital community.

Figure 4.2 The Syntax Cat

We have already briefly touched upon Hambspeak (in Chapter 3), which is the feline language variety used in the Facebook group *This Cat is Chonky*. There is not much that we can say about Hambspeak. The rules laid down for this group are written in a mix of uppercase and lowercase letters, there are specific spelling conventions and special characters, and the rules use group-specific vocabulary. Only group members can see the posts and read the comments.

Rules of the Facebook group This Cat is Chonky
NO CHONK SHAMING
tHe ULTIMATE siN.
You hAth'st CHONK SHAMED? YOU BANISHED TO H E C C. no chonks to cuddle you there. hâ hâ.
2 NO OWNER SHAMING
we wiLL P R O T E C C our CHONK guarDians.
You W I L L be sat on.
3 BE NICE <3
fEELING like a < B Ü T T H Ø L E > today? G O   A W A Y !
Don't be condescending, judgy, or incite arguments. Don't like a post? Then scroll away! If you are a NASTY POOPLOOP you will be coughed up out of this group like a disgusting hairball.
4 DON't DO POLITICS OR MEDICAL ADVICE. A N Y of IT.
!! (R E S I S T) the URGE !!
even iF med advice is well-meAning, its UNWANTED. Y O S ! that includes "spay/neuter" comments/pØsts.
wE aren't VETS – you probably aRen't either. Your "aDviCe" starts "fiGHts".

... and nobody wants your p o l i t i c c in a thicc cat group. you pööp lööp.
5 ADMIN/MODS ARE HERE TO (* H E L P ! *)
Please tag/message us W H E N :
-Someone did a R U D E / break rules
-You think a post shouldn't be in the group
-You have any group related problem/question
-You wanna say hi :)
We need your help to keep C H O N K Y sâçrēd.
(BLOCCING ADMIN/MODS IS STRICTLY FORBODDEN)
(Facebook Group This Cat is Chonky)

Then there are cat accounts whose varieties might be mistaken
for LOLspeak at first glance, like the purrieties used by Cheddar or
Queen Pinky on Twitter. We have already met Cheddar in his role as
a guardian and healer for his human owner (in Chapter 1) and Queen
Pinky (Figure 6.13), the translator of a Hambspeak sentence into her
purriety (in Chapter 3).

The way language is used by Cheddar and Queen Pinky looks
like LOLspeak, with the misspellings, non-standard grammar, and
baby voice. Yet, there are differences: there are the internet-related
changes with the development of technology and the change of the
Internet since the beginning of the LOLcats in the early noughties;
then, the purpose of the ICHC website and the LOLcat Bible project
differs from the social media channels, with different target audiences
and communities. The main differences, however, are the different
contexts in which the cat-inspired idiolects and LOLspeak occur. Cat-
inspired idiolects are used to talk about the everyday life of cats, while
LOLspeak serves humorous purposes on image macros. And unlike the
users in the ICHC universe, the cat account holders on Twitter do not
refer to their varieties as LOLspeak.

In fact, the varieties do not yet have a name at all. In my survey,
done in 2019, a respondent pretending to be a cat said that their native
language was 'Cat', and in July 2020 the cat account holders of Queen
Pinky and Cheddar told me in online conversations that they would
name the language variety after their cat as in 'cat name-isms' or 'cat
name-ese' rather than seeing it generically as LOLspeak. For lack of
another name, we could take up the cat account holders' suggestions
and categorise the varieties tentatively as 'individual catisms', or
perhaps better – if we think as dialectologists – we could call them
'cat-inspired idiolects'.

To be fair, LOLspeak also consists of many feline idiolects, but texts like the LOLcat Bible have been crowd-monitored for correctness and the image macros and their captions on ICHC have been upvoted or downvoted, and, thus, a regulatory effect has already impacted on LOLspeak. In what relation to LOLspeak the cat-inspired idiolects have developed is impossible to say, and whether or how much people have been influenced by LOLcats and LOLspeak is also unknown. When I asked cat account holders about where they learned their language, Cheddar's answer was: 'I dunno ware I lerned it. I just lerned it!'

The question as to the inspiration for the cat-inspired idiolect is much easier to answer: cat account holders just want to give their cats a distinctive voice and write posts and comments the way they imagine their cats would sound. For example, Queen Pinky has been given a lisp in addition to the modification of words with a phonetic spelling and the use of the meowphemes ('meow', 'mew', 'purr', and more) when a word is phonetically similar.

Generally, Cheddar's and Pinky's spelling is phonetic, like 'oo' for [uː], as in 'yoo' for 'you'; 'w' for [ɹ] and [l], as in 'twy' for 'try' and 'wike' for 'like'; 'd' for [ð], as in 'dey' for 'they'; or 'f' for [θ], as in 'fink' for 'think'. 'Meow' is sometimes used for 'I' and 'you', and there are some specific words like 'owies' for pain. As for syntax, the suffix '-s' is added in the first person to the verbs 'to think' and 'to say' as in 'meow finks' (I think) and 'I ses' (I say), and the past tense tends to regularised by adding '-ed' to the verbs as in 'the waps bited her' (the wasp bit her), sometimes – but not always – resulting in a double marking of the past tense, like in 'I gotted' (I got) as opposed to 'I maked' (I made). The form of the verb 'to be' is 'be' in the first person singular and the third person singular and plural, as in 'I be bwave' (I am brave), 'he be a big ant' (he is a big ant), 'he be sitting' (he is sitting), and 'dem zombees be twikking yoo' (those zombies are tricking you), or it is missing entirely as in 'dat funny' (that is funny). In negated sentences, the auxiliary verb may be missing like in 'she not understands' (she does not understand).

Humour does play a role because a life with cats can be funny, as Cheddar (Figure 4.3) shows in his very own #CheddarPoetry. But neither the posts nor the images are created as image macros, unlike LOLcats.

I was only fwee monffs old
Wen I firs climed a twee.
I runned up and climed lots hi,
Den cwied come look at me!

Mama wached and be amazed,
I showed off jus for her.
Den she skooped me off da bwanch,
And I began to purr.

#CheddarPoetry
#BabyCheddar
#ThrowbackThursday #tbt

6:15 PM · Jun 25, 2020 · Twitter Web App

Figure 4.3 Cheddar poetry

I was only fwee monffs old
Wen I firs climed a twee.
I runned up and climed lots hi,
Den cwied come look at me!

Mama wached and be amazed,
I showed off jus for her.
Den she skooped me off da bwanch,
And I began to purr.

#CheddarPoetry
#BabyCheddar
#ThrowbackThursday #tbt

Sources Used in This Chapter

🐾 Adger (2019) for syntax
🐾 Austin and Irvine (2020) for cat photos
🐾 Bartram (2019) for LOLcats

🐾 Brubaker (2008) for LOLcats
🐾 KnowYourMeme.com (2007) for LOLcats
🐾 Thibault and Marino (2018) for LOLcats
🐾 Miltner (2012, 2014) for LOLcats and LOLspeak
🐾 Dash (2007) for LOLspeak
🐾 Fiorentini (2013) for LOLspeak
🐾 Gawne and Vaughan (2012) for LOLspeak
🐾 Herring (2012) for LOLspeak
🐾 LOLCatBible (2008) for LOLspeak
🐾 McCulloch (2019) for LOLspeak and ludlings
🐾 Crystal (2010, 2018) for ludlings and linguistic terms in the glossary
🐾 Brown and Miller (2013) for linguistic terms in the glossary

Examples and Quotes Used in This Chapter

🐾 'LOLcat' (2007) for LOLcat
🐾 'kitteh' (2007) for kitteh
🐾 KnowYourMeme.com (2007) for quote on 'cat'
🐾 LOLCatBible (2017) for Ceiling Cat Prayer
🐾 LOLCatBible (2008) for LOLspeak
🐾 'LOLspeak' (2010) for LOLspeak
🐾 Adger (2019, pp. 9–10)
🐾 Fiorentini (2013, pp. 92, 103)
🐾 Gawne and Vaughan (2012, pp. 102–103, 105, 118) for LOLspeak quotes on (linguistic) research
🐾 Thibault and Marino (2018, pp. 473–474) for the quote on 'reductio ad cattum'
🐾 Cheddar on Twitter
🐾 Turtlecat on Twitter

Suggestions for PURRther Reading

🐾 Adger (2019)
🐾 Gawne and Vaughan (2012)

5

Virtual Furever Homes

The contemporary Internet was designed, in no small part, for the dissemination of cute pictures of cats.
(Zuckerman, 2008)

For people in the animal-related digital spaces, a furever (forever) home is a place where people adopt unwanted animals. love them, and take care of them for the rest of their lives. In the virtual world, cats have found a furever place to stay on the Internet. Not surprisingly for cat owners and cat lovers, the cat symbolises the development of the Social Web. Cats shape the Internet and cause the technological advancements of Web 2.0, as a media scholar has said, tongue in cheek.

Our aim in this chapter is to find out more about the digital spaces the cats inhabit, and we are looking for research within and outside linguistics to get as much insight as possible into the phenomenon of the cats' virtual furever homes and their communities. With the keywords 'cats' and 'Internet', we discover findings in media studies, digital humanities, and anthropology.

We see that we need to consider also the developments of technology and the concepts of digital communities. The evolution of the participatory culture of Web 2.0 and the possibilities to create content have had implications for how people form networks and come together in the online world. In this chapter, we focus on the different online communities, the cats' virtual furever homes, and their stories but leave the topic of computer-mediated communication, the cats' 'multimeowdality', for Chapter 6.

Concepts Discussed in the Chapter
🐾 participatory culture

- online communities
- communities of practice
- affinity spaces
- light communities
- online narratives
- small stories
- shared stories
- typology of cat accounts
- microcelebrities
- influencers

Terms from the Clawssary

affinity space community of practice digital humanities discourse analysis light community media studies meowlogisms shared story small story translanguaging

5.1 Cats and Pawticipatory Culture

With Web 2.0, we've embraced the idea that people are going to share pictures of their cats, and now we build sophisticated tools to make that easier to do. (Zuckerman, 2014)

The development of digital cat-related spaces is closely bound up with the development of technology and the evolution of the Social Web. Researching the serious issues of political activism, censorship, and social media, media scholar Ethan Zuckerman, whose quotes we find in this chapter, has chosen the phenomenon of the cat on the Internet – of all phenomena – to show the connection between technological advancements, user-generated content, and political activism.

Zuckerman has, in fact, put forward the Cute Cat Theory about censorship and social media, basically claiming that cute cat pictures help political activism. The tools created for sharing cat images on the Social Web can also be used by political activists in countries with strong censorship. He says that blocking people's access to cute cat pictures, that is, blocking a Web 2.0 site, means spending political capital and making people actually more aware of situations that governments would rather be suppressing.

In media studies as well as in digital humanities, we find the spotlight on the cat in some research. Media studies investigates the effects of the media, including the mass media, from the angle of sociology, history, psychology, semiotics, and critical discourse analysis. Digital humanities is an interdisciplinary field combining the various fields of humanities with digital technologies. Both disciplines provide us with information on cats' virtual furever homes.

Research in the digital humanities has shown when the cats arrived on the Internet and how they have contributed to its development. Even though cats were only explicitly identified with the Internet in the noughties, they are now so intertwined with the Internet and its history that it seems they were there from the beginning. For us, cats are simply part of the Internet and 'the suite of online rituals' whose origins we have forgotten. Contrary to the initial belief about computers to be special-purpose tools for calculations in the 1980s, the functions of the Internet are social. Instead of focussing on their jobs, people have always used computers for social things unrelated to their jobs, and the cat has come to symbolise this social aspect:

Cats are a symbol of pointless online sociability
(White, 2020)

An important factor is the relation between technology and com- munication because technology makes online communication possible and shapes communication. Online communication technology can be divided into three historical phases, into the pre-Web, Web 1.0, and Web 2.0. The pre-Web era, lasting from 1983 to 1993, is characterised by its text-only mode, specialised stand-alone servers, specialised proprietary reader software, and people with technological savviness. People could communicate with typed text only via e-mail and group conferencing, in Usenet newsgroups, in game multi-user dimensions or dungeons, and an early form of synchronous chat. Internet users were predominantly male.

Web 1.0, the period between 1994 and 2004, came into existence with Tim Berners-Lee's World Wide Web, which was made public in 1991 and was integrated into a browser in 1993. The browser – called Mosaic – could work with both text and graphics and made it easy for people to go online. Virtual worlds were created, and people could chat in audio and video. There was the chat client ICQ, instant messaging, and text messaging on mobile phones. More people had access to the Internet, and more and more female users went online. By 2000, there were as many female as male users.

In that period, chats, discussion forums, wikis, and weblogs appeared. There was Usenet, forums, IRC, BBS, and listservs. As opposed to today's possibilities, communication tended to be text-only. As we have seen in Chapter 4, this is the era when people used cats in forums and started to talk about their cats in forums, like rec.pets.cats on Usenet.

Coined as a term in 2004, Web 2.0, the phase that we are in now, is characterised by participatory information sharing, user-generated content, social platforms, blogs, microblogs, social network sites, and media sharing sites. Examples for early social network sites are AOL Instant Messenger, MSN Messenger, blogs, LiveJournal, and MySpace. The fact that data is transmitted much faster now makes it possible for us to use video, audio, graphics, and text on a single platform, like Facebook, Twitter, Instagram, or YouTube. With Snapchat, WhatsApp, and TikTok, more social media platforms have appeared. We go into the interactive multimodal platforms in Chapter 6.

With all the new technological possibilities, the mode of communication has now become multimodal, which means we can share our cats in different ways on one and the same platform: images, videos, text, GIFs, audio, and whatever mode technology allows us to use. Whether we still use Web 2.0 or already 3.0 or even 4.0 is being debated, and new developments are found in the areas of artificial intelligence, machine learning, and natural language search. For our purposes, the number following the word Web is not important. What is relevant, however, are the developments and how they affect our communication with each other.

Cats, by the way, have been playing an active role in the development of technology, and the strong link between cats and the geek culture of the Internet is exemplified by a Google experiment. Researchers in Google's deep-learning division used a cat image to train a computer to recognise cats. The neural network was indeed able to generate a cat image itself without being told how to do it. Considering the recent development of technology and artificial intelligence, we have to widen Zuckerman's quote below with 'Web 3.0 was developed for computers to create their own cat pictures'.

Web 1.0 was invented to allow physicists to share research papers.
Web 2.0 was created to allow people to share pictures of cute cats.
(Zuckerman, 2014)

In White's (2020) light-hearted book linking cats to the evolution of the Internet, the section *Purr-ticipatory Culture* gives the example of cat memes to illustrate the concept of participatory culture. Users take cat images and ideas for captions from each other, change them, and share them. On the Web, people collaborate with each other to create content, to communicate with each other, and so on. In other words, there is a culture of participation. The idea of participatory culture as an enabler for democracy is perhaps just wishful thinking by some academics and the media. The means for serious discussions are there, but people prefer cat images, just like Zuckerman says.

When we connect the development stages of the Internet to cats, we can divide the Internet also into three historical phases, namely into the webcam and personal blog era, the meme era, and the celebrity cat era. The first phase, the webcam and personal blog era from 1995 to 2004, corresponds to Web 1.0. In that era, cats came into the online world via webcams and personal blogs. The bandwidth was not strong enough for videos as we know them now. There was the *KittyCam*, a webcam in an office in California taking a picture every two minutes and showing the cat Kitty – or not – depending on whether she was in front of the camera or not. There were websites like *Cat of the Day*, which posted a cat picture every day, together with a short text.

The second phase, from 2005 to 2011, is the meme era, in which cat images and cat videos appeared online on image sharing sites like 4chan. The year 2005 marks the beginning of YouTube, the home of many cat videos. From a cat-related point of view, it is definitely worth mentioning that YouTube was promoted to investors with a cat video. YouTube was initially intended for people to share homemade videos showing their everyday life, but it has become a channel for professional video makers. The professionalism of the videos can be seen in the examples of the earliest famous cats, such as Maru, Surprise Kitty, Keyboard Cat, and Henri le chat noir.

These cats also mark the beginning of the third phase, the celebrity cat era, starting in 2012 and still ongoing. Often with their own media manager, celebrity cats have an extremely large number of followers and make money with their channels. The YouTube Partner Program, the monetisation programme of Google, also has the category *Cat Partners*. In terms of technological development and communication, Google/YouTube offers *Super Chat & Super Stickers*. Fans pay for these stickers so that they can highlight their chat messages and profile pictures, and chat messages with paid-for profile pictures will stay on top longer, Google says. The channel of Simon's Cat, for example, offers its subscribers loyalty badges to be used next to their names in comments and live chats, then custom emoji to be used in comments and live chats, and exclusive wallpapers to catify their mobile devices.

The latest phase of the Internet can be related to blockbuster economics: the Web has become a huge marketplace dominated by a few blockbuster companies, and while many niche products are offered too, these are situated in what is referred to as the long tail. In terms of cats, this means that the appearance and popularity of the celebrity cats is due to the Internet's maturing as a marketplace. A few – or more than a few – celebrity cats gather much more of the attention than the vast number of other online cats. We can apply the Pareto Principle to the cats as the 'Purreto Principle'.

The Pareto Principle suggests that 20 percent of the online cats should get 80 percent of the attention [...] the social media channels of superstars like Grumpy Cat and Lil Bub have subscriber counts that vastly dwarf those of channels belonging to the large number of would-be celebrity cats out there (White, 2020)

Regardless of how we categorise and name the development stages of the Internet, technological innovations have been influencing communication. Different technological possibilities have enabled cats – or rather their human owners – to extend their ranges to the online world via different means, modes, and channels.

Two thoughts are to be added here: the first is that not every online cat strives to be a celebrity cat; the second is related to the view of the cat as the symbol of 'pointless online sociability', a view expressed by some but not shared by all. Chapter 11 shows the various reasons of people to have or to follow a cat account. Without giving too much away at this stage, making one's cat famous does not seem to be a reason to have a cat account – at least not for the respondents of my 2019 survey on attitude and perception. As for the second thought, while looking at online cats may be regarded as a pointless online sociability, some real benefits of, say, watching cat videos have been shown in research.

There are also examples of participatory culture in linguistics. In the noughties, the BBC Voices project was run to provide a snapshot of the linguistic landscape across the UK. People were asked to share their words and thoughts on language use, and more than 8,500 contributions were made online via the (now archived) website www.bbc.co.uk/voices/. The British Library holds 283 recordings of the Voices project in their *Accents and Dialects* collection, which can be accessed online. Together with the recordings, we get linguistic descriptions on the keywords, spontaneously elicited words, phonology, and grammar.

The Englishs Dialects App is another example of participatory culture. The project was launched in January 2016 as an app for iOS and Android mobile devices free to download for people willing to participate in dialect research. The crowdsourcing approach has paid off, and now a corpus of English is available with dialect variants of 47,000 participants and audio recordings of 3,500 people reading a text passage. While cat-related words do not feature as keywords in the corpus as such, we can still find out more about the pronunciation of the vowel in 'cat' and, thus, make inferences as to the pronunciation of the word 'cat' in the various regions of England. Additionally, we can participate ourselves via the app in a dialect quiz and in the reading passage even if we come from outside the UK.

A more recent example of participatory culture in dialectology is a Twitter survey done by the Tweetolectology project. When the maps for female and male cats (see Chapter 2) were put online, Twitter users were asked to participate in a survey to compare today's language use with the results of the SED. Maps with today's usage of the terms for female cats recorded in the SED are one of the results of people's participation. For the words 'queen(cat)/queencat', 'tabby(cat)/tib(cat)', 'sheder/she(cat)', and for 'no specific term' (Figures 5.1–5.4). The shades on the maps indicate how much a given term is used in a region in the UK.

Another aspect of participatory culture in linguistics – and in research as a whole – is the online availability of data, which allows researchers to access the data and use it for their own research. This approach of open data and open science has made it possible for us to include the cat-related words of the corpora and the related statistics in Chapter 3. Yet there are legal and ethical issues we need to think about when we share and use data online. These legal and ethical requirements for fieldwork and data collection concerning data protection and privacy protection are dealt with in Chapter 8.

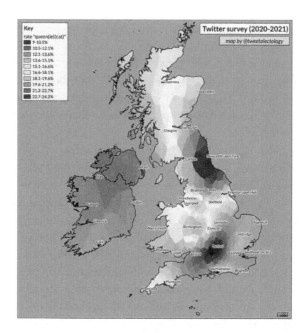

Figure 5.1 Queen(ie)(cat)

5.2 Cats and Digital Ranges

Post hier [...] je lolcats. [Dutch]
Post here [...] your lolcats [English translation]
Taken from Excerpt 4.17 Question-free Friday (Dutch community)
(Dailey-O'Cain, 2017)

In Chapter 1, we touched upon the notion of digital spaces or third
places where people meet to catch up on each others' news and hang
out to communicate with other like-minded people. Just like in real
life, these third places exist in the virtual world, and there are different
types of digital spaces. The issue we are addressing now is how to
categorise these spaces in the online world. Different terms have been
suggested, such as 'communities of cultures and subcultures', 'digital
affinity spaces', 'virtual communities', and 'communities of practice'.
The relevant point is that we can find examples for all these categori-
sations in the cat-related digital spaces, such as a virtual community
that sent out the call for LOLcat postings on their 'Question-free
Friday'. 'Question-free Friday' refers to their community practice of
always including a question in the posts – except on Fridays.

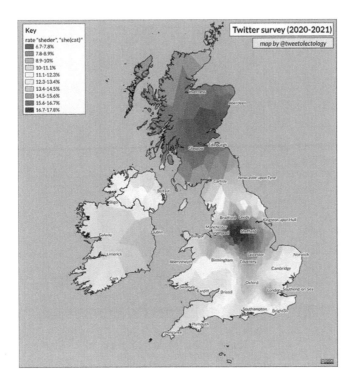

Figure 5.2 Sheder/she(cat)

From digital anthropological research on influencer culture, we can take up the notion of the community as a culture of shared ritualised habits. People form populations online and congregate in distinct groups practising ritualistic habits in their specific communities of cultures and subcultures. Generally speaking, these online rituals are the typical platform-dependent social media conventions of communication, media consumption, sharing, and sense making. The view of anthropology and sociology is that rituals in media and communication function socially to regulate the existing social order.

In the cat-related digital spaces, we can see the cultures and subcultures with their ritualised habits. Groups form around specific cat-related hashtags, in the more complex networks of followers and followings of cat account holders, or as special cat-related interest groups. Following this approach, we can classify the groups we find in the digital spaces based on how they are formed: specific hashtags,

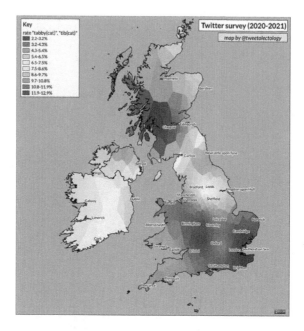

Figure 5.3 Tabby(cat)/tib(cat)

networks of followers and followings, and special-interest groups. The subcultures are not separate entities but may overlap, and cat account holders are often part of more than one community and (sub)culture. Social network analysis, which we look at in Chapter 10, provides us with a data mining tool to graphically display the networks and the density with which people are connected.

With Murrli's cat account, I belonged (and still belong) to various subcultures at the same time: to the subculture around academics with cats, then to a network of (mostly) black cat account followers and followings on Instagram, and to the special interest group of @black_cat_crew, which has taken up the cause of promoting the welfare of black cats.

Regarding cat-related cultures on social media, we must not forget the cat-related influencer culture consisting of the likes of Grumpy Cat, Simon's Cat, Smoothie the Cat, and other famous felines. Digital anthropology provides a definition of what constitutes an influencer, and we take this definition when we discuss the types of cat accounts in Section 5.4.

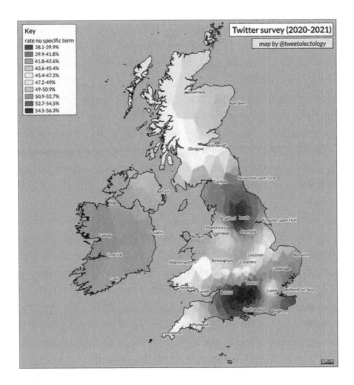

Figure 5.4 Cat: no specific term

Linguistic research works with the concepts of communities, which includes virtual communities and communities of practice, and digital affinity spaces. In their definitions, there is a basic difference between communities and spaces: a community implies a more stable grouping, while a space indicates a more fleeting grouping. This separation into stable and fleeting helps us to categorise the cat accounts.

In order to call a group of people a community, we need to find signs of a space that is created, maintained, and controlled by community members, as well as evidence for matters related to authority, dominance, submission, rebellion, and cooptation. Research on computer-mediated communication provides us with a list of six criteria that our groups of cat accounts need to fulfil to be communities.

By definition, we should be able to observe (1) active participation and a core of regular participants; (2) a shared history, purpose, culture, norms, and values; then we should be able to recognise (3) solidarity, support, and reciprocity; (4) criticism, conflict, and means for conflict resolution; (5) a self-awareness of the group as an entity distinct from other groups; and, finally, (6) emerging roles, a hierarchy, governance, and rituals.

Virtual communities and communities of practice are subtypes of communities. When communities form online, they are referred to as virtual communities because the space where they meet is a virtual one. A community of practice refers to people coming together to work towards common goals. Linguistic research usually gives the example of a workplace or classroom to illustrate the nature of a community of practice.

When we cannot find evidence for the six criteria, we talk about an affinity space, which means that the formation of the group is non-lasting. Just like in communities, people also come together in an affinity space because of common interests, causes, lifestyles, or activities, yet, the connection between the members in the affinity space is loose. In sociolinguistics, the term 'light communities' has been suggested to refer to groups that emerge when people form a solid group around a common topic for the time of an event and then dissolve it again when the event is over. An example for such a process is people going to a pub to watch a football match. During the time of the match, these people form a robust group with similar behaviours, intimate closeness, and emotional bonding. After the match, the group disperses.

Among the many groupings in the cat-related digital spaces, we take the @black_cat_crew, Cats Protection, the space around #AcademicsWithCats, and a Twitter thread around a tweet by football club FC Bayern Munich during a football match to illustrate virtual community, community of practice, affinity spaces, and light community, respectively.

The cat account @black_cat_crew on Instagram is an example of a virtual community. When we go to its feed, we can, in fact, observe the six criteria for a community in action. Around the posts by @black_cat_crew, a core group of people comment actively and on a regular basis, and the common purpose is to raise awareness for black cats, to share calls for adoptions of black cats, and to simply have fun with the regular use of specially created hashtags, such as #BCC_AdoptBlackCats, #BCC_BirthdayCat, and season-specific hashtags, like #BCC_BCAD_2020 – the acronym BCAD is short

Figure 5.5 #BCC_Halloween2020

for Black Cat Appreciation Day – and #BCC_Halloween2020 (Figure 5.5). There is a lot of solidarity and support for owners whose cats are ill or have crossed the rainbow bridge; followers are asked to share in the joy or grief. In the comments, followers refer to their shared history and mention black cats that have died.

Since the beginning of the @black_cat_crew more than 2,000 images ago, group-specific rituals and roles have been emerging. It sees itself as different from other cat-feature accounts. Features, as the posts are named, are created by so-called crew members, and there are honorary members too. Additionally, there are @black_cat_crew angels, the term referring to crew member cats that have died. Making use of Instagram as a multimodal platform, @black_cat_crew have created their very own logo and stickers, which they put on their images to give the posts an additional visual identifier (Figure 5.6).

Cats Protection is a large charity in the UK helping around 200,000 cats and kittens every year in their local volunteer-run branches, each with their own social media presence. Cats Protection and its branches are not a pure online community but a blended form of online and offline groups. When we look for the criteria for communities, we find Cats Protection to be an organisation with its organisational culture,

Figure 5.6 Logo of the black_cat_crew

history, values, hierarchy, solidarity, support, reciprocity, and self-awareness as a group. As a community of practice, they communicate and cooperate to find new homes for cats in the real world as well as online. While the main charity and the individual branches have individual social media accounts, they are clearly connected in the way they frame their postings and in the way they are visually represented. Followers interact with them and often share the posts of cats up for adoption.

The space of academics with their cats is loose and fleeting, and when we apply the criteria for a community, we find that the space of academics with cats does not fulfil all criteria. We have evidence for active participation and a shared culture, with students and staff posting images of their cats with captions related to university and research life. However, the other criteria are not met: there is no real core group of regulars, group formation is fleeting, and there are no procedures for regulating group member relationships. While a historical relationship of academics and cats can be illustrated, for example with the paw prints on a manuscript dated 1445, the history of the groupings around the space of academics with cats is not shared among the people interacting with the posts. Therefore, the space of academics and their cats is not a community but an affinity space.

For affinity spaces, we can still look for features of community, but it is not necessary to find evidence for all the features laid out in the research. Only an ideal affinity space has all the features, and the more features a given space provides, the closer it comes to being an 'ideal' affinity space. An affinity space (1) forms around a common endeavour; (2) offers a shared space for everyone without segregating people into a hierarchy of 'newbies' and 'masters'; (3) allows members to create new features; (4) encourages, offers, and uses (new) knowledge inside and outside the space; (5) offers various forms and routes for participation and status; and (6) has a vague boundary between leaders and followers, with no hierarchy.

In the space of academics with cats, we find a common interest in cats and simultanously in university and research matters. We see that staff, students, and others share the space equally without categorising or labelling others, that there is no hierarchy, and that participants make use of the the technical possibilities offered by the social media channels. People congregating in the academics with cats space not only create new content and meaning with their vernacular photos, GIFs, videos, memes, or emoji but also search and share knowledge on academic and other matters. To be really exact here, not all the features are specific to academics with cats; it is the social media platforms that encourage the formation of an affinity space like academics with cats and the use of various channels for participation.

The hashtag #AcademicsWithCats was created on Twitter in 2014 when the blog and Twitter account *Academia Obscura* popularised the hashtag with the 'Academics with Cats Awards' for the best images in the categories of academics and their cats: research, writing, teaching and outreach, and research assistants. The awards were covered by *Times Higher Education* and *The Guardian*. In the space of academics with cats, cats are shown 'helping' with marking, researching, and teaching, or taking part in online meetings, like Mikey and Schiller (Figure 5.7), who 'support' their owner's work as 'supurrvisors'. The majority of cats feature on people's personal accounts rather than on their own feline accounts. There are exceptions, though: university cats, like Rolf at Warwick or the Augsburg Campus Cat, have been given their own accounts to interact with staff, students, and other followers.

The space of academics with cats has extended from posting cat images related to the hashtag to light-hearted feline takes of academia and research in general. One example from 2021 is the paper 'Are cats good? An important study' in the *Journal of Catological Science* published by 'Cat-related Science Publishing' (Figure 5.8), written during a period of lockdown in Australia in September 2021. The tweet advertising this paper went viral, with more than 2,500 retweets, 721 quotes, and almost 9,000 likes.

Figure 5.7 Mikey and Schiller, supurrvisors

Another cat-related tool available to purrify academia is the R software programming package CatterPlot, which shows cat-shaped points instead of circles and squares. The (s)catterplot in Figure 5.9 visualises the answer to the question 'On which platforms do you follow cats?' from my July 2019 survey. In the scatterplot, the x-axis shows the answers choices Facebook (1), Instagram (2), Twitter (3), YouTube (4), and 'don't follow cats' (5), and the y-axis displays the number of respondents (n = 195). We do not interpret the results at this point because all the details of the July 2019 survey are described in Chapter 11.

On a sidenote, the affinity space of academics with cats shows that real cats are behind this purrification of academia. The cat Prince S (Figure 5.10) is one of the cats mentioned in the 'Are cats good? An important study' paper, and the R package CatterPlot was essentially inspired by Turbo (Figure 5.11), a former cat of the software developer. The name CatterPlot itself is a meowlogism using the meowpheme 'cat' to refer to the term scatterplot, which is a statistical tool for graphic data visualisation.

When a cat unexpectedly interferes with a sporting or other public event, the cat not only makes the news but also triggers a cat-

Cat-related Science Publishing

Journal of Catological Sciences

J Cat Sci **2021**; 5(2):1

Are cats good? An important study

Patrick J Owen[1] and Severine Lamon[1]

[1] Deakin University, Institute for Physical Activity and Nutrition (IPAN), School of Exercise and Nutrition Sciences, Geelong, Victoria, Australia

E-mail: p.owen@deakin.edu.au

Received 30/09/2021
Accepted for publication 30/09/2021
Published 30/09/2021

Abstract

Cats have four legs. Cats can purr. However, science does not know if they are good. Therefore, we shought to determine if cats are good. This was a consensus opinion study between the two scientists. Sensitivity analyses were not considered. Results demonstrated that cats are good. Limited sample size and use of anecdotal evidence may have been limitations. In conclusion, it appears that cats are good. Puur puur puur.

Keywords: cat, good, important, study

1. Introduction

A cat is a four legged creature (Cat et al. 900BC). Purring is odd, but most people can just deal with it. Asking too many questions regarding purring is not recommended. No studies have examined if cats are good. Therefore, the aim of the current study was to determine if cats inherently good.

2. Methods

This was a consensus opinion study between two scientists (PJO, SL). Both were asked if cats were good. If consensus was not achieved, a series of egg-and-spoon races were held each Sunday morning until opinions aligned. Sensitivity analyses are a good idea, but beyond the scope of this scientific endevour.

3. Results

Collectively, 100% of opinions suggested that cats were good. No egg-and-spoon races were held.

4. Discussion

The current study showed that, when compared to robust study designs, a two person consensus appeared satisfactory for identifing that cats are good.

A previous autoethnographical study by Catlady et al. (2009) attempted to answer a similar question to the current study, yet the authors were only able to conclude that cats were not 'not good'. This double negative was less than helpful and may in part explain why cats do not currently have voting rights in the majority of developed nations.

5. Conclusion

Cats are good. Future studies may benefit from asking cats for their opinion.

Acknowledgements

The authors wish to thank their cats.

References

[1] Cat, Cat & Cat. 900BC *Journal of Catology* 3 112-4
[2] Catlady, Catfriend & Catboy 2009 *Cats & Friends* 5 14-53

Figure 5.8 Are cats good? An important study

related digital space. Strictly speaking, the digital space already exists because of the event and the people involved; the cat only hijacks the event and the digital space.

For our categorisation of such cat-related interactions, the concepts of virtual community or affinity space do not fit because the shared interest in the event has a clearly delimited timespan with a beginning and an end. Yet we can apply the term 'light community', which

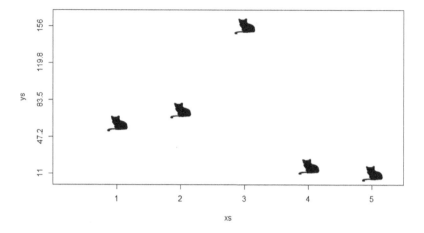

Figure 5.9 Catterplot

Figure 5.10 Prince S

linguistic research has come up with for exactly these types of interactions.

In a light community, people – strangers, acquaintances, and friends alike – congregate only for the time of an event and disperse again at the end of the event. They come together because of a shared focus,

Figure 5.11 Turbo – the real cat behind CatterPlot

like an object, a shared interest, a person, or an event. The shared focus is triggered by a specific prompt and is limited in space and time. While the event is taking place, people display similar behaviour because they experience a certain closeness to each other. At the end of the event, the light community dissolves again.

In the case of the posts around the hashtag #MiaSanMiau, we have a light community. Like other football clubs, FC Bayern Munich has encouraged the formation of virtual spaces on social media. To show to others online, people supporting Bayern Munich use the hashtag #MiaSanMia (Bavarian variety for German 'Wir sind wir', 'we are who we are'), the club's motto. When a cat crossed the football pitch during Bayern Munich's Champion's League match in March 2018, Bayern supporters tweeted about it, changing the usual hashtag to #MiaSanMiau ('Wir sind Miau'). Throughout 2018, the hashtag #MiaSanMiau, together with memes of the players and cats, was used by the club itself and by its supporters. A news article in Spanish on the website of T13 in Chile even describes the creation of the hashtag and shows the tweets, including the translanguaged German–English version #MiaSanMeow ('Wir sind Meow', 'We are Meow'). By the way, the cat was elected FC Bayern Munich's player of the match in a popular vote on Twitter (Figure 5.12).

Who is your Player of the Match vs @besiktasEnglish ?
#BJKFCB

Thiago	12%
Wagner	6.6%
Cat	68.2%
Müller	13.2%

@FCBayernUS

Figure 5.12 Cat is player of the match

5.3 Cats and Online Narratives

Another way to approach the cat-related digital spaces is to look for stories and use mediated narrative analysis. The mediated narrative method interprets online interaction as narratives because, in their posts and comments, people tell and share stories. To be as complete as possible in our analysis of the cat-related spaces, we should take a nexus approach, which combines frameworks from various fields, like mediated discourse analysis, critical discourse analysis, social semiotic approaches, and interactional pragmatics.

With the mediated narrative analysis, we look for small stories and shared stories in our cat-related digital spaces and take into account the contextual and multimodal aspects of online interaction. That means that we are not searching for traditional stories but for brief, open-ended, easily shareable stories focussing on ordinary everyday life experiences. Social media is an ideal place for sharing small stories in multimodal manners. In this section, we are concentrating on the narrative element, leaving multimodality for Chapter 6.

A shared story fulfils four narrative characteristics that refer to how the story content is created. In a shared story, several people contribute to the narration (co-tellership) by producing and reproducing the story content across multiple posts, reposts, and comments (distributed linearity). Additionally, they connect their contribution to the others by referring to the other texts (intertextuality) and assume a common ground with the other participants in the story. Put non-scientifically, we have several authors writing, copying, rewriting, and adding their bits in their own posts on their own channels. The outcome of that sharing is one common story.

Once we have identified the small and shared stories, we analyse them. The analysis is done on three levels, starting with the content of the story on Level 1, the contextual characteristics of the story on Level 2, and the wider socio-cultural contexts with their ideological implications on Level 3. On the content level, we ask about which parts of the story are taken up, how are the characters represented, whose words are heard, which resources are used to connect one text to another, which stereotypes are stated, and which knowledge is assumed. On the level of contextual characteristics, we go into the structure of the story, the position of the story contributors, the previous use of the material, any changes in meaning, and the community norms and rights. On the socio-cultural level, we look for what the story tells us about the privileges of one story version over another, how the story teller shapes and evaluates the master narrative, how in-groups and out-groups are created, which shared knowledge the story requires to understand the intertextual references, and in whose interests the story lies.

To illustrate the approach, we take the story of Millbrooks Minnie, a rescue cat found with horrendous injuries in June 2019. The case of Millbrooks Minnie was reported in the national and international news. The Minnie story is composed of a number of small stories. Written in 2021, the post on a fundraising page below sums up Minnie's story from beginning to happy ending:

Cat Castle is raising money for the RSPCA Millbrook Animal Centre
So more cats like Minnie can be saved for RSPCA (England and Wales) because of how they cared for Minnie

Story
On the 2nd of June 2019, RSPCA Millbrook was informed a severely abused 9 month old cat was found in Woking, UK. The tiny tortoiseshell cat had burns all over her body, unable to stand and signs of sexual abuse. After spending several days at the vet, she was released into Millbrook's care and called Minnie, because of her size. They cared for her wounds, helped her go to the toilet and showered her with love. Minnie slowly started to walk again. After a few weeks, she was placed with a foster, Maureen, who continued working with Minnie and help build her confidence. On the 8th of October,

more than 4 months after she was found, she left for her forever home with us at Cat Castle.
(Cat Castle)

Minnie's story is a shared story because it fulfils the narrative characteristics of co-tellership, distributed linearity, intertextuality, and the assumption of common ground. To start with the last of these four characteristics, the common ground is the love for cats and the abhorrence of animal abuse.

In Minnie's story, there are at least two main story tellers, namely the RSPCA and Cat Castle. There are other story contributors, too, such as the news media and people who share content related to Minnie. In June 2019, several videos showing Minnie's improvement were posted after the initial tweet, and quotes of the people immediately involved in Minnie's treatment were included.

Next, we have evidence for distributed linearity as Minnie's story has been shared across channels, posts, and reposts. The public Minnie story started on 3 June 2019, when the RSPCA appealed for information on social media and included an image of the cat in their tweet (Figure 5.13). The tweet linked to the news post on the RSPCA website.

URGENT APPEAL, PLEASE SHARE – @RSPCA_official appealing for info after severely abused cat found in Woking. The cat, who has been named Minnie, had burns all over her and signs of sexual abuse. More info here: https://news.rspca.org.uk/2019/06/03/rspca-urgent-appeal-after-severely-abused-cat-found-in-woking/@surreylive
(Tweet by RSPCA Press Team)

People shared that tweet and left replies sending their love to the cat and condemning the cruelty. Because people asked about Minnie's health, the official RSPCA as well as the Millbrook RSPCA branch posted regular updates on the cat's condition using first the hashtag #MinnieUpdate and then #MillbrooksMinnie together with photos and videos. After Minnie's recovery and rehoming, her new humans at Cat Castle have been sharing updates on her, such as Minnie being befriended by another cat in the household or Minnie coming for cuddles, using the additional hashtag #LoveWins. Images and videos of Minnie are still posted on a regular basis.

The Minnie story at Cat Castle has been widened to include the other rescue cats living at Cat Castle, and the pinned tweet on the account 'The Tails of Cat Castle' contains a slideshow of all the rescue

URGENT APPEAL, PLEASE SHARE - @RSPCA_official
appealing for info after severely abused cat found in
Woking. The cat, who has been named Minnie, had
burns all over her and signs of sexual abuse. More info
here: news.rspca.org.uk/2019/06/03/rsp... @surreylive

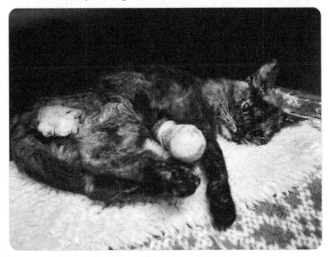

10:17 AM · Jun 3, 2019 · Twitter Web Client

Figure 5.13 Milbrooks Minnie: appeal for information

cats at Cat Castle and their stories. On 'International Minnie Day'
on 2 June 2021, Cat Castle asked people to share their cat stories in
line with the hashtag#LoveWins (Figure 5.14):

join us this International Minnie Day and share your own #lovewins story of
your own furbaby/babies. We want to hear them all! Make sure to tag us so
we can reshare and show that love truly is all around and conquers everything
🐾 #TailsOfCatCastle #MillbrooksMinnie
(Cat Castle)

We also find intertextuality in Minnie's story. Posts link to videos,
to articles in the news media, to previous posts, and more. The
overarching hashtag on Twitter is #MillbrooksMinnie, and people
often used the phrase 'Minnie update' to signal that there was new
information on Minnie. Some people briefly changed their profile
picture to Minnie's image to show their support and solidarity.

The Tails of Cat Castle #lovewins #ambassacats @catcast… · Jun 2   ···
join us this International Minnie day and share your own #lovewins story of
your own furbaby/babies. We want to hear them all! Make sure to tag us so
we can reshare and show that love truly is all around and conquers
everything 🐾 #tailsofcatcastle #millbrooksminnie

Figure 5.14 Milbrooks Minnie and #LoveWins stories

In the cat-related digital spaces, there are many more stories, with
most of them sharing moments of the cats' and people's everyday
lives. We come across non-account-specific 'good morning', 'have a
nice day', 'good evening', and 'good night' stories and account-specific
stories when the cat account holders tell their followers a regularly
occurring type of story.

Rolf at Warwick University is another good example of a shared
story. On Rolf's Twitter account, the regular updates of the cat's life
at home and at university, written by 'my American human' and 'my
English human' are called 'Rolf Report' and are labelled with the
respective day's date. Additionally, the account features Rolf poetry

written by followers. Another follower works on the #RelaxWithRolf playlist on Spotify.

Shared stories provide us with a lot of linguistic data and many verbal, visual, and audio-visual multimodal elements. We have taken up elements of discourse analysis and semiotics throughout the book, and we take the mediated narrative approach to help us with categorising the cat accounts we use for data sampling (Chapter 8) and for statistical insight (Chapter 10).

As for the contextual level, both Minnie's and Rolf's stories are generally embedded in the cat-related digital spaces but also reach outside the cat spaces into the wider realm of the news media. Cat stories in the media are quite a common occurrence, and a search on online news aggregator portals yields many articles related to cats.

Typical cat stories in the news include the story types of cat heroes, unbelievable cats, cruelty to cats, cat companions, feral cats in colonies, homeless cats in shelters, internet cats, show cats, cats and human health, or cats and business. In the media, we have certainly come across cats helping a human (cat heroes), runaway cats returning home after years of absence or cats travelling for miles hidden in the motor block of a car (unbelievable cats), cats as companions, and cats suffering from abuse. The most common types in the news media are related to heroic cats, to unbelievable cats, and to abused cats.

Regarding the socio-cultural level, we have already seen in Chapter 1 how far the cativerse extends in human society. The perception of animals has changed from commodities to sentient beings. Animals are now perceived as companion animals rather than pets, and in the UK, the status of animals as sentient beings has effects on animal welfare laws.

5.4 Cats and Their Stories

In the cativerse, cat accounts have different aims, post about different topics, and attract different audiences. Some cat accounts are raising awareness for causes while others are having fun, and others again are monetising their account. The common ground for all cat accounts, and indeed the cat-related digital spaces, is the cat and the love of animals in general, all of which their stories reflect. When we apply the narrative lens, we can see that they all tell small stories and that their stories differ somewhat in content.

Dividing the cat accounts based on the different types of stories is a step towards our analysis of language variation in the cat-related digital spaces (Chapters 9 and 10), and the account categoristion plays an important role in the stage of data sampling (see Chapter 8).

The four types of cat accounts we are going to look at below have already been mentioned briefly in Chapter 1: for-profit celebrity cats, working-for-cause cats, individual cat accounts, and collective cat accounts. A workable categorisation is based on the accounts' main small stories, their main aims, and their main content. Other factors helping us to decide in which category to put cat accounts are how professionally managed the accounts are in terms of public relations strategies and marketing concepts, as well as whether the account is used to make money with the cat's celebrity status, and whether the account features the same cat(s) or shows many different cats.

Numbers do not really help us with a division into account types because we do not really have figures to work with, apart from the statistics given by the social media platforms. These statistics can be taken as key performance indicators to identify influencers – and in the case of cats – 'cat influencers' or 'petfluencers'. Influencers have already been researched, and we have criteria for influencers, as a community, but for the many other non-influencers, these criteria are not really available.

The cat accounts belonging to the type of 'for-profit celebrity cats' fulfil the criteria of influencers. In marketing literature, they are sometimes referred to as 'cat influencers' or 'petfluencers'. Marketing identifies influencers by using the interaction rate, which refers to the number of likes, comments, shares, and followers. Digital anthropology provides more criteria for an influencer. Influencers have a high-follower to low-following ratio, sparingly use metrics – such as likes, comments, and views – provide advertorials in the content, and use a business account with more options instead of a personal account.

Additionally, influencers are more than just famous; they are micro-celebrities. Microcelebrities have attracted online fame with a loyal fanbase of followers and boost their audience engagement by sharing minute details of their lives. Influencers practise microcelebrity in that they are actively pursuing their celebrity status as opposed to people, memes, pets, icons, and more that have become viral by chance. In our categorisation of cat accounts, we must remember that not every form of internet celebrity is a microcelebrity. People, memes, and pets have become (in)famous celebrities in viral social media posts by chance without using the practice of microcelebrity.

As the name 'for-profit celebrity cats' already implies, the main aim of for-profit celebrity cats is to make money for their owners. To be fair, the owners did not always open the cat account to monetise their cats, yet the cats' celebrity status has attracted advertising and sponsoring. For-profit celebrity cats have a very large follower base and are known to the news media worldwide, which is why they are attractive for product endorsements and have consumer goods named after them. Generally, the images of the cats are very professional – as are the accounts themselves, which are based on a strategic social media concept. For-profit celebrity cats are often present on several social media platforms. While the posts of celebrity cats attract many likes and comments, the celebrity for-profit cats rarely interact with the followers.

The second type of cat accounts are the 'working-for-cause cats', and their aim is to support charities, organisations, or public institutions. The cats 'work' as community outreach cats or lend their images and online voices to public campaigns. The general feline popularity on social media is used by the working-for-cause cats to support causes and to raise awareness for serious issues. These cat accounts also have a large follower base and attract media attention, although on a lesser scale, national rather than international, than the for-profit celebrity cats. The cat account holders show their cats in their environment and write the captions in support of the issue at stake. The working-for-cause cats usually interact with their followers.

The third type are the 'individual cat accounts'. They are cat accounts for normal moggies – and pedigree cats – whose owners have opened accounts to have fun or to present their cat to the world. The individual cat account holders consider the cats as their family members and show their cats in everyday life. Images are mostly vernacular photos, which show the users' and cats' everyday lives. The individual cat accounts are the largest group of cat accounts. The follower base can be small or large, and there is a lot of interaction between cat account holders and followers.

The fourth type are the 'collective cat accounts'. Collective cat accounts feature different cats and focus on people or organisations who charitably work with many cats. Examples of collective cat accounts include accounts featuring a specific type or breed of cat or the accounts of cat charities. Collective cat accounts can have a large follower base, and there is usually frequent interaction between the account holders and their followers.

The categorisation into these four account types is, of course, largely theoretical. First, the social media status of cat accounts as petfluencers is fluid, and it is difficult to say why some cat accounts go viral and – perhaps more importantly – stay viral, thus achieving microcelebrity status, while others do not. Second, the aim, and thus the small stories, of the cat accounts is not a fixed entity. As cat account holders, we can change the focus of our posts and have our cat support an issue in addition to providing fun and showing our cats as part of our lives.

Another categorisation with a different perspective sees cat account holders as 'Fame Hound', 'Cat Herder', 'Busy Beaver', or 'Lone Wolf'. Rather than small stories, the focus here is on the motivations of cat account managers and on microcelebrities on social media as a marketing factor. The findings are based on in-person interviews, with questions on the drive and motivations for managing a cat account, the choices of visual and textual content, the cat persona, and relationships with other cat account managers.

This account typology divides cat accounts based on the desire for recognition and interaction on social media. A Fame Hound is a cat account holder who is interested in fame through their cat account rather than in establishing a social connection with others. For a Cat Herder, the cat account's main aim is to establish social connections, and fame is not important. A Busy Beaver is looking for recognition, interaction, and social connections through their cat accounts. A Lone Wolf is neither looking for fame nor for social interaction on social media.

On a feline sidenote, several cats were involved in the research on cat account managers and microcelebrities: MauMau (Figure 5.15), Honey (Figure 5.16), and Puff Marx (Figure 5.17).

Sources Used in This Chapter

🐾 Leaver et al. (2020) for influencers, communities of cultures and subcultures

🐾 Burgess et al. (2019) for social media rituals

Figure 5.15 MauMau, research assistant

🐾 Blommaert and Varis (2015) for online communities

🐾 Dailey-O'Cain (2017) for digital spaces

🐾 Gee (2005) for affinity spaces

🐾 Holmes and Wilson (2017) for communities of practice

🐾 Podhovnik (2018) for meowlogisms and communities

🐾 Page (2018) for online narratives

🐾 Georgakopoulou (2021) for narratives and social media

🐾 Mahler (2020) for language in dog-related digital spaces and communities

🐾 Shamayleh (2019) for the typology of cat account managers

🐾 Shamayleh and Arsel (2020) for cats as petfluencers and strategies for visual and textual content creation

🐾 White (2020) for development of the Internet and participatory culture

🐾 McCulloch (2019) for development of the Internet

🐾 Zuckerman (2008, 2014) for participatory culture and Cute Cat Theory

🐾 Brügger (2016) for digital humanities

🐾 University of Leeds (2014), for BBC Voices

🐾 Leemann et al. (2018) for English Dialects App

🐾 Brown and Miller (2013) for linguistic terms in the glossary

🐾 Crystal (2018) for linguistic terms in the glossary

Figure 5.16 Honey, research assistant

Examples and Quotes in This Chapter

- 🐾 Zuckerman (2014)
- 🐾 Cats Protection (2020) for information on Cats Protection
- 🐾 Wright (2015, 2017) for #AcademicsWithCats
- 🐾 Lock (2015) for Academics with Cats Awards
- 🐾 Owen and Lamon (2021) for the paper 'Are cats good? An important study'
- 🐾 13/AFP (2018) for Bayern Munich FC
- 🐾 Deportes FC Bayern US (2018) for Bayern Munich FC
- 🐾 Dailey-O'Cain (2017, pp. 126-127)
- 🐾 Herring and Dainas (2017, pp. 3, 7–8)
- 🐾 White (2020, pp. 7, 93)

The RSPCA, the largest animal welfare charity in the UK, has kindly allowed the use of Figure 5.13.

Figure 5.17 Puff Marx, research assistant

Suggestions for PURRther Reading

- White (2020)
- Seargeant (2019)
- BBC (2014)
- British Library (2021)
- Page (2018)
- Leaver et al. (2020)

6

Multimeowdality

🐱 🐈 😺 😸 😹 😺 😼 😽 🙀 😿 😾
(Cat emoji)

When we decide to put something on social media, we have to make several choices: which technological device to use, which platform to post to, what to write, how to write it, which visual elements to include, who to tag, which hashtags to use, and which of these not to do. We are almost spoilt for choice when it comes to visual elements representing cats. Our choices are not entirely free but are mediated by technology and curated to some extent by the social media platforms. Social media platforms encourage us to share everyday moments of our lives and to interact with other people. With their various prompts, the platforms offer us specific ways to create textual, visual, and audio content. The different apps for mobile devices, like smartphones and tablets, on the one hand, and laptop and desktop PCs, on the other hand, also create a different user experience for us.

In this chapter, we are looking at the interplay of textual and visual elements in social media and are approaching our multimodal cat sharing through the lenses of computer-mediated communication (CMC) and computer-mediated discourse (CMD). In Chapter 5, we saw that an analysis of computer-mediated interactions requires an interdisciplinary approach that combines methods from various fields, which is why we are taking up CMD and multimodality in this chapter to add to a well-rounded description of how we talk about our cats online.

The cats in the examples show us that, on interactive multimodal platforms, the traditional division of discourse analysis into spoken and written forms of text has to be widened to include more modes than text. Digital discourse has evolved from text-only discourse to multimodal interactions with text, audio, video, emoji, stickers, and more on a single social media platform. In the cat-related digital spaces, our cats have purred their way into all the modes that make up multimodality in CMC. Welcome to multimeowdality 😻 🙀 😹!

Concepts Discussed in the Chapter

🐾 multimodality
🐾 computer-mediated communication (CMC)
🐾 computer-mediated discourse (CMD)
🐾 computer-mediated discourse analysis (CMDA)
🐾 CMC modes
🐾 semiotic modes
🐾 graphicons
🐾 media coactivity
🐾 constraints

Terms from the Clawssary

🐾 CMC mode 🐾 critical discourse analysis 🐾 discourse 🐾 discourse analysis 🐾 faceted classification tool 🐾 graphicons 🐾 interactive multimodal platforms (IMPs) 🐾 media coactivity 🐾 mode of discourse 🐾 semiotic mode 🐾 semiotics

6.1 Caterwauling in Multimeowdal Manner

text, audio, video, emoji, stickers, GIFs, and more

Cats have expanded their range to multimodality with their digital caterwauling, and we can use them as prime examples when we outline the developments of technology and the impacts on communication possibilities. To understand the connection between technological developments and multimodal communication, we go into computer-mediated communication and its linguistic sub-field computer-mediated discourse in this chapter.

Computer-mediated discourse (CMD) is the part or sub-category of computer-mediated communication (CMC) studied by linguistics.

When we analyse CMD, we talk about computer-mediated discourse analyis (CMDA).

Simply put, with CMC we have the technical side: it refers to the technical aspect of communication in which the message exchange is digitalised at some point. 'Computer-mediated' means the technical devices, their hardware, software, and the user interfaces of communication platforms and channels. Here, 'channel' refers to the technical devices we use to interact, like our tablets, smartphones, and keyboards.

The linguistic side is covered with 'discourse' and 'discourse analysis'. 'Discourse' has two meanings in linguistics, either referring to a continuous stretch of (mostly spoken) language, on the one hand, or a style of language, such as legal discourse or digital discourse, on the other hand. 'Discourse analysis' is the study of patterns in how the discourse is organised linguistically. Alternatively, we could also say CMDA looks at how we talk and write about our cats online and create our meaning with textual, audio, and visual elements.

Research on CMC has provided us with tools to work with, namely the CMDA toolkit and the faceted classification tool. Both tools give us a framework with which we can analyse the multimodal aspects of cat-related digital discourse. The first CMDA toolkit, finalised in 2004, was originally designed for text-only discourse. At the time when the CMDA toolkit was established, technology did not offer multimodal interaction, and communication was mainly done by using text. To incorporate the new technological developments in CMC and CMD, the CMDA toolkit now incorporates multimodality as an additional feature.

The CMDA toolkit covers the five levels of structure, meaning, interaction management, social phenomena, and multimodality. For each level, we are given the issues and phenomena to look at and the methods to apply. When we want to study online discourse, we can choose the levels and use the respective methods. As we are focussing on multimodality in this chapter, we do not touch on structure, meaning, interaction management, and social phenomena.

Just to mention very briefly, we look at orthography, syntax and morphology, identity, multilingualism and code-switching, and language use on individual social media platforms in other chapters of this book (Chapters 3, 4, 7, 9–11).

The newly added level in the CMDA toolkit is multimodality, which has become an integral part of CMC. On the interactive multimodal platforms, we can choose the modes to communicate with. On one and the same platform, we can use the CMC modes of text, audio, video, and graphics. Examples of such interactive multimodal platforms are Facebook, Instagram, YouTube, and Twitter, the four social media platforms we look at in Chapter 9.

The CMDA toolkit shows us which aspects we can consider in an analysis of CMC in cat-related digital spaces and gives us a concept of multimodality with five general CMC modes, namely text, audio, video, robot, and graphics. The concept outlines the connections of the CMC modes to show how we communicate on interactive multimodal platforms. Here we leave out the robot mode because we are not dealing with human–robot or robot–robot communication in cat-related digital spaces. For our purposes, therefore, we modify the tool to ignore the element of robot.

For the technical aspects of multimodality, we use the faceted classification tool. This tool helps us with our description of CMC in the cat-related digital spaces by providing us with a list of medium and situation factors to consider. Medium factors are synchronicity, one- or two-way message transmission, persistence of transcripts, characters allowed per message, modes of communication, anonymous messaging, private messaging, filtering, quoting, and the order in which messages appear. The situation factors include the participation structure, participant characteristics, purpose, topic or theme, tone, activity, norms, and code.

Both tools are very easy to apply. For the cat-related digital spaces of our choice, we find out which textual, audio, video, and graphics elements are made available on the respective multimodal platforms and list these elements for the respective CMC mode:

- text
  post/tweet, reply/comment, share with comment, chat, group chat, direct message
- audio
  audio tweet, messenger audio call
- video
  videos (one-way, two-way, synchronous, asynchronous), reels/stories/fleets (temporary), messenger video call
- graphics
  photos, memes, meme-like photos, GIFs, emoji, stickers

On Facebook, for example, we have the textual elements of posting, replying/commenting, sharing with comment, chatting, group chatting, and direct messaging. The audio elements Facebook offers are audio calls on messenger, and we find live videos, videos, stories, and messenger video calls in the video mode. As for graphics, there are photos, memes, meme-like photos, GIFs, emoji, and stickers.

In a multimodal environment, we are dealing with two kinds of modes: CMC modes and semiotic modes. CMC modes are in their essence technology, which shapes communication by putting constraints on what is possible. Examples of CMC modes are emails, messaging, or video conferencing. Research sees CMC modes as sociotechnical constructs with online messaging protocols, around which we have constructed our social and cultural practices. The semiotic modes refer to the different ways in which we create meaning, like text, audio, and visual elements. The CMDA toolkit provides us with a way to combine both types of modes: For each CMC mode, we can analyse the various semiotic modes.

To illustrate how CMC modes and semiotic modes are connected, we take the example of online meeting platforms. Interaction on platforms like Zoom or Microsoft Teams has become quite frequent since the onset of the Covid-19 pandemic. Cats have been playing their part in online meetings, too, as the many stories in the spaces around academics with cats have shown. Figure 6.1 shows a screenshot of Wicht, Purr Reviewer 2, zoombombing an online guest lecture I attended on the platform Microsoft Teams.

Figure 6.1 Wicht zoombombing an online lecture

For a first overview, we take the situation factors offered by the faceted classification tool, like participation structure, participant characteristics, purpose, topic or theme, tone, activity, norms, and code. By filling in the fields for the situation factors, we can describe the zoombombed online lecture:

- Participant structure: by invitation only, one-to-many, small number of active speakers
- Participant characteristics: cat, members of staff, students, invited guests
- Purpose: professional, academic, informative
- Topic: satirical media in Austria, cats
- Tone: formal, friendly
- Activity: online lecture interrupted by cat
- Norms: of university, of online lectures
- Code: spoken German, occasional English word

In the next step, the CMDA toolkit comes into play, and we look at which CMC modes are used in the zoombombed online lecture. Microsoft Teams is an interactive multimodal platform that offers its users a number of modes for communication. During the zoombombed online lecture, the following CMC modes were used:

- Text: chat, direct messages
- Audio: audio stream
- Video: two-way video, gallery of participants in split windows
- Graphics: emoji, GIFs, stickers, photographs, video clips

At one point in the online lecture, Wicht placed himself in front of the camera and watched the split windows displayed on the computer screen. In situations like these, the cat very often becomes a cue for interaction. Here, too, the participants immediately reacted to the cat's presence: the visible participants displayed positive emotions like smiles and 'aaw' and used the emoji buttons directly in the gallery windows, the current speaker mentioned the cat, and other non-visible participants left messages like 'Gaaadse' (German for 'cat') and clicked on the emoji buttons, which are offered as an available reaction to the message. At the same time, students posted on Twitter in English and created a meme from the screenshot (Figure 6.2) adding the caption "'Ah yes, my most prized possession...'".

Figure 6.2 Meme created from screenshot

The best part of every online lecture? When @Meow_Factor brings in Wicht
for a few glorious seconds
(Tweet by @ifeomamoiraikea)
We want Wicht. Wicht and Wicht only'
(reply by @c_pschorr)

The CMC modes used in that online lecture were mainly video and
audio in the online lecture, as well as text and graphics in the chat.
The cat-induced interactions, thus, happened on the verbal level in
spoken as well as written language, on the non-verbal level of gestures
and facial expressions, and as 'liking' with reaction buttons and
emoji on the graphics level. The semiotic modes are text, nonverbal
communication, and 'liking' using graphics.

The study on meowlogisms (see Chapter 3) provides examples of
CMD occurring in a cat-related digital space on Instagram (Figure
6.3). The study analyses the captions and comments of three accounts
of black cats on Instagram, focussing mainly on the description of
the genre characteristics, with its typical spelling of words, use of
specific words, genre-specific conventions, and typically used hashtags.

Figure 6.3 Sample Instagram post

However, it is an analysis mainly based on text. While the study does not ignore the inherently multimodal nature of an Instagram post with its combination of image, caption, comments, likes, and emoji, the analysis does not specifically address the fact that different modes are used by the cat account holders and how these modes have affected the discourse in the particular cat-related digital space.

The sample post (Figure 6.3) illustrates the elements analysed for the study on meowlogisms: a black cat in the shared image, a caption with text, hashtags, emoji, and comments with emoji:

Enjoying myself on #SundayFunday #Cats #BlackCatsRuleTheWorld #BlackCatsOfInstagram #BlackCatsClub #meow😻 #OldCatsofInstagram #Panther #Garden #Black
(Meow.Factor)

While there is no meowlogism in this particular post, it shows the cat as the author of the post ('myself'), the response to the cat ('Have fun Murrli'), emoji reaction, emoji together with text, and the hashtags typically used in that particular digital space ('#blackcatsruletheworld').

This meowlogisms study has served as a starting point for a wider, more comprehensive description of CMD in cat-related digital spaces, namely this book. To give a rounded overview of CMD in cat-related digital spaces, we look at the various CMC modes and semiotic modes in cat-related digital spaces, and in our description of purrieties, we are considering the textual as well as the visual elements in the various chapters.

While we have already discussed textual elements, the graphics mode with its visual elements is still waiting for our examination. The visual elements important for cat-related digital spaces comprise emoji, emoticons, modified and unmodified images, memes, GIFs, and videos. The visual elements are also referred to as 'graphicons'.

6.2 Caterwauling with Graphicons

Social media provides a variety of visual elements for us. They include not only the more 'obvious' ones we choose to use as part of our messages, like emoticons, emoji, GIFs, stickers, images, and video. These are the graphicons. Visual elements also comprise the predetermined elements, like the design of the social media platforms, the templates, and the reaction buttons, such as the 'like' button. Cats have their place on all of them, as we can see in the descriptions of emoticons, emoji, stickers, and GIFs below. Although we have already talked about memes, vernacular photography, and videos in Chapters 1 and 4, we take them up again here to show them in their connection to multimodality.

Before we go into the each of the different types of graphicons, we take a look at their general functions. A linguistic study of Facebook posts and comments has analysed the use of graphicons in the comments section from public Facebook groups. The analysis goes into how often emoji, emoticons, stickers, GIFs, images, and videos occurred and how they were used to create which meaning. Six main functions have been identified, namely mention, reaction, tone modification, riffing, action, and narrative sequence. The list below explains these functions:

🐾 Mention: comments that refer to the graphicon explicitly
🐾 Reaction: the use of a graphicon as an emotional response to previous content
🐾 Riffing: a humorous elaboration or play on a previous comment or graphicon; can also be a parody

🐾 Tone modification: a graphicon accompanying the text and modifying its content; a cue as to how the comment should be interpreted

🐾 Action: the use of a graphicon to portray a physical action

🐾 Narrative sequence: a series of consecutive graphicons telling a story

Important from a cat-related point of view, the study includes data collected in Facebook groups of cat afficionados. Out of the eight public Facebook groups, two groups are cat-related, namely CatGIFs and Grumpy Cat Memes. To give the exact figures, the data comprises 24 threads with 2,888 comments and 975 graphicons collected between January 2014 and May 2016. On Facebook, the order of graphicon frequency is as follows, from most frequent to least frequent: emoji – emoticon – image – sticker – video – GIF. When looking at this result, we should keep in mind that the Facebook of 2014 to 2016 did not support all graphicon types.

As for the functions, the order ranging from most frequent to least frequent is this: reaction – tone modification – mention – riffing – action – narrative sequence. In other words, the emoji is the most common graphic icon and is used for all functions, while other graphicons have more specialised functions, and reactions are the most commonly displayed function in the Facebook group.

In the study, one observation refers directly to cats: on the level of a thread in Facebook groups, prompts with cats attract responses with personal photos and positive emoji:

> Prompts containing cats were more likely than other prompts to be responded to with personal photos and/or positive reaction emoji.
> (Herring and Dainas, 2017)

I have noticed the same effect of cat prompts on people in a professional setting. On the platform Slack, a multimodal communication platform for businesses, cats in the postings make people share cat photos and use more graphicons. In a Slack community of university students and staff, cat postings have hijacked a channel normally reserved for official administrative tasks and topics. When students introduced themselves with cat photos, two faculty members joined in and left posts with their own cats (Figure 6.4). As we can see in the image of Lemmy and Moritz, many reactions with graphicons and likes followed.

Figure 6.4 Lemmy and Moritz say hi on Slack

Lea
Ok, now I have to join with the picture! 😃 Lemmy says hi to you all! 😎 🤘
Tanja
And of course I also have a cat, which happens to look very similar to Lea's 🐱

The development and use of visual elements in social media are tied
to the technical developments and ease of use of devices. In the early
days of online interaction, technology was limited to text only. In text
messaging, for instance, we used emoticons as graphic elements to
give additional meaning to our message. While, in the early stages,
we would have needed a certain computer savviness to put a caption
on an image to create macros, we can easily make memes, GIFs, and
videos with the apps we have now. With smartphones, it also very
easy to take photographs and to share them online.

To approach multimodality in the cat-related digital spaces, we
start with the question of which CMC modes the cat account holders

use in their interactions and what meaning the individual visual elements add. The CMC concept, provided by research on CMDA, is part of the CMDA tool and guides us in our analysis of the visual modes, and research in sociology and anthropology helps us with studying online photography.

Among the modes in the CMC concept, two are visual communication modes, namely video and graphics. Here we also take into account the medium factors of synchronicity and asynchronicity and the situation factor of participant structure (one-way, or two-way). The interactive multimodal platforms often offer both types of videos, the synchronous live broadcast and the recorded video, as well as the one-way and two-way video.

For us, this means that we categorise the cat-related digital spaces likewise into whether cat account holders interact with each other per synchronous video in a one-way or two-way interaction or per (asynchronouos) graphics. The CMC mode of video is used in settings like live online lectures or video calls that are synchronous in nature, which means that the participants are present at the same time. Videos added to posts, like Instagram stories, Instagram reels, and TikTok videos, are recorded and uploaded to the interactive multimodal platforms as part of a post and are asynchronous because we do not need to be logged in at the same time, and we can classify those as graphics.

Interactive multimodal platforms like Instagram and TikTok also offer synchronous video. Users can watch live videos, click on emoji reaction buttons, and interact with others, including the host accounts, via chat.

For the graphics mode, the CMC concept distinguishes, first of all, between static and dynamic graphics. Static graphics include drawings and photographs. Dynamic graphics can be navigable, like avatars, or not navigable, like GIFs and recorded videos. With the CMC concept, thus, we have a very useful way of classifying the various visual elements in our cat-related digital spaces. Simply put, we categorise the visual elements of our posts into (recorded) videos, GIFs, emoji, image memes and meme-like images, profile pics, and other unmodified pictures.

To analyse recorded videos, we apply the medium and situation factors of the faceted classfication tool in the same way as done for the synchronous video with the medium and situation factors. Rolf, the

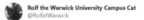

Figure 6.5 Rolf in Birdland

Warwick University Cat, uses both recorded videos and unmodified photographs in his tweets. The example in Figure 6.5 is a smartphone video accompanied by the tweet explaining what Rolf is up to in the video, and Figure 1.1 (in Chapter 1) is an unmodified photograph of Rolf showing him in an office at Warwick University.

Rolf report 13 March: Here's a very short film. After my usual big breakfast, I like to hang out in Birdland, my observation point high up in the eaves of the house. I get up close to the velux windows which makes my ear flap back & I have a thorough wash. Then I'm chilled. Rolf x
(RolfatWarwick)

Another example is Professore Mauz (Figure 6.6), a ginger tom with his own page on Facebook. On this page, snapshots of Mauz's daily life are shared via videos and photos but are not accompanied by a textual post. The mode of communication is, thus, graphic only.

Caterwauling with Photographs

The CMC concept's division of graphics into the various subgenres is just the first step in our analysis. Once we have an overview of which types of graphics are used, we can go into more detail

Figure 6.6 Mauz grooming in a cardboard box

regarding the content and meaning of the individual types of graphics. For photography and memes, sociological research on online cat photography gives us an approach based on an analysis of cat photos on the social media platform Reddit.

In addition to the category modified/unmodified, we can divide the photographs into glamorous commercial photographs and vernacular photos, as in a study on cat photos on the subreddit *r/cat* on Reddit. The decisive factor here is how the cats have been portrayed. Unlike ornamental commercial photography, vernacular photography not only shows cats as sentient beings with their individual personalities but also portrays the warm and meaningful relationship between humans and cats.

Unmodified Photographs
The first step we take, then, is to divide the images in our data into modified and unmodified photographs and then into commercial and vernacular photos. In the second step, we categorise the photos based on the content of the photos.

The *r/cat* study used a qualitative approach to the photos to define the categories and found four main types. In the subreddit *r/cat*, there are cat portraits, cats displaying juvenile play and behaviour, cats

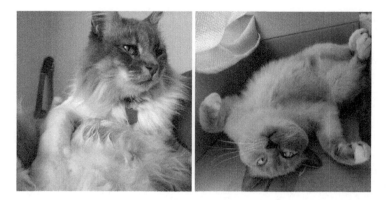

Figure 6.7 Cat pawtraits of Gaia and Skylar

in undignified or unusual poses interpreted as human-like, and cats together with humans. Portrait-style photos show cats as the central figure looking at the camera, like Gaia and Skylar in Figure 6.7 from a Twitter account in Chile. Then there are images which focus on the juvenile features of cats. Regardless of their ages, our cats retain some juvenile behaviour throughout their lives, which is a fact we like to share and see. The third type of photos, often posted for humorous purposes, presents our cats posing and acting in human-like ways, and the fourth type of photos refers to images in which cats are in the centre and humans are fully or partially visible, like the photo of Fred (Figure 6.8), who comes from the digital space of academics with cats and is one of the many cats helping research by sitting on the keyboard.

To see how we can study photographs in their connection to multimodality, we are briefly sneaking into the dog world for *Mission Impawssible?*, the title of a study on multimodality in dog-related spaces on Reddit. As briefly mentioned in Chapter 1, dogs have their own digital spaces and their own language varieties, like doggo lingo and pupper talk. *Mission Impawssible?* looks at the relationship of photographs with the use of pupper talk in dog-related subreddits. The mission undertaken by *Mission Impawssible?* is to find out if we are more likely to use pupper talk when the photos are cuter.

The element of cuteness plays an important role for account holders and followers. Cuteness is linked to the animals' faces, to their ages, and to their human-like behaviour. *Mission Impawssible?* statistically

Figure 6.8 Fred and human

measures the perceived cuteness of dog photos and looks at whether there is a statistically relevant connection to pupper talk.

For its statistical approach, *Mission Impawssible?* categorises the photographs based on three cuteness variables and accordingly analyses the textual comments establishing the percentages of pupper talk in the comments. The three cuteness variables refer to the visibility of the dog's face (visible/partially visble/averted), their ages (young/adult), and their behaviour (dog-atypical human-like/not dog-atypical human-like). The analysis has shown that the more the dog's face is visible, the more pupper talk has been used in the sample, while age and human-like behaviour do not affect the usage of pupper talk. Here, *Mission Impawssible?* inserts a word of caution because other factors, like the type of subreddit and the community practices, also affect the use of pupper talk.

On a methodological sidenote, *Mission Impawssible?* uses descriptive statistics and inferential statistics to describe the dog-related subreddits. We will come back to using statistics in linguistics in Chapter 10.

Figure 6.9 Balou, canine research inspiration

To give credit where credit is due, we analyse an image of Balou (Figure 6.9), the dog who partially inspired the *Mission Impawssible?* study. The image of Balou is an unmodified photograph showing the dog in a snapshot of his everyday life. It is vernacular because it presents Balou as a sentient being and expresses a warm and meaningful relationship with his owner. It is a portrait-style photograph with the dog in the centre looking at the camera. The dog's face is fully visible.

Back now in the feline ranges of the digital world, the visibility of the cat is a factor we can use to categorise photographs. A citizen science experiment for a school fair has studied the effect of eye visibility on our perception of cuteness. To test the claim that the cutest photos have two visible eyes, a nine-year-old cat owner asked people to select the cutest photos of his cat Milis (Figure 6.10) in a series of photographs. The tweet describes the set-up:

A few weeks ago he [Colin] read some guides to taking cat photos and one of the recurring suggestions was to include both eyes in the frame
He thought some of the cutest photos of cats have no visible eyes and wanted

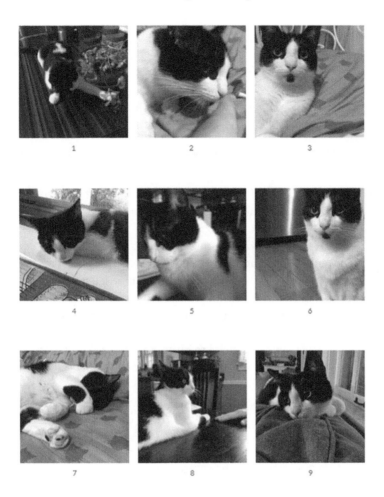

Figure 6.10 Cuteness factor of Milis

to test this advice empirically. He designed an experiment that needed 9 photos of Milis: 3 with both eyes visible, 3 with one eye visible, and 3 with no eyes visible
(Colin's Father on Twitter)

The call for participants was posted in the linguistics space of #AcademicsWithCats on Twitter, and 5,000 people took part in the online survey. The results of the survey show that the cutest photo has both eyes visible. The second and third cutest photos, however, do not show the eyes.

The cat cuteness experiment, by the way, is a typical example for the purrticipatory culture and the affinity space of #AcademicsWith-Cats, which we came across in Chapter 5.

Memes and Meme-Like Images

The fact that an adorable kitty can perfectly capture a funny and relatable moment is on another level of funny.
(Reader's Digest Editors on www.rd.com/list/hilarious-cat-memes-youll-laugh-at-every-time/)

With the LOLcats of Chapter 4, we have already got to know a typical cat meme. Cat memes have gone beyond the realm of LOLcats into mainstream culture and across the age groups. Cat memes are discussed in the media with an older demographic profile, as the quote from *Reader's Digest* indicates. When we search 'cat meme' images on Google, one of the first search results is an article from *The Daily Bayonet* listing the cat memes that trended the most in 2020. Among them are the 'women yelling at cat memes', the 'surprised cat memes', the 'high cat memes', 'cute cat memes', 'crying cat memes', and the 'thug cat memes', all of which are given variations with the captions and dialogues assigned by people. *The Daily Bayonet* calls the cat meme a treasure.

the 2020 cat meme world has brought us more treasure. This treasure is to make us laugh and forget our tensions for a while
The Daily Bayonet on https://dailybayonet.com/best-cat-meme-2020/

As already mentioned in the sub-section on photography, the CMC concept differentiates between unmodified and modified photographs. Modified photos comprise memes and meme-like images. When we study the modified photos in the cat-related digital spaces, we find modified images that are not memes, although they look like them at first glance. The definition of memes says that memes are virally spread and show variation, and not all modified photos fulfil the criteria of a meme.

The OED defines the meme as an image, video, or piece of text that is passed on from on person to the next and to which people may add their own elements. A meme is humorous, is copied and shared rapidly, and there are often slight variations to it. In terms of modes, this means that memes can be visual as well as textual, like the 'keep calm' meme in the quote in Figure 6.11.

Figure 6.11 Keep calm and meow on

Keep calm and meow on
Keep calm and cat on
(Text memes)

The phrase 'keep calm and carry on' is a really well-known visual as well as textual meme. A quick Google search has come up with feline variations for the 'carry on' bit: there is 'meow', 'cat', 'purr on', 'hiss', 'hiss on', 'every day is Caturday', 'enjoy Caturday', and many more. With a meme, we show that our communication is intended as humour, and we can easily create memes now with apps.

In the year 2020, the 'Dolly Parton Challenge' went viral after the singer Dolly Parton posted an image macro composed of four pictures of herself with 'LinkedIn', 'Facebook', 'Instagram', and 'Tinder' as captions as a parody on how we present ourselves on the social media platforms: professional on LinkedIn, with friends and family on Facebook, living our best life on Instagram, and dating on Tinder. Many people took up the challenge and created their visual memes using the hashtag #DollyPartonChallenge. In the memes, the four

Figure 6.12 Hosico and the Dolly Parton Challenge

captions stay the same, only the four photos change. Here, the criteria for memes are fulfilled as there is humour, the meme was rapidly shared and copied, and people added their own variations to it.

Cat account holders, too, joined in and posted feline versions of the challenge, sometimes as the 'Dolly Purrton Challenge'. The cat Hosico, a petfluencer from Russia with 1.9 million followers on Instagram, participated (Figure 6.12) and posted his version on his social media account.

Not all modified photos fall into the category of memes because they do not fulfil all the criteria of memes. While clearly intended as humour, the modification is not based on a virally spread image with slight variations. But, perhaps more importantly, the meme-like photos still convey the personal meaningful relationship with the

Figure 6.13 Queen Pinky and her official royal photograph

human owner and are not solely used as fun objects. The cat Queen
Pinky (shown in Figure 6.13), who we met in Chapter 4, is meme-like
with the crown pasted on her head to indicate the royal status she
enjoys in the eyes of her owner and her followers.

Caterwauling with Drawn Graphics

Static graphics include emoticons, emoji, and stickers, which we add
to our messages to show our attitude and emotion. A recent study
looking at the use of emoji and stickers on Facebook Messenger sees a
change throughout time in our use of emoticons, emoji, and stickers.
With the advent of emoji, emoticons lost in popularity, and their
meanings and functions shifted to make place for emoji. The same
is perhaps happening now that stickers are becoming more popular.
Emoticons, emoji, and stickers have developed slightly different
functions, which means that changes are taking place in how we use
them. An additional issue we should keep in mind is that there may
very well be cross-cultural differences in how we use the graphicons.

Emoticons

The word emoticon is a blending of 'emotion' and 'icon'. Emoticons
have been used since the 1970s and consist of ASCII characters.
The abbreviation ASCII is short for 'American Standard Code for

Information Interchange' and refers to a standard character encoding
for electronic communication that ensures that we can read digital
text across the world and across devices.

The Oxford English Dictionary defines an emoticon as a

representation of a facial expression formed by a short sequence of keyboard
characters (usually to be viewed sideways)
(Oxford English Dictionary)

A cat represented in emoticons looks like this: =^.^= or >^.^<.
The sequence of keyboard characters depends on our choice of
whiskers, eyes, and nose. By the way, the platform Wikihow gives good
instructions for beginners on how to create cats with our keyboard,
including an instruction for the more complex cat:

```
    \      /\
    )    ( `)
   (    /  )
    \  ( __)|
```

People have gone beyond the simple one-line emoticons and have
created more elaborate ASCII art, like Figures 6.14 and 6.15. The
abbreviation 'SJIS' within Figure 6.14 stands for 'Shift Japanese
Industry Standards' and refers to ASCII art.

We have been adding emoticons to our posts in at least four
possibly overlapping functions. With emoticons we express emotions,
especially non-seriousness, lightness, and humour; we use them to
mimic non-verbal signals; we emphasise or downplay the force of our

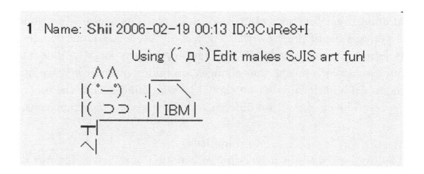

Figure 6.14 ASCII cat

Figure 6.15 ASCII box pawty

utterances; and we use them as punctuation marks. The meanings of some emoticons have broadened, like the smiling face emoticon ':)', which has widened its meaning from happiness and positive attitude to sincerety and politeness.

Emoji 🐱🐱

=^.^= converting to 🐱

We still use emoticons today, but depending on the app and on our settings, emoticons can be automatically converted to emoji. For us, emoji express the same functions as emoticons but are visually more expressive and have a stronger impact on us. We find emoji more useful, interesting, fun, easy, and informal. We use emoji to keep the conversation going, to make fun of other graphicons ('riffing'), and to narrate events. The emoji in the quote below tell the story of James Bowen and Streetcat Bob from their meeting to writing the book and making the movie.

🐱🐱📱🐾🎸🎤✍️📗🎬🎞️🎥 Congratulations James Bowen & Bob (comment of Facebook)

The word 'emoji' is a borrowing from the Japanese language consisting of 'e' for 'picture' and 'moji' for 'letter' or 'character' and refers to a small digital image or icon used to express an idea, emotion, and more in electronic communications While the word 'emoji' resembles the word 'emoticon' in form and meaning, the resemblance is probably coincidental, according to the OED. Emoji are encoded as part of the text and are governed by the Unicode

Consortium. They are standardised, and conventions of emoji use in communication have developed: We often use emoji in clusters, like in this comment:

Yay 🐱 🐱 🐱 😺 😺 😺🐾 🐾 🐾
(Comment on Instagram)

As cats have made quite an impact on emoji, cat emoji get their own section, and we have a more detailed look at them there.

Stickers

they used stickers to express their personality, e.g., through sending [...]a cat character to 'express my inner cat'.
(Konrad et al., 2020, p. 25)

The word 'stickers' has been taken to represent the little images that are added to the posts similar to the adhesive labels in the real world. In terms of technology, online stickers are cut and pasted as image files and are not encoded as part of the text as emoji are. For us as users, the difference between stickers and emoji is that stickers are platform- and channel-dependent and may have to be bought, while emoji are standardised and free and are usually available across platforms. There is no such standardisation for stickers, and stickers may be a commercial commodity. The sticker in Figure 6.16, though,

Figure 6.16 Cat laptop sticker

Figure 6.17 WhatsApp stickers of Daisy

displaying a cat typing on a laptop, is freely available via Wikimedia Commons.

Not being governed by a ruling body when it comes to stickers means that we can create our very own stickers and sticker packs with the many apps available for the operating systems of our mobile devices, like the stickers of Daisy in Figure 6.17. While we can use many stickers for free, we may also have to buy the stickers if we want to use them, as we can see in the example of the Simon's Cat YouTube channel. The commercial side to the stickers is certainly worth mentioning because the stickers are huge business with an enormous revenue.

Stickers are created and spread very quickly, and they are much more diverse than emoji. Additionally, stickers can be based on actual events and can represent real people and companies, all of which is actually forbidden for emoji standardised by Unicode. Because stickers are not standardised, we do not use stickers in such conventions as we do emoji.

The function of stickers is to help interpret the message and to express complex emotions. Especially in Asia, stickers have become very popular, and some communicative functions have been established. For the users, stickers express how they wish to be perceived by others and are used instead of text for greetings and closings in text messages. We add stickers to our messages to convey fun and emotions, to illustrate what we write, and to 'riff' on other graphicons.

Recent research on graphicons has identified the types of functions for emoji and stickers. While the functions overlap, stickers are perceived as louder and convey more than emoji: in addition to expressing emotion, emphasising the message, softening the message, acknowledging the message, clarifying a joke, making conversation fun, adding cuteness, responding quickly, and responding with a graphicon to another graphicon, stickers convey something specific, make others laugh, relate to others, are playful and flirty, start or end a conversation, and express our personality.

Caterwauling with Dynamic Meows

A black cat sharpening its claws with a nailfile.
A widespread GIF

The word GIF is short for 'Graphic Interchange Format'. GIFs are files that contain still or moving images and often show exaggerated expressions of emotions with which we can illustrate our reactions. When we add animated GIFs to a message, we usually do that as a reaction to another message. Research on GIFs has found that GIFs express more emotions more intensely. Adding GIFs is quite easy as all we have to do is to use a platform where GIFs can be used, search for GIFs in a database (often provided on the social media platform itself), and add a suitable GIF to our own message. Like stickers, we can make our own animated GIFs to share online.

6.3 Caterwauling and CMC

For discourse in general, the textual, audio, and visual possibilities to interact on interactive multimodal platforms make us deal with the phenomenon of media coactivity. Media coactivity means that we can do many things using different modes on one and the same platform, which is likely to have an impact on how we produce our messages and process the discourse – or how we send and receive communication. It also means that multimodal interaction is a competition for the users' attention.

The cat-related digital spaces we look at in Chapter 9 are located on interactive multimodal platforms. Instagram, Facebook, Twitter, and YouTube are multimodal with text, audio, video, and graphics available for us to create meaning. Facebook offers us our own homepage with the newsfeed, friending, messaging, stories, photos and videos, pages and groups, events, and more. Facebook's Messenger allows us to communicate via text message, voice or video call and to send photos videos, stickers, and GIFs. The textual, audio and video, and graphics features of Instagram include the photo and video sharing feed, direct messaging, group messaging, stories, reels, IGTV, and messenger across Instagram and Facebook. Twitter's features include the timeline, tweets, photos, videos, live videos, GIFs, direct messages, and fleets, and Twitter was testing audio message tweets in March 2021. YouTube features videos, commenting, livestreams, and community interactions on channels, including chats.

The platforms put technical constraints on our online communication. Not just in the cat-related digital spaces but also on the platforms in general, these constraints impact the type of message we can send, our behaviour in turn-taking, and the order in which we see posts in our timeline or newsfeed.

Our posts are affected by the given infrastructure of the social media platforms, which offer us specific formats with their templates, layout, and architecture and use algorithms that organise the content posted. Using various prompts, social media platforms curate our content and steer us towards sharing-the-moment stories, which are a specific type of story-telling, Even though the platforms stress the importance of real-life representations and authenticity, the algorithms rely on likes, views, and other metrics to feed us the content we are assumed to like or 'care about'.

Studies on influencers, also called microcelebrities, have shown that influencers post the types of visuals and text that appeal most to their followers and are ranked high by the algorithms, and the more their content is viewed, the more money is involved. The effect is that content is no longer created freely and individually but rather shaped by the social media platforms to be monetised as much as possible. If we aspire to become microcelebrities, we will copy the methods of successful influencers, post the same kind of content in the same way, and use the templates provided by the social media platforms, like graphicons and various CMC modes.

The way we can post is predetermined by the social media platforms. When we look at where the photos and texts are located in each individual post, we see the differences between the platforms. On Facebook and Twitter, the text is first and the photo or video comes second, while on Instagram and YouTube the image or video comes first, and the caption or description is placed underneath. Other examples of a predetermined post types are Twitter, which limits tweets to 240 characters and allows a maximum of 2,400 tweets and 1,000 direct messages per day, and Instagram, which sets the maximum of hashtags at 30 hashtags per post.

The CMC modes also constrain the flow of our conversations as turn-taking is shaped by the setup of the platforms. Twitter, for example, displays the tweets in a way that makes us feel part of a discussion between participants. We can easily read other people's comments even if they are not directly replying to us. Replies to tweets we have commented on or have liked show up in our newsfeed as tweets.

Facebook's newsfeed works differently as it displays only the post but not the comments. Comments are indicated by notifications and, if many of our friends have liked or commented on a post, the algorithms may move that particular post to the top of our newsfeed. Instagram works similarly to Facebook in that we only see the posts but not the comments in our newsfeed. For likes and comments on our own posts and comments we have left, we receive notifications, but, we do not see other people's comments on another user's post unless we actively return to that post. On YouTube, we are allowed to comment on a video if the channel owner has switched the comments section on. Depending on our settings, we receive notifications when someone has interacted with our comments. Likes and dislikes are anonymous.

The newsfeed, too, has an influence on communication and community building. While Twitter allows us to toggle between top posts and latest posts, Twitter's algorithm may still decide to show other tweets in our timeline and suggest content to us. On Facebook and Instagram, too, the feed is determined by technology. On Facebook, the default setting for the placement of posts is influenced by our connections and our activities. While we can adjust the settings more to our liking, there is no chronological order to the posts, and after some time, the settings return to the default. The Instagram feed always shows us the images in the order determined by Instagram's technology, and we cannot choose between 'top' and 'most recent posts' but are shown the content Instagram's algorithms decide on.

This predetermined feed is a technological constraint on communication. Twitter's and Instagram's algorithms, for example, look for signals to decide which post to show in our feed and in which order. Twitter's signals are based on a tweet's popularity and network interaction with a tweet, and Instagram's signals include the 'likelihood you'll be interested in the content, the date the post was shared', and 'previous interaction with the person posting'. In that way, the algorithms constrain our communication behaviour and our network- and relationship-building because technology decides whose posts we see first.

6.4 Caterwauling and Its Emoji

How does the Unicode Consortium choose which new emoji to add to the Unicode Standard?
One important factor is data about how frequently current emoji are used. Patterns of usage help to inform decisions about future emoji. The Consortium has been working to assemble information about how frequently various emoji are used and is making that data available to the public. (Unicode Consortium, 2019)

An informative source for everything emoji-related is the website www.emojipedia.org. We only need to type 'cat' into the search field, and Emojipedia provides us with information about the cat emoji, what they mean, when they were adopted by Unicode, what they are called, and how they appear on different mobile devices. The site gives links to further data, such as the exact number of the proposal made to Unicode and the files, which are open access. For the cat face emoji shown in Table 6.1, www.emojipedia.org links to the proposals made to Unicode. The Table 6.1 is based on the proposal of 2009.

Apart from the names of the cat face emoji, there is one difference between what was proposed and what was finally included. The 2007 and 2009 proposals to Unicode contained one cat emoji and nine cat face emoji. In Unicode's Emoji Version 1.0, however, there are 10 cat face emoji, and the names have been changed. The additional cat-face emoji is the grinning cat face with open mouth. In its Emoji Version 1.0, the Unicode Consortium rolled out all emoji approved between 2010 and 2015, and we can now choose from 11 cat-related emoji to communicate online: one cat and 10 cat face emoji. Table 6.2 shows the emoji together with their names and the meanings originally given to them. As we have seen above, the emoji meanings have changed.

Depending on the mobile device and on the social media platform, cat face emoji – and of course the cat emoji itself – have a different appearance. We can see the differences in Table 6.3, which gives us the platforms and the symbols.

Multimeowdality

Table 6.1 *Proposal of cat face emoji to Unicode in 2009*

Code Point	Symbol	Name & Annotations	Internal ID
U+1F381		CAT FACE WITH OPEN MOUTH Temporary Notes: Happy	e-348
U+1F382		HAPPY CAT FACE WITH GRIN Temporary Notes: Forms a pair with e-333. Hee hee hee	e-349
U+1F383		HAPPY AND CRYING CAT FACE Temporary Notes: Forms a pair with e-334. Tears of joy	e-34A
U+1F384		CAT FACE KISSING Temporary Notes: Forms a pair with e-320. Kissing action	e-34B
U+1F385		CAT FACE WITH HEART-SHAPED EYES Temporary Notes: Forms a pair with e-327. Heart-shaped eyes (in love)	e-34C
U+1F386		CRYING CAT FACE Temporary Notes: Forms a pair with e-339. Crying (one or two tears)	e-34D
U+1F387		POUTING CAT FACE Temporary Notes: Forms a pair with e-33D	e-34E
U+1F388		CAT FACE WITH TIGHTLY CLOSED LIPS Temporary Notes: Smart confidence	e-34F
U+1F389		ANGUISHED CAT FACE Temporary Notes: Forms a pair with e-321	e-34G

In case we are interested in which of the emoji are the most frequent, we can go the Unicode webpage and check out the ranking of emoji. Emoji are put into various groups depending on how their frequency relates to the top emoji – the face with tears of joy. As it turns out, quite a number of cat face emoji are in one of the ten most frequent emoji groups. The smiling cat with heart-eyes and the grinning cat

Table 6.2 *Cat-related emoji in Emoji Version 1.0*

Emoji	Emoji Name	Original Emoji Meaning
	Cat (also known as Domestic Cat, Feline, Housecat)	A domestic cat, beloved as a pet. Generally depicted as a light orange cat with stripes in full profile on all fours facing left, with its long tail held upright.
	Cat Face (also known as :3, Kitten, Kitty)	Meow! A friendly, cartoon-styled face of a cat, looking straight ahead. Generally depicted as a yellowish-orange cat face with pointed ears and whiskers. May be used with a more affectionate tone than the full-bodied Cat, though their applications generally overlap.
	Cat with Wry Smile (also known as Smirking Cat)	A cartoon cat variant of Smirking Face. Often used to convey flirtation or sexual innuendo.
	Cat Face with Tears of Joy (also known as Happy Tears Cat, Laughing cat)	A cartoon cat variant of Face with Tears of Joy. Widely used to show something is funny or pleasing.
	Weary Cat (also known as Scared Cat, Screaming Cat)	A cartoon cat variant of Weary Face. May convey various feelings of frustration, sadness, amusement, and affection. Often playful in tone.
	Pouting Cat Face (also known as Grumpy Cat)	A cartoon cat variant of Pouting Face. Also resembles Angry Face. Sometimes used to represent the internet meme and celebrity Grumpy Cat.
	Crying Cat (also known as Sad Cat)	A cartoon cat variant of Crying Face. May convey a moderate degree of sadness or pain.
	Smiling Cat Face with Heart-Eyes (also known as Heart-Eyes Cat, Loving Cat)	A cartoon cat variant of Smiling Face with Heart-Eyes. Often conveys enthusiastic feelings of love, infatuation, and adoration (e.g., I love/am in love with this person or thing).
	Grinning Cat Face with Open Mouth (also known as Happy Cat, Smiling Cat)	A cartoon cat variant of Grinning Face. Often conveys general pleasure and good cheer or humour.
	Grinning Cat Face with Smiling Eyes	A cartoon cat variant of Grinning Face with Smiling Eyes. Often conveys general happiness and good-natured amusement.
	Kissing Cat Face with Closed Eyes (also known as Kissing Cat)	A cartoon cat variant of Kissing Face with Closed Eyes. Commonly conveys sentiments of romantic love and affection.

Table 6.3 *Cat emoji on different platforms*

Platform	Cat Emoji
Google	
Twitter	
EmojiOne v2	
Firefox OS Emoji	
OpenMoji	

Table 6.4 *Cat emoji frequency*

Emoji	Group
	5
	6
	8
	8
	8
	9
	9
	10
	10

face with tears of joy are the two most popular cat face emoji (Table 6.4).

From a feline point of view, it is quite fascinating to see that there are so many cat-related emoji. Human face emoji have cat face equivalents, but there are no dog face equivalents. One reason could be that the Internet culture is very much connected to Japanese culture. Many technological advances and the corresponding aesthetics and symbols have come from Japan, and from a Japanese point of view, the inclusion of cats and cat-related symbols and pictograms is no coincidence. Cats have always had a special place in Japan and in Japanese popular culture, and cats have indeed played a role in the development of emoji.

In 1970s Japan, teenage girls used the cute way of 'kitten writing'- or 'koneko ji' in Japanese. In the kitten writing style, the writing is done in large and rounded characters, often with decorations with hearts, stars, and cartoon faces. In turn, kitten writing became part of the cute – or 'kawaii' – culture, Japan's youth culture. With the very popular anime TV series and video games like *Sailor Moon*, *Super Mario*, and *Pokémon*, 'Cool Japan' has come to culturally influence the western world and has given us not just 'Hello Kitty' but also the cat emoji.

Structural use of emoji to indicate the end of this chapter

Sources Used in This Chapter

- Mahler (2020) for pupper talk on Reddit
- Spitzberg (2006) for CMC
- Androutsopoulos (2006, 2014b) for CMC
- Herring (2019) for development of the Internet and CMDA
- McCulloch (2019) for development of the Internet
- Emojipedia.org (2020a), Unicode Consortium (2007) for Unicode Consortium
- Seargeant (2019) for Unicode and emoji; also Japanese culture
- Herring and Dainas (2017) for graphicons and multimodal interaction
- Konrad et al. (2020) for graphicons
- Google (2020) for stickers
- Page (2018) for mediated narrative analysis
- Georgakopoulou (2021) for mediated story-telling
- Brown and Miller (2013) for linguistic terms in the glossary
- Crystal (2018) for linguistic terms in the glossary

Examples and Quotes in This Chapter

🐾 Colin McGowan and Kevin B McGowan have kindly shared information on Colin's Cute Cat Experiment

🐾 Cats Protection (2020) for information on Cats Protection

🐾 Emojipedia.org (2020b) for cat emoji

🐾 Emojipedia.org (2020c) for cat face emoji

🐾 Unicode Consortium (2019) for most frequent emoji

🐾 wikiHow (2020) for ASCII cat

🐾 The cat sticker was taken from Idil Keysan for the Wikimedia Foundation, CC BY-SA 4.0 <https://creativecommons.org/licenses/by-sa/4.0>, via Wikimedia Commons

🐾 Simon's Cat (2021) for stickers

🐾 Herring and Dainas (2017, pp. 3, 7–8)

🐾 Konrad et al. (2020, p. 25)

🐾 Table 6.1 is based on the Unicode Consortium (2009)

🐾 The emoji in Tables 6.3 and 6.4 are used under the following licenses:

  – By Google, https://github.com/googlei18n/noto-emoji/tree/v20 18-08-10-unicode11/svg/emoji_u1f408.svg, Apache License 2.0, https://commons.wikimedia.org/w/index.php?curid=76890255

  – By Twitter, CC BY 4.0, https://commons.wikimedia.org/w/index.php?curid=80932960

  – By Emoji One, CC BY-SA 4.0, https://commons.wikimedia.org/w/index.php?curid=37427936

  – By Mozilla, CC BY 4.0, https://commons.wikimedia.org/w/index.php?curid=59726901

  – By OpenMoji, CC BY-SA 4.0, https://commons.wikimedia.org/w/index.php?curid=69428538

Suggestions for PURRther Reading

🐾 Herring (2019) for CMDA tool and multifaceted classification tool

🐾 Seargeant (2019) for emoji

7

Meow and More

Exercise 3: In Britanny [...] the mother spoke Breton to the dog because it was [a] farm dog, but she used (in her view) the more sophisticated language, French, to the cat because it was a pet. If you live in a multilingual speech community you might like to make notes on which language people use to their pets and why.
(Holmes and Wilson, 2017)

Which language or language variety do we use when we talk to cats and other pets? This is the question asked by the quote above, taken from an introductory book to sociolinguistics. As for me, I use German even with pets living in English-speaking countries. Despite my proficiency in English, German feels more natural to me in these situations, and I switch codes when I talk to an animal. My cat account online, however, is mainly in English. Why I use more than one language and what this says about me are sociolinguistic questions, and this chapter will look at them in detail.

From a sociolinguistic point of view, cat-related digital spaces are a rich resource for examples of sociolinguistic variation and phenomena. As sociolinguists, we are interested in what our language choices say about our social background, and we look at why we make a particular choice, on the one hand, and how our uses of language are perceived by others, on the other.

In this chapter, the cats in the cat-related digital spaces lead us to the areas of code, code-switching, bilingualism, and multilingualism. They stray once more to technology to show how it affects multilingual online discourse, and then they patrol with us the field of how we use language to construct our identity. Cat account holders from around the world use different languages and language varieties not

Figure 7.1 Wicht, Purr Reviewer 2

just to communicate with each other but also to construct their cat identities. The cat account holders' linguistic practices give us insights into identity and identity creation in cat-related digital spaces.

In addition to English, the cat-related examples for this chapter come from a variety of languages, namely Croatian, Danish, Dutch, Farsi, French, German, Russian, Slovenian, Spanish, and Turkish. And there are some examples from Japanese and Korean too.

On a sidenote for this chapter, my cat Wicht, Purr Reviewer 2, has commented on the manuscript, and I have left his comments where he inserted them on his way across the keyboard (Figure 7.1). His 'remarks' are a tongue-in-cheek example of the code of a real cat.

Concepts Discussed in the Chapter

- 🐾 bilingualism
- 🐾 multilingualism

- 🐾 code
- 🐾 domains of language use
- 🐾 multilingual online discourse
- 🐾 code
- 🐾 code-switching
- 🐾 transnational communication
- 🐾 networked multilingualism
- 🐾 polylanguaging
- 🐾 translanguaging
- 🐾 identity
- 🐾 identity construction

Terms from the Clawssary

🐾 code 🐾 code-switching 🐾 inter-sentential switching 🐾 intra-sentential switching 🐾 metrolingualism 🐾 monolingualism 🐾 multilingualism 🐾 polylanguaging 🐾 social network 🐾 social variable 🐾 sociolinguistics 🐾 speech community 🐾 style 🐾 translanguaging

7.1 The Meow Code

meow – miau – miaou – miao – мяу – νιάου – mijav – miyav – mauw
(English, German, French, Italian, Russian, Greek, Slovenian, Turkish, Dutch)

There are many ways to say and write 'meow'. While English tends to be the lingua franca on the Internet, other languages are very much present too. In our conversations in the cat-related digital spaces, we often use more than one language, not just because we want to say 'meow' in various languages but because we are bilingual or multilingual.

Research has shown that more people are bilingual or multilingual than monolingual. Even in apparently monolingual countries where a single language is spoken by the majority of the population, there is a substantial group of speakers of other languages, which means that societies are multilingual rather than monolingual. Societies become multilingual for various reasons. Depending on the circumstances, some people choose to learn and speak another language, while others, however, are forced to do so. Education, culture, politics, religion, economy, and natural disasters play a role in people's willingness or necessity to move to a region with a language different from their own.

Many cat-related digital spaces are multilingual. In Chapter 2, we came across the 2019 survey in which cat account holders shared their words and endearments for cats in English. There, we looked at the lexical variation in the English language from a regional dialectological point of view, with the wordlist and the localities in which the words occur. The same survey also provided us with data that illustrates the multilingual side of the cat-related digital spaces. As we can see in the list below, there are many words for 'cat' and endearments for cats. The survey respondents shared their words in a number of different languages: Croatian, Danish, Dutch, Farsi, French, German, Russian, Slovenian, Spanish, and Turkish. For each language, the words for 'cat' are listed first and the endearments come second.

🐾 Croatian
maca, macketina, mace, macak
Maca, mac
🐾 Danish
Kat
(no endearment shared)
🐾 Dutch
poes, kat, miauwbeest, kattenbeest, poeswoes, tijger, poezel, poezenbeest, poes, poeswoes, kitty, poesje, kat, hongermonster, beest, poezel, vreetzak, rotbeest, snertkat, kachel, snertbeest, zeurder, zeurbeest, snurkie, tijger
miauwwauw, poes, poezel, poeswoes, snoepie, tijgertje
🐾 Farsi
(no word for 'cat' shared)
baboshy
🐾 French
chat, chaton, chatte, greffier, Mademoiselle, matou
haton, chatoune, ma pépette
🐾 German
Boga, Büsi, Chätzli, DaMüizn, Depp, Dicker, Fellknäuel, Fellmonster, Fellnase, Fetti, Flauschi, Fluffi, Gadse, Gata, Hauskatz, Kater, Katerlein, Katerli, Katz, Kätzchen, Katze, Katzen, Katzer, Katzerl, Katzetatze, Katzi, Katzilein, Katzili, Kotz [koːts], Le Miez, LeMüiz, Mäusi(s), Mautzi, Miau, Miaui, Mietz, Mietze,

Mietzekatze, Mietzi, Miez, Mieze, Miezekatze, Miezmiez, Mini-
panter, Minitiger, Minki, Mitzi, Mizi, Monster, Muck, Muschi,
Mutz, Mutzi, Mutzie, Mutzikatze, Mutzili, Mutzmutz, Müüzn,
Muzi, Muzili, Müzn, Panter, Pengling, Pinguin, Schatzi, Schnuffi,
Schnurrler, Schnurrli, Stritzi, Stubentiger, Süße, Traktor
Baby, Brummbärchen, Bubu, Depp, Dickerchen, Doofie, Eierbär,
ein richtiger Boga, Fellknäuel, Fellknäuelchen, Fetti, Flauschball,
Flauschi, Flauschmonster, Gadse, Herzilein, Hübsche, Katerlein,
Katerli, Katz, Kätzchen, Katze, Katzerl, Katzerle, Katzi, Katzilein,
Katzili, Knauschi, Maunzi, Mäuschen, Mausi, Mauzn, mein Baby,
mein Großer, Miau, Mietz, Mietzekatze, Mietzi, Mietzie, Mietzi-
Maus, Miez, Mieze, Mieze-kätzchen, Miezekatze, Miezmiez, Mutzi,
Mutzie, Mutzili, Mutzmutz, Mutz-Mutz, Müüzn, Müüzntatzen,
Muzi, Muzili. Schatzi, Schatziiii, Schlafmütze, Schmusi, Schnugi,
Schnurli, Schnurrbärtchen, Schnurrer, Schnurrler, Schnurrli,
SchnurrliMaus, Stinker, Süße, Tiger, Wuschibaby
🐾 Russian
кошка, кошечка, киса, киска (f), кот, котик (m), котёнок,
котька, котечка
киса, киска, котик
🐾 Slovenian
maček, mačka, mica, muc, muca, muci, mujc
buci, cartek/cartika, lepotica, lev, muci, princesa, princeska, zver
🐾 Spanish
gatito, minino, mino
gatito, guapo, minino
🐾 Turkish
kedi, kedicik, kediş, minnoş, pisi pisi, pisi, pişik, tatlış
apşik, aşkım, birtanem, canım, canlarım, cüce, eşek sıpası, eşek,
guzelim, güzelim, iblis, kızım, kuzum, minnoş, oğlum, paşam, pisi
pisi, sarman, tatlışlarım, tekir, tüy torbalarım, yavrularım

The respondents who shared these words are bilingual or multilingual. As we will see later when we talk about networked multilingualism of cat-related digital spaces, it does not matter how well we know
a language to be considered bilingual or multilingual. What matters
is that we use other languages.

To find out more about language variation, we turn to sociolinguistics as it is the field that deals with social language variation and

looks at our choice of language, referred to as 'code' in the case of another language and 'variety' in the case of a dialect.

We all have a linguistic repertoire at our disposal, which consists of all the languages we use as well as of the regional and social varieties of a language. We may be monolingual, bilingual, or multilingual, and which particular code or variety we use depends on certain social factors, like the situation or context we are in. In the cat-related digital spaces too, the linguistic repertoire of cat account holders affects their communication with their followers.

As Murrli, I used a number of codes in the posts and comments in my cat account on Instagram. While I interacted mainly in English, I commented in German to followers from German-speaking countries. As my linguistic repertoire comprises more foreign languages, I had Murrli occasionally switch to other languages, like Italian, Russian, and French, for comments to a cat shelter in Italy, to the Russian cat Henry, and to a French cat. As Murrli, I used meowlogisms, but no other purrieties because they were then not part of my linguistic repertoire. Now they are.

In any case, why we use certain codes in certain situations and what our code choices say about us are questions that sociolinguistics answers. Several social factors influence our code choice, and there are specific patterns in our language use. When we apply the sociolinguistic concept of 'domains of language use', we can identify these specific linguistic patterns in a community.

The domain of language use is a general concept that shows the typical interactions between typical participants in typical settings. To find the domains, we examine who is usually involved in the communication, where the communication takes place, and what the participants talk or write about. For many communities, domains typically consist of family, friendship, religion, education, and employ-ment, which have proved relevant when it comes to describing patterns of code choice.

Sociolinguistic research describes a way in which we can identify the patterns of language use. We take five categories, namely domain, addressee, setting, topic, and variety/code and, with these as a guide, we can describe the domains of language use and more insight into the choices of code/variety people make in a community. This simple categorisation is useful when we are trying to find out which codes or varieties are important in a community, on the one hand, and when

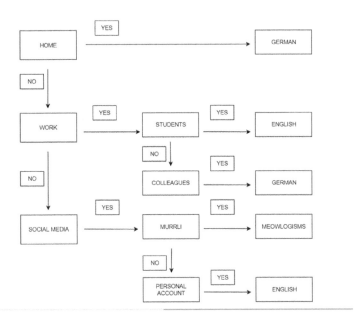

Figure 7.2 Domains of language use – flowchart

we are comparing code choice patterns across linguistic communities, on the other hand. We can easily adapt and extend the model depending on our findings and our needs, for example, to account for multimodality (Chapter 6).

1223wwwwwwwwwwwwwwwwwwwww
(Wicht, Purr Reviewer 2)

Leaving aside now the multimodal aspects of computer-mediated discourse, we apply the domains of language use to the cat-related digital spaces. One method of visualising the patterns of language use is a flowchart. A simple diagram using yes/no choices can be drawn to identify the domains and to list them together with the codes that are appropriate in a particular domain. The flowchart in Figure 7.2 shows my choices between German, English, and meowlogisms, with the domains of home, work with the sub-domains of students and colleagues, and social media with the sub-domains of Murrli and personal account.

Instead of a flowchart, we can also visualise the domains of language use in a table that uses columns for the main categories, like domain,

Table 7.1 *Domains of language use – table*

Domain	Addressees	Setting	Topics	Variety/Code
a specific cat-related digital space	existing followers of accounts	a specific social media channel	a particular weekday	catspeak
	potential followers		a particular hashtag	meowlogisms
			a specific image	English other languages graphicons

addressees, setting, topic, and the varieties or codes used (Table 7.1). For the cat-related digital spaces, a general categorisation looks as follows. The domain is 'cat-related digital space', the addressees are 'existing and potential followers of accounts', the setting is 'specific social media channel', and the topics are 'a particular weekday, a particular hashtag', or 'a specific image', and 'the variety' or 'code' used include the various purrieties and meowlogisms (discussed in Chapters 3 and 4), and graphicons (discussed in Chapter 6).

Taking the example of the cat Horst (Figure 7.3) on Instagram, we apply this general categorisation to a specific account and a specific post. For the owner of Horst, the domain is a black-cat digital space, the addressees are Horst's followers, the setting is the cat account @horst_the_hero, the topic of this particular post is Horst on Panther Thursday, and the code used consists of English, of meowlogisms as a variety of English, of specific hashtags (mainly in English), of emoji, and of the image itself. When we consider the graphics mode (see Chapter 6), the image is an unmodified photograph of the vernacular type portraying the cat in a human-like way, with the cat wearing a cap.

The man 🐾 The myth 🐾 Horst 🐾 The legend 😺 Happy Panther Thursday
🐈‍⬛ Happy Purrsday 💜 my pawfriends 🐾
.
.
.
#blackcat #blackcatstellall #derp #weeklyfluff #cutie #grumpy #fatcat #catsdoingthings #meow #meowed #simonscat #gato #Kater #coolcat #boopmynose #cats_of_instagram #herocat #picneko #helmet #catswearthings #mondaymood #horstthehero #crazycat #neko #funnycat #cat #9gag
@horst_the_hero

Figure 7.3 Horst the Hero on Instagram

In this post, Horst uses the English translation of German 'Der Mann, Der Mythos, Horst, Die Legende', which is the writing on the cap Horst is wearing in the image. By including the phrase 'Panther Thursday', sending good wishes, and inserting emoji as well as the meowlogisms 'Purrsday' and 'pawfriends', Horst uses the typical codes for the digital space he is in. In digital spaces related to black cats like Horst's, Thursday has not only turned into 'Purrsday' but has also become 'Panther Thursday', which is the day on which users post images of their black cats and wish others a 'Happy Panther Thursday'.

Horst's post is a typical example of the domain 'black cat on Instagram'. When we look at it in more detail, we find out how much the factors of participants, setting, and topic affect the code choice of Horst. From the information provided on his profile page, we know that Horst lives in Germany, has 64,200 followers on Instagram, and is a cat living with three other cats. The topic of Horst's account is cats and black cats, and the code/variety includes meowlogisms and other cat-related words and phrases.

The setting is the photo-sharing social media platform Instagram, which means that communication consists of a visual element, namely the image, then the caption, and then the comments. With the intent of reaching an international audience, Horst's owner has chosen to communicate in English instead of their native German and has assigned to Horst the code of 'Denglish', which is a blending of 'Deutsch' and 'English', because 'a Saxon accent is inevitable for Horst sometimes', as Horst's owner told me. In the comments on the post, the language is mainly English, but there are also interactions in German.

The categorisation of codes and domains is not always clear-cut, and people switch codes within a situation or domain as we can see in the example of Horst: code-switching can be related to a particular addressee, which is the case in my interactions with Horst, when we use German. We may switch between languages when we want to show that we belong to a particular group or we have the same native language as an addressee. These switches are related to identity and the relationship between participants. The concepts of identity and the role of a speaker are complex, as we will see in Section 7.3.

To find out more about bilingualism in a society, we can also look at the media, which function as a formal institution and reflect the existing linguistic practises of that society. While this approach to media takes us back to the offline world, it is relevant for the digital spaces too. When we study the relationship of bilingualism and the various forms of media, we consider questions like (1) whether we are dealing with societal or impersonal bilingualism, (2) which media genres and which patterns of usage we can identify, and (3) what we can say about the relationship between bilingual practices and social identities.

The first question we address is whether the bilingual interactions are societal or impersonal. If the bilingual interactions reflect the bilingual practices of the society of the people involved, bilingualism is societal. If, however, bilingual practices are not part of the society and words from other languages are simply used without necessarily understanding them, bilingualism is impersonal.

In the case of Horst and Murrli, the bilingual practices are societal as both languages, German and English, have their place and function in German-speaking countries. German is the official language and English is the most commonly taught foreign language in schools. According to Eurostat, the statistical office of the European Union, English is taught in 96.2% of secondary schools at the lower level, which makes the vast majority of the population in German-speaking countries at least bilingual.

Figure 7.4 Bilingualism with Tippy and Pekoe
'A window to the world for Tippy and Pekoe #cat #Katze #gatto #chat #micia #γατα #кошка #neko'

In the cat-related digital spaces, there are also examples of impersonal bilingualism, namely when a cat account holder uses hashtags in various languages. Instagram, for example, offers us the use of up to 30 hashtags in a post, and to appear in as many Instagram searches and to be included by as many algorithms as possible, we can add versions of the hashtag #cat in other languages. We could write the caption for Tippy and Pekoe's (Figure 7.4) image as follows: 'A window to the world for Tippy and Pekoe #cat #Katze #gatto #chat #micia #γατα #кошка #neko'. We write the hashtag #cat in German, Italian, French, Greek, Russian, and Japanese. In this case, my English-Japanese bilingualism is impersonal because I do not know Japanese but I use the Japanese word 'neko'.

Next, we go into which media genre our bilingual or multilingual dwellers of the cat-related digital spaces fall into. Sociolinguistic research has found five groups of media genres, namely (1) talk between media professionals and the public, (2) performance genres, like movies and popular music, (3) advertising, (4) various non-fictional genres of written discourse, and (5) computer-mediated interaction. There are cat-related examples for all these genres, especially for advertising, non-fictional genres, and computer-mediated interaction. Computer-mediated interaction is also referred to as networked multilingualism – a concept which we take up in more detail in the section Section 7.2.

Bilingual practices in sports commentaries are quite common. The quote below is a cat-related example taken from a live commentary of a football match in Germany in 2008. It is a literal translation of the English idiom 'It's raining cats and dogs'. While this example is not really an example of bilingualism, it still shows an awareness of English.

Es regnet Katzen und Hunde wie der Brite sagen würde
German, a literal translation from English 'It's raining cats and dogs, as a British person would say'
(football live commentary)

The genre of commercially driven media is quite a fertile ground for bilingual practices, and we notice a flourishing bilingualism in commercially driven formats, like popular music, advertisements, or lifestyle magazines. In advertising, words from other languages are typically included to create a certain image. The commerce-driven media and the advertising machinery behind them see us as consumers and use other languages in their ads. For example, French is considered elegant, and German is seen as effective. In German-speaking countries, English is omnipresent in advertising.

A cat-related example provided by a commerce-driven media is the advert of cat food producer Perfect Fit (Figure 7.5), which I came across on Facebook in 2019 while using an Austrian IP address. The advertising slogan 'Happy Miau-o-ween!' is English together with the German–English meowlogism 'Miau-o-ween' for 'Halloween'. Originally a US import, Halloween has now entered Austrian culture, and regardless of whether Austrians celebrate the event or not, the slogan 'Happy Halloween' is meaningful, which in turn makes the meowlogism 'Miau-o-ween' easy to understand.

When we consider patterns of usage, we find billingual practices and social identity to be closely connected in the cat-related digital spaces. The expression 'patterns of usage' refers to when and how

Figure 7.5 Happy Miau-o-ween!

much we switch between languages. In sociolinguistics, we study to what extent we use languages or language varieties that are associated with a particular culture to create a social identity. Sociolinguistic research has found that people use a second language as an attention-seeking device or as a symbol for a certain group membership.

In the cat-related digital spaces, a particular code-switching pattern is noticeable: whenever users take on the identity of their cats on social media, they use catspeak purrieties. In the English-language social media, taking the cat's voice is signalled by the use of meowlogisms or other catspeak purrieties. Whether meowlogisms or other purrieties are used depends on the other cat account holders in the network, on the one hand, and on the account holder's proficiency in English, on the other hand, in case they are non-native speakers of English. Non-native speakers of English tend towards meowlogisms because meowlogisms are easier to create and to understand.

Meowlogisms and other catspeak purrieties are a symbol of group membership and an expression of taking on the identity of a cat. Olly the Cat (Figure 7.6) and HumanAl on Twitter exemplify this identity-related code-switching pattern: while the Twitter account is in the cat's name, the human behind the account also posts occasionally. Olly's tweets are in catspeak, and HumanAl's tweets are in English.

Yooz vewy gud to mama
Gibz her snuggols fwom me and HumanAl.
We luvz yoo lotz.

Twitter Web App

Figure 7.6 Olly the Cat

Yooz vewy gud to mama
Gibz her snuggols fwom me and HumanAl
We luvz yoo lotz.

(Olly and HumanAl)

For francophone cat-related digital spaces, a recent study analysing 100 accounts on 'Touitoui' or 'TwiTwi' (Twitter) has identified several patterns in French that indicate the cat's voice: francophone cats use a childlike tone together with a formal register. Cats use euphemisms like 'la grande sieste' (the big nap, which means death) and formal register like 'prédater' (to predate), 'prestance' (stature), and 'outré/scandaloutrage' (outraged). The cats refer to themselves as 'pôtichats', which is the feline spelling of 'petits chats' (small cats). Cats show a fake politeness and use specific 'that'-constructions. The study also showed that people pick up the norms from core accounts in the various cat-related digital spaces. In the quote below, we find specific spelling, 'z'humains' for 'les humains' (humans); specific vocabulary ('la Blouse' for 'vet', 'mamychats' (mummy cat), 'papychats' (daddy cat); and the meowlogism 'minoustre' for 'ministre', which is formed by the French word 'minou' (kitten).

« z'humains », le vétérinaire est « la Blouse »
« Minoustre des mamychats et papychats »
(www.20.minutes.fr)

7.2 The Meow World

üöp´ßüüüüüüüüüüüü
(Wicht, Purr Reviewer 2, walking across a German-language keyboard)

When people from different countries are in contact with each other, communication becomes transnational. The cat-related digital spaces are a prime example for such a transnational communication, which extends and operates across national boundaries and languages. Transnational communication makes looking at language variation in the cat-related digital spaces a multilingual endeavour. These linguistic practices are called 'networked multilingualism'.

Sociolinguistic research on multilingualism in computer-mediated discourse uses concepts such as 'metrolingualism', 'polylanguaging', and 'translanguaging' to describe the linguistic diversity on the Internet. Metrolingualism looks at how, in modern cities, users manipulate their linguistic resources across languages and ethnicities. Translanguaging refers to the way multilingual users use their languages across all modalities with code-mixing, code-switching, translations, and transliterations, while polylanguaging means that users employ any linguistic form that best expresses their aim without caring about how well they know the other languages. An example of translanguaging with English in German is the verb 'extempurrieren', created from English 'purr' instead of the syllable 'por' in 'extemporieren' (to improvise on the stage).

Aber "extempurrieren" würd mir eh besser gefallen
(alephi8 on Twitter) – Austrian dialect of German
Aber "extempurrieren" würde mir ohnehin besser gefallen. – Standard German
But I would like ‚extempurrieren' better anyway. – Translation into English

The concept of networked multilingualism refers to two connected processes of networks on the Internet. On the one hand, we are digitally connected to other people, and on the other hand, we are situated in a global network. With the Social Web spanning the whole world, users come together from various geographic and social regions to communicate. While we can easily communicate online with people in various languages, we are constrained at the same time by the network technology we have available. Our communication is shaped by keyboard-and-screen technologies, by our access to network resources, and by orientation towards networked audiences. Different languages use different writing systems; there may not be a standardised writing system for language varieties; and there may be a mix and match of orthographies used for specific effects.

For example, the orthography of German is standardised and does not display regional accent variation. German spelling is, therefore, changed to show these accent variations. Users in Austria, for example, often refer to 'Gaadse' in various spellings for German 'Katze' (cat). Occasionally, dialectal spellings occur in postings by official organisations and companies, like the Austrian Railway Company ÖBB. The word 'Gaaadse' appears on the official Facebook page of ÖBB in a post that shows a passenger's cat travelling outside its carrier. The post itself includes a dialectal spelling of words and dialectal grammar of Austrian German, and, most notably in capital letters, the word 'GAAAAATZE'.

Was wir sagen sollten: Es warad weng da Transportbox! Aber samma sich ehrlich: GAAAAATZE😻 😻
(Österreichische Bundesbahnen (ÖBB) on Facebook) – Austrian dialect of German
Was wir sagen sollten: Es wäre wegen der Transportbox! Aber sind wir ehrlich zu uns selbst: Katze! 😻😻 – Standard German
What we should say: It would be because of the carrier! But let's be honest with ourselves: CAAAAAAT😻😻

Another example shows how users can play with different scripts. Gaston, a French cat account on Twitter (Figure 7.7), uses French language characters and French orthographic writing for English words in a Twitter conversation. Later on in the conversation, another linguistic process typical for bilingualism takes place, namely intra-sentential code-switching, which means that the language switch from English to French occurs within a sentence.

Figure 7.7 Gaston

Châle aïe bi in your book, dir @Meow_Factor?
Gret, Madame. You ar heu goude numan. Aïe apprécie.

Shall I be in your book, dear @Meow_Factor?
Great, Madame (madam). You are a good human. I apprècie (appreciate).

   The network resources we have at our fingertips make an endless
stream of linguistic material available to us. Our exposure to other
languages offers us the possibility of increasing our linguistic repertoire, maybe only by a phrase or two, maybe more. We include phrases
and spellings from other languages in our own posts regardless of how
well we know the other language or whether we know it at all. Horst,
for example, uses the hashtag #고양이, which, according to Google
Translate, is 'cat' in Korean. Yet, the cat account holder does not
know Korean. Tools like Google Translate make it possible for us to
use other languages and other scripts just by copying and pasting, as
I have done with the example of 'cat' in Arabic.

قطة
(Arabic for 'cat' as offered by Google Translate)

   A cat account from Japan uses the hashtags #ねこ #猫 #kissa
#고양이 #cat #gatto #katze #chat #Meow #猫のいる暮らし

#🐈🐾. While we recognise some of the words, we cannot read all of them – unless we know all the languages. As mentioned above, various online tools make it possible for us to simply copy and paste and get results. The online tool Google Translate shows us that the non-western characters in the hashtags of the Japanese cat account are mainly Japanese characters (Figure 7.8). One hashtag remains the same in both fields of the translating tool, which indicates that Google Translate does not recognise this hashtag as Japanese and leaves it untranslated, so another round of copying and pasting of just this untranslated hashtag is needed. On its own, the hashtag is recognised as Korean (Figure 7.9).

As we can see, the hashtags all refer to cats and are English with #cat and #Meow, French with #chat, German with #katze, Italian with #gatto, Finnish with #kissa, Korean with #고양이, and Japanese with #ねこ, #猫, and #ねこのいる生活. Google Translate offers those of us who cannot read Japanese or Korean scripts the transliteration as #Neko #neko, #neko no iru seikatsu for the Japanese and #goyang-i for the Korean. Machine translation, however, does not translate or interpret the emoji #🐈🐾, which in Unicode are 'cat' with the code points U+1F408 and 'paw prints' with the code points U+1F43E.

On a sidenote, the study on graphicons we came across in Chapter 5 also used Google Translate connected to Facebook's *translate this* function for comments in unknown languages and/or checked with native speakers. This method of translating worked fine.

Another issue related to keyboard-and-screen technology is the use of keysmash – the smashing of fingers against the keyboard to indicate an intense feeling, like 'ajfköjafklsdöfjkföjföjklföjs'. In a keysmash, very common letters are those of the middle row of the keyboard followed by those in the top row. The characters in our keysmash depend on the keyboard that we are using. In my keysmash above, the presence of the letter 'ö' (umlaut) indicates that my keysmash has originated on a qwertz keyboard, which is the typical layout of a German-language keyboard.

Likewise, when our cats walk across our keyboards, the characters pawed in depend on the keyboard type. In *Because Internet*, a book on internet language, we find the example 'tfgggggggggggggggggggggggdzzzzz zzz', which was produced by the cat Eliza on her way across the keyboard. This example has been included in the book to show the

Figure 7.8 Using Google Translate

Figure 7.9 Google Translate Korean

differences in a keysmash. If Eliza had walked across my German-language keyboard, the 'z' at the end would be a 'y'. Likewise, the comments by Wicht, Purr Reviewer 2, which appear in various places in this chapter, have been produced on a German-language keyboard. The occurrences of 'z', 'y', umlauts, 'ß', and special characters like '<' (in connection with 'a', 's', 'x', and 'y' in the example below) are indicators of a different keyboard – not only in keysmashes but also in texts of cats walking across the keyboard.

<AAAAAAAAAAAAAAAAAAAAAAAAAAAAAAAAAAAAAAAAAAAAAA
AAAAAAAAAAAAAAAAAAAA
>>>>>>>>>>>>>>>> ASXAYYYYYYYYYYYYYYYYY
(Wicht, Purr Reviewer 2)

Networked audiences, too, shape our communication online. On the social media platforms, we have built up a network of friends (on Facebook) and followers (on Instagram and Twitter), people with whom we share our posts and who we see as a semi-public audience. Although we know some of our followers in person, we have got to know others online only. The contexts in which we have come across our followers are different, something sociolinguists call 'context collapse'. Context collapse means that both our online and offline networks – with their different socio-demographics and different relations – co-exist in the virtual network.

The different backgrounds of the network audiences mean that, if we have a multilingual network, we make choices regarding our linguistic practices and decide which language to use. Linguistic research has shown that users whose native language is not English but who have an international network nevertheless use English for their status updates. English is seen as the common denominator for the entire

Figure 7.10 Bilingual Russian–English cat Henry

network. Replies may be in other languages – as we have already seen in the example of Horst, where Horst's owner and I use German. Other languages of the linguistic repertoire may also be used for posts intended for a sub-audience of the network.

The owners of Henry, the ginger cat from Moscow, use mainly English in the captions of Henry's photos on Instagram, yet switch to Russian when the issue is a local one relating to Moscow and Russia. Judging from the code choice, Henry's humans divide their 131,000 followers into worldwide followers and local Russian followers. Calendars featuring Henry and fellow cat Raymond are offered to a worldwide audience in English, whereas their stay in a cat hotel in Moscow is described first in Russian and then in English (Figure 7.10). The English version, however, is shorter because it does not include the promotion presented in Russian, probably for the simple reason that people from outside Russia would not use a cat hotel in Moscow.

Генри и Райми сейчас живут в отеле @_ пока в квартире доделывают грязные ремонтные работы. Ребята привыкли и вовсю играют. Поэтому ещё немного погостим и поедем домой. Спасибо хозяйки отеля Алене, за такой радушный приём! Ребята вкусно кушают, их чешут, с ними играют и даже подстригли коготки. У Алёны тоже есть котики @_ посмотрите, какие хорошие!

Друзья, если вы уезжаете в отпуск или как я затеяли ремонт, и вам нужно отдать ваших котиков гостиницу, то отель @р самый лучший и комфортный для котят вариант.

Прекрасный сервис, очень удобное расположение и уверенность, что с котятами всё будет прекрасно!

❗ Используя промокод "henrykingcat" вы можете получить скидку от 15 до 20 % (в зависимости от номера) на проживание вашей кошки в отёле @_

Henry and Ray are currently living at @_ while the apartment is being finished with dirty renovations.🐾🔨
The guys are used to it and are playing with might and main. 🖤 So we'll stay a little longer and go home.😊
Thanks to Alena, the owner of the hotel, for such a warm welcome! The guys eat deliciously, they are scratching them, they are playing, and they even cut their claws. Alena also has cats @_ look how good they are!
(Henry King Cat)

7.3 The Meow Identity

zhu'
(Wicht, Purr Reviewer 2)

When we open a social media account for our cats, we often take on their identity and use linguistic means to do so. Identity is language in use, as sociolinguistics says. The concept of identity is at the core of sociolinguistics, which is why we take a closer look at identity and identity creation. Sociolinguistics sees language positioned at the interface between our inner personal world and the outer social world. Language in use means two things: first, we create our identities in our interactions with others as we position our self socially in relation to them, and second, we can analyse linguistic forms to say more about identity creation.

One approach looks at identity at the intersection of language, culture, and society through what is know as 'socio-cultural linguistics'. This interdisciplinary approach offers us a combination of different research fields drawing on five principles: the emergence principle, the positionality principle, the indexicality principle, the relationality principle, and the partialness principle.

The emergence principle says that our identities do not pre-exist as such but rather emerge as we create them in our interactions, especially through our use of language. The positionality principle states that our identities are based on macro-level demographic categories, like our age, gender, and social class, then on local identity categories, like groups important in our environment, and finally on any temporary positions we take in our interaction with others. The indexicality principle relates to what we associate with a specific linguistic form, which can include social categories and specific identity categories, such as education or intelligence.

The relationality principle looks at identity as a phenomenon of relation. Our identities do not stand on their own but become meaningful when we see them in relation to other positions and other people. We construct our identities along the lines of sameness and difference, of genuineness and artifice, and of authority and powerlessness.

Finally, the partialness principle means that different processes are at work when we construct our identities. We may create our identities on purpose and deliberately in some ways, while, in other others, the process is habitual and we are not conscious of it. In other ways again, our identity evolves as an outcome of other people's perceptions, and ideological beliefs may also affect our identity creation. To sum up the socio-cultural linguistic approach, identity creation is not a simple binary decision of 'this is me and that is the other' but a rather complex process that encompasses a number of different conscious and subconscious factors.

The same is true for the online world in general and for cat-related digital spaces in particular. They provide us with multiple opportunities for social interaction and, in turn, identity construction. In fact, the digital spaces offer us easy ways to have not just one but various identities. With us crossing between offline and online realities, our identities can even be fluid, shifting from one to another in a short span of time or space.

In the cat-related digital spaces, we continuously switch from our human identity to a cat identity and back, a fact that illustrates the emergence principle, which says that identity emerges in inter-action. The cat-related digital spaces are a prime example of online identity creation. When we open accounts for our cats in addition to our own personal accounts, we often take on the identity of our cats in these accounts and post on issues from the cats' point of view.

We can see all the socio-cultural linguistic principles at work when we construct our online cat identity: our cat identity emerges through our online interaction (emergence principle), then we place ourselves in the group of online cat lovers (positionality principle). Additionally, we use the linguistic forms typical of cat-related digital spaces (indexicality principle), and we experience that we are not alone in pretending to be our cats. While saying there is safety in numbers does miss the point, the sheer number of cat accounts on social media as well as the use of purrieties in the media give us a sense of legitimacy and authority for our cat-inspired endeavours (relationality principle). Finally, we make a conscious decision about our identity, but at the same time, our identities are shaped by other, less conscious factors, like our cultural backgrounds (partialness principle).

Using language variation for identity construction is not unique to cat-related digital spaces. Sociolinguistic research has found that language, together with other social practices, is actively used to construct identities and that people assign specific meanings to specific linguistic features. A specific linguistic feature, like intervocalic [t] or [ʔ] in 'kitty', carries with it meanings, like social characteristics and social groups, which people can use to construct different identities.

Language variation has also been observed in other digital spaces. This is true for the digital communities where people have been noted using different language variations. Social variation in digital discourses exist when people adopt different identities. A study on the use of African American Vernacular English in tweets has shown that stylistic elements like specific spellings are used to construct a very specific persona.

As stated in the positionality principle, cat account holders want to show that they are part of the cat-related digital spaces, and the cat-inspired language varieties are a sign of belonging. Chapter 11 shows how the cat account holders and followers perceive the purrieties and what they think about them.

As the example of cat-related digital spaces illustrates, we actively use language to construct our cat identity, and we can observe both style-shifting and code-switching. The change of identities from human to cat – from personal account to the cat account – is a conscious choice, which is usually accompanied with a conscious shift in language use – a shift in style and a code switch. Cat account holders use either meowlogisms or catspeak purrieties, all of which are cat-inspired linguistic forms. These forms are recognised as cat-specific by their followers, and, thus, the forms take on an indexical meaning.

[Purrieties]...are part of the unique culture that is social media cats. (Respondent 121)

Sources Used in This Chapter

🐾 Androutsopoulos (2007, 2015) for bilingualism and networked multilingualism

🐾 Holmes and Wilson (2017) for bilingualism and multilingualism

🐾 Bucholtz and Hall (2004, 2005) for language and identity

🐾 Drummond and Schleef (2016) for language and identity

🐾 Darvin (2016) for language and online identity

🐾 Ilbury (2020) for language and online identity

🐾 Herring and Dainas (2017) for using machine translation in multilingual threads

🐾 McCulloch (2019) for keysmash

🐾 Eurostat (2018) for English in the EU

🐾 Truan (2022) for francophone Twittersphere

🐾 Brown and Miller (2013) for linguistic terms in the glossary

🐾 Crystal (2010, 2018) for linguistic terms in the glossary

Examples and Quotes in This Chapter

🐾 Holmes and Wilson (2017, p. 23)

🐾 Horst the Hero: Instagram post

🐾 Gaston le Chat: Twitter post

🐾 Österreichische Bundesbahnen ÖBB: www.facebook.com/unsere OEBB/photos/a.178554505507321/1989338784428875

🐾 Alephi8: https://twitter.com/alephi8/status/1331176109954699265

🐾 McCulloch (2019, p. 6)

- 🐾 Henry: www.instagram.com/p/CHiDNQCnbXf/?utm_source=ig_web_copy_link
- 🐾 Olly and HumanAl: Twitter post
- 🐾 Example in French: www.20minutes.fr/arts-stars/culture/2702019-20200123-20-minutes-enquete-touitoui-potichats-communaute-tres-feline-twitter

Suggestions for PURRther Reading

- 🐾 Ilbury (2020)

8

Going on Pawtrol

The survey *Cat-inspired Online Language* is part of my ongoing research called *Purrieties of English*, in which I research how online cats speak on Facebook Twitter, Instagram, and Youtube.
(Introduction to the online survey in 2019)

When cats go on pawtrol, they go around their territory, inspect it, and, if necessary, protect it. We do something similar when we do fieldwork for linguistic research. We select our area, then go out and study it, and we protect people's privacy when we research their language.

In this chapter, we look at how to do linguistic research using the cat examples from the original research done for this book. The cats lead us through the issues of data collection, cat account selection, cat-related wordlists, and the surveys done.

While in scientific writing the theoretical background usually comes first, we switch that order in this chapter and go into the empirical part before turning back to the underlying design and method of the research. Our pawtrol takes us to the methodological decisions we have to consider in linguistic research and describes sampling methods and data collection.

Throughout our research, we need to think carefully about protecting our research participants and about keeping our research ethical. We touch on the laws in place to protect people's privacy and data, on the one hand, and on ethical guidelines established for researchers, on the other.

Concepts Discussed in the Chapter

🐾 research methodology

🐾 qualitative research
🐾 quantitative research
🐾 data collection
🐾 surveys
🐾 data sampling
🐾 data protection
🐾 privacy protection
🐾 ethics

Terms from the Clawssary

🐾 API 🐾 CMC mode 🐾 data scraping 🐾 Github 🐾 Python
🐾 quantitative linguistics 🐾 R 🐾 sampling 🐾 web crawler

8.1 Pawtrol: Checking Cat-Related Digital Spaces

Love the idea for the study!
(Respondent 3 in the January 2021 Survey)

Often, it is a personal interest that steers us towards certain topics we want to know more about. In the case of this book, my fascination with language and my love for cats have met and come to fruition. Yet the process, from having a vague idea of 'there is something out there' to arriving at scientifically sound explanations or descriptions of the phenomenon of language varieties in cat-related digital spaces, has taken a lot of time, which I spent observing, taking notes, jotting down and discarding half-baked ideas, formulating and revising research questions, revising the ideas again, collecting data, analysing data, and drawing conclusions – always making sure to use a suitable scientific method.

My observation of cat-related digital spaces started in 2014 on Instagram, Facebook, cat blogs, and news media. I started writing down ideas in a research journal and documenting my fieldwork in a publicly accessible blog called The Meow Factor, which eventually led to the publication of the journal article 'The purrification of English' in 2018.

The approach I took with 'The purrification of English' and have also taken with the original research data for this book is called 'linguistic ethnography', a research method used to gain insights into a different culture and community without preconceptions. It is an especially suitable method if we want to study how members of a community construct their identities. With my cat account for Murrli, I became part of a specific digital space within the spaces of #BlackCat on Instagram and started taking informal notes.

In 'The purrification of English', I view cat-related online interaction as a social process that takes place on Instagram, and I describe how three black-cat account holders and their followers communicate and which linguistic practices they share. Based on what I observed online, my research question developed from which cat-related language exists on Instagram to a question with a more focussed scope: which meowlogisms occur in the captions and comments of selected cat accounts of black cats? The aim of my research was to find out more about the range of meowlogisms and the different spellings, but not on quantifiable variables.

In other words, the focus of my study lies in discourse practices with which the cat account holders construct their identities. The sampling was a sampling by theme (the hashtag #BlackCat), a sampling by phenomenon (the occurrence of meowlogisms), and a sampling by individual (three selected black cat accounts and their followers). I collected screen data after asking the humans behind the three cat accounts for permission to use their posts for my research. To protect the users' privacy, I changed the cats' real names in the publication.

The data collection itself involved the simple method of copying and pasting the posts of the three cat accounts and the comments of their followers over a one-month period. Despite copying and paste being a straightforward procedure, it is quite time-consuming to search for each individual post, open each post in a separate window, select the caption and all the comments, and copy them into a .doc file. This .doc file was then imported into QDA Miner Lite, a software programme for qualitative data analysis.

To analyse all the captions and comments, I used the method of coding, which refers to the cyclical process of reading, interpreting, assigning codes to words and phrases, categorising, and repeating this cycle as often as needed to make sense of the data. To illustrate this method, we can look at the hashtags that have been used by the three cat account holders and their followers. Depending on my interpretation, the hashtags #JustUsOldCats, #TongueOutTuesday, #CatnipTimes, #KitnipBox, #CrazyCatLady, and #InstaCat_Meows have been coded as cat-specific, days, general, people, kittens, and sounds, respectively.

As it happened, looking at the language used in the three cat accounts triggered ideas for further research questions, such as which meowlogisms exist on Twitter and Facebook, which topics are discussed in cat-related digital spaces, which language variants exist in the cat-related digital spaces across the social media platforms, why people use purrieties, why people take on the identity of their cats in cat accounts, what different types of cat accounts exist, and the overall question of to what extent purrieties are fully-fledged transnational internet dialects. I have followed up on these questions in this book.

The research on purrieties is exploratory, which means that we explore a new territory, and because we are dealing with communities of people, the method of linguistic ethnography is appropriate, with its systematic observation and the use of screen data as well as user-based data. Guided by my previous research on meowlogisms, I decided to sample more cat accounts. The focus is still on a qualitative description of how users interact and construct their identities in cat-related digital spaces, but at the same time, there is the possibility to compare the different cat accounts based on online-specific categories of variables, like 'social media platform as place' and 'type of cat account'.

We are dealing with the variables of genre, namely the different social media accounts, and with different types of cat accounts, which are described in Chapter 5. To prepare for the sampling of screen data, a diagram with 16 cells was created with the intention of filling each cell with four participants (Table 8.1). The variables in the diagram, 'social-media platform' and 'type of cat account', are different from the socio-demographic variables usually found, like age, gender, or ethnicity, because the cat-related data is collected online and the accounts were cat accounts.

To protect the privacy and anonymity of the cat account holders, pseudonyms were usually taken instead of their real names. Therefore, all names of the cats in the diagram (Table 8.2) have been pseudonymised with generic cat names. A Google search of 'most popular cat names' provided extensive lists of names, like the one provided by a US pet insurance company. For that list, the company claims to have looked through more than one million quotes in 2020 to come up with the most popular cat names in the United States.

Table 8.1 *Diagram used for sampling*

	Twitter	Instagram	Facebook	YouTube
for-profit celebrity cats	🐱🐱🐱🐱	🐱🐱🐱🐱	🐱🐱🐱🐱	🐱🐱🐱🐱
for-cause working cats	🐱🐱🐱🐱	🐱🐱🐱🐱	🐱🐱🐱🐱	🐱🐱🐱🐱
individual cats	🐱🐱🐱🐱	🐱🐱🐱🐱	🐱🐱🐱🐱	🐱🐱🐱🐱
collective cat accounts	🐱🐱🐱🐱	🐱🐱🐱🐱	🐱🐱🐱🐱	🐱🐱🐱🐱

In the US, the top five names for female cats are Luna, Bella, Lucy, Nala, and Kitty, and for male cats they are Oliver, Leo, Milo, Simba, and Max. The substitutes for the original names of the cats come from these lists. With these new generic cat names, no account can be identified. Lilly, for example, is a common cat name, and any reference to, say, Lilly and #FluffyFursday does not give clues as to who the real cat is – even if an image of Lilly (Figure 8.1) were to be included.

Data collection from the accounts of pre-selected individuals is called 'sampling by individual'. Sampling by individual is done when our aim is to look at the discourse practices of these individuals and their followers. Some cells have been filled with the same cat, which means that this cat has a social media presence on more than one platform. Even when a this is the case, the captions differ and there are different followers as the various platforms attract different audiences. Four cells have remained empty, namely the cells of individual cats on YouTube. In the sampling phase, it turned out that the YouTube channels of the pre-selected individual cats do not attract

Table 8.2 *Sampling*

	Twitter	Instagram	Facebook	YouTube
For-profit celebrity cats	Maverick Jack & Sebastian Simon Bagheera	Maverick Real Georgie Simon Princess	Jack & Sebastian Georgie Cat Henry Mac	Georgie Mimi Zeus Cat Simon
For-cause working cats	Larry Bandit Loki Oscar	Flame Captain Buddy Treasury	Felix Cookie Dexter Oreo	Prince Cat Luna Bear Biscuit
Individual cats	Willow Buddy Max Shadow	Dolce Grizzly Midnight Walter	Daisy Ginger Rascal Kitty	
Collective cat accounts	black cats Mr TV cat rescuer professional cats	cat cafe black cats per day black cats feature another cat rescuer	cat fair Mr TV cat rescuer other black cats	cat video compilation Mr TV cat rescuer another cat rescuer

Figure 8.1 Lilly on #FluffyFursday

comments and, thus, do not provide the type of linguistic data we used for our analysis.

For the actual data collection, a more practicable way of gathering the screen data was necessary because copying and pasting is not efficient. Computers offer a way out with data scraping, and the open-source programming languages Python and R, for instance, can be used for data scraping. Though ready-made scripts are available for both programmes, we need to have some knowledge in Python or R to make the scripts work for our purposes. There are introductory books for linguists, for example *Python for Linguists* and *Statistics for Linguists: An Introduction Using R*, as well as online tutorials.

For the data from the cat-related digital spaces, I used two computer solutions: one is the Python module Instaloader and the other is a programme called Facepager, which is a ready-to-use tool running under Windows, Mac OS X, and Linux. Both solutions fetch publicly available data using APIs and webscraping. Python, Instaloader, and Facepager are open-source resources available on

Table 8.3 *#JellyBellyFriday: Output generated by Instaloader*

Tweets
AT LAST!!! We made it to #JellyBellyFriday again 🐾🐱🐾 That's worth a roll right?! 💚🐱💚#fridayfeeling
💚 #catlovers #catstagram #catsofinstagram #ragdoll #ragdollcat #ragdollsofinstagram #kitty #dailykitty #catslife #catoftheday #instacats #instameow #lovecats #ragdolls #catlover #worldofcats #fluffycat #moggymob #rescuecatsrule #bestmeow #catloversclub
Happy Friday fur-friends!🐾 #jellybellyfriday #catsofinstagram #cats #catsoftwitter #fluoof #TheBestBelly
Sadly #Luna has gone over the rainbow bridge. Her heart has been #reunited with her family and the love & memories they shared will linger forever. #RunFree sweet Luna Ginger Tabby Cat

www.python.org and www.github.com and come with documentation guiding the user through the steps.

After deleting any metadata, like geotags or other identifying details, the data was converted for use in Windows as an Excel file (Table 8.3) and then imported it into QDA Miner Lite, the qualitative data analysis tool used for the study on meowlogisms. I deleted the metadata because I did not plan on including it in my research and because the General Data Protection Regulation (GDPR) requires us to only collect the data that we actually use.

The data itself was collected over a one-month period in August 2018 on the social media platforms Instagram, Twitter, Facebook, and YouTube. In the case of Instagram and Facebook, the data includes not only the captions but also the comments left by followers. In total, Instaloader and Facepager collected 4,910 posts: 491 posts with many comments from Instagram, 1,593 tweets from Twitter, 426 posts with many comments from Facebook, and 2,400 comments from YouTube.

On a sidenote, TikTok also has very interesting cat-related digital spaces, yet I did not consider collecting data from there. Our research always has some limitations, which is fine as long as we are aware of them and can give reasons. In our case TikTok did not feature much on my horizon in 2018 because it the platform only recently started operating.

The screen data (the 4,910 posts) was complemented by user-based data, which was collected in two qualitative online surveys via Microsoft Office Forms on www.forms.office.com. The first survey was conducted in July 2019, and the second in January 2021. After doing research for my meowlogism study of 2018, I wanted to find out what cat account holders and followers think of purrieties and why they use them or choose not to. In July 2019, the questionnaire with 23 questions was shared online.

(1) Cats on social media

    (a) Do you follow cats on social media platforms?
    (b) On which social media platform do you follow cats?
    (c) How often do you react to posts of other cats?
    (d) In addition to your personal account, do you have an account for your cat?
    (e) How often do you post in your cat account?
    (f) Which social media platforms do you use with your cat?
    (g) Why do you follow cats on social media?
    (h) Why do you have an account for your cat?
    (i) What do you like about the online cat-related digital spaces?

(2) Catspeak

    (a) What do you think about the way cats communicate with each other online?
    (b) What do you think about so-called meowlogisms?
    (c) What do you think about LOLspeak?
    (d) How likely are you to use cat-inspired word play in your social media posts? (Rank from 0 to 10)
    (e) Why are you likely/not likely to use cat-inspired language in your posts?

(3) Words and phrases

    (a) How likely are you to use the pronouns 'I', 'my' or 'mine' when you want to indicate that your cat is writing the post? (Rank from 0 to 10)
    (b) Which hashtags do you usually include in your posts?
    (c) What is your favourite cat-inspired wordplay?
    (d) Which example of your posts in a cat community would you see as typical?

(4) Demeowgraphics

(a) To which gender identity do you identify the most?
(b) Is English your native language?
(c) What is your native language (if answer to previous question was 'no')?
(d) Where do you come across the English language?
(e) What would you like to add?

This survey is a 'language attitude and perception study', a type of survey used in sociolinguistics to find out more about attitudes towards languages, dialects, accents, new words, and new pronunciations. The questions are mostly open, inviting the respondents to give precise and personal answers.

The January 2021 survey intended to specifically address the question of why we have a language for our cats and why our cats 'talk the way they do'. In the questionnaire itself, I share my thoughts with the participants to comment on.

(1) Why did you choose to give your cat an account on social media?
So many cats have their very own account on social media. You may know that my cat Murrli had her very own Instagram account and was friends with many other cats. People have told me that it's fun to have a cat account.

(2) Why does your cat talk the way he/she does?
In my research I have noticed two basic kinds of cat language: catspeak and meowlogisms. Catspeak is perhaps similar to how babies speak. Using meowlogisms means that we use 'regular English' on the whole but try to include 'meow', 'paw', 'purr' as often as we can, as in 'purrhaps', 'pawticipate', and 'meowsic'. My theory is that our choice of language depends on which cats we follow, which language they use, how comfortable we feel with our choice of cat language, and, perhaps, what is more fun for us. It is an individual choice.

(3) How would you describe your cat's language?
I am asking this question to make sure that I 'have got the cat language correctly'. Catspeak tends to use phonetic spelling and a specific grammar, like irregular plurals; third-person 's' for I, as in 'I sayz; z' for 's'; and so on. Meowlogisms include examples like 'purrhaps', 'pawty', 'ameowzing', 'pawsome'; there are words

Figure 8.2 Survey shout-out on Twitter

like 'panther' and 'void' (black cat), 'tortie' with 'tortitude' (for tortoiseshell cats); there is the 'tabby troop', and so on.

(4) Which comments – if any – would you like to leave?
You may have more insights into catspeak that you would like to share. As for me, writing about cat language and linguistics is a lot of fun. And it is also a way to honour my cat Murrli, who was the inspiration behind my research.

The sampling for the survey of 2019 was done via an invitation on my social media accounts. The link to the survey was shared on my personal social media accounts on Twitter (Figure 8.2), Facebook, Instagram, and LinkedIn. To encourage people to pass the link on to others, my shout-out uses some specific cat account practices. I address the cat directly, use a meowlogism, and, with the word 'Dreamies', use a cat-specific food-related term:

Calling on all my cat friends: could you get your humans to fill in my survey, purrlease? Does not take long. Virtual Dreamies coming your way. (Link to online survey)
(Meow_Factor)

The shout-out on Twitter received 16 comments, 20 retweets, and 44 likes. Twitter analytics say that this tweet was seen 4,531 times and that people interacted with it 168 times via likes, shares, and clicks on the tweet and profile. All in all, 195 people filled in the questionnaire in the first survey. In January 2021, I directly contacted nine cat account holders who use catspeak in their social media activities.

The results of my research on screen data and user-based data, namely, which linguistic practices were found in the analysis of the scraped data and how respondents answered, are presented in Chapters 9–11 respectively.

8.2 Pawtrol: Prepurring for Linguistic Research

Example of a Research Question: ... does the following sound or the formality of the context make a difference to how often [t] alternates with [ʔ] in a word like 'kitten'
(Hazen, 2014, p. 14)

Linguistics is defined as 'the science of language', which implies that we use scientific methods to study language and adhere to scientific principles. Before going on pawtrol, we need to ask ourselves the questions of what we want to find out, how we are going to find out what we want to find out, why we want to find out what we want to find out, and where we will find out what we want to find out. The book *Research Methods in Sociolinguistics: A Practical Guide*, from which the example of a research question in the quote above has been taken, gives examples from research projects and provides a 'how-to' guide.

To narrow down our choices, we look at previous research dealing with language in digital spaces. Research on this topic is related to the following areas: variation and change, impact of digital media on language use and interaction between participants, identity and online relations between participants, linguistic diversity, multilingualism and code-switching, and globalisation and mobility. We have already come across these areas in previous chapters of this book.

The research question we want to answer shapes all our further decisions in the research process. Researchers spend some time on framing and – in most cases – narrowing down the research questions. Ideally, our research question is based on what has been done before, adds something new to existing research, is realistic in its scope, and is clear and simple. The research question is usually stated at the beginning of a research paper and is formulated either as a so-called falsifiable or as an interpretative question.

Falsifiable means that the answer can be proven wrong with quantitative empirical testing, and a falsifiable question can be answered with yes or no. Interpretative, on the other hand, refers to a question that is open to qualitative interpretation and is answered by building a case. The answer to an interpretative question cannot be proven wrong. Interpretative questions tend to be formulated as open questions. The two methods are complementary in the research cycle and can be used together to give a fuller picture.

Knowing the differences between the methods is important because there are implications for the results as far as generalisability is concerned. When done correctly, quantitative research results can be generalised for the whole of the population and states whether something is the case (true) or not (false), but it does not explain why. Qualitative research, on the other hand, provides explanations and descriptions, but the results cannot be generalised. While giving insight, the research results are only valid for the data sampled.

To apply this explanation to cat-related linguistic research, we take the study 'The purrification of English' as an example: The research question 'Which meowlogisms are used?' is asked to show which specific linguistic practices, namely the meowlogisms, occur in a specific black-cat community on Instagram. The question is open, and the answer of 'Meowlogisms are formed by using meowphemes and occur in this black-cat-related digital space' cannot be falsified, which means that, as a researcher, I have to build a case for my argument with words and do not use quantitative testing and rely on numbers. The results of the research are lists of meowlogisms used in that community as well as findings and explanations generated by the data.

How to ... Find Cat Data

I am glad you are researching us and our language!
(Respondent 40; a cat who made their hooman take the July 2019 Survey)

In the section above, we have seen that the research question has implications for our survey design, sampling, data collection, and data analysis. Regarding the language in cat-related digital spaces, we also deal with the specific type of computer-mediated communication (CMC) and computer-mediated discourse (CMD). We have already come across the multimodality of CMD (Chapter 6).

As researchers, we usually look for what has been done before in the field and how it has been done, which is a useful approach in most cases. For cat-related language in digital spaces, this way does not really work because, first, 'traditional' sociolinguistic studies focus on spoken language and not on the written language, as our research does. Second, in the case of digital sources, it is difficult to gather background information on the social context, on the participants in a communication, and on socio-demographics. Third, we have an enormous amount of data available in the digital spaces, which exceeds the data in traditional studies by far.

These differences between traditional and digital studies have an impact on the decisions to take and the methods to choose because we have to adapt the existing models of data collection and data analysis. One sociolinguistic how-to suggests using both qualitative and quantitative methods and adapting existing sociolinguistic methods to digital spaces, which is why both ways have been taken into consideration for the research on the purrieties.

Additionally, we have to take two decisions before we collect data in digital spaces: first, whether we see CMC as a text or a place and, second, whether our data is screen data or user-based data. The categorisation of screen data and user-based data is fairly straightforward. Screen data is data that is produced and collected on screen, and user-based data is data that we collect when we ask users directly in interviews. The question of whether we regard CMC as text or place is slightly different and depends on our view of online interaction. We either see the Internet as a repository of text or as a social process happening in a digital environment.

Both viewpoints are, of course, possible in sociolinguistic research, but the research focus is different. We are looking either at specific linguistic practices in a large dataset and seeing how these practices are used by different groups of people (CMC as text) or at how specific people interact online in a specific context (CMC as place). The decision we take has an impact on our data collection and data analysis.

Next, we move on to the issue of online observation. Systematic online observation helps us find out what the participants talk about, how often they interact with each other, who the core members and the peripheral participants of a cat-related digital space are, and which typical linguistic features they use. When we carry out online observation, three main options are open to us: revisiting, roaming around, and trying out. Revisiting means that we go to our selected target on a regular basis and take field notes on the usual activities and possible changes. Roaming around implies that we explore by visiting websites and the utilities they offer, like threads, profiles, and sections. Trying out relates to us actively using the options, such as search, statistics, and tags. What all three options have in common is that during the online observation, we take field notes and make screenshots to document our observations.

The next step to be taken is the actual data collection. Here, we come back to our decision on whether we use screen data or user-based data. When we look at screen data, we collect the writing that people have produced online. Various methods are on offer, depending on technology, on the one hand, and on our IT savviness, on the other hand. An easy way to get the data is to simply copy and paste or to download pages in HTML. While this method is easy, it can be very time-consuming, especially if we are looking for large quantities of data. Another possibility is the use of data scraping tools, like web crawlers, APIs, and scripts. The advantage of data scraping is that we can obtain large amounts of data, but we need to have some IT skills to use the tools.

Data collection is strongly connected to data sampling. When we select the sample of data, our research question comes into play again because it decides where and how we collect our data. Data sampling depends on certain sampling criteria: random sampling, sampling by theme, sampling by time, sampling by phenomenon, sampling by individual or group, and sampling by convenience. In terms of cat-related digital spaces, the sampling methods can be described as follows: in a random sample, we scrape, say, tweets from the last two years tagged with #BlackCat and then select tweets at regular intervals or use a randomiser tool for selection. A certain randomness gives every #BlackCat tweet an equal chance of being selected. While this method makes our data representative and generalisable in a statistical sense, we lose the context of a conversation.

Sampling by theme refers to the selection of data organised on the basis of a selected theme in a forum or of threads in a post. If we decide to look at the theme of academics with cats, our sample would then consist of, for example, complete threads by different users focussing on the life of academics with cats, and our sample would include, for example, the cat Noodles (Figure 8.3) doing his cute bit to keep his owner away from researching and marking.

Instead of themes, we could also choose time as the selection criterion and collect data from a particular online forum at regular time intervals. If our study wants to look at the development of linguistic practices in a particular cat-specific forum in the last 10 years, sampling by time will be the appropriate method.

Sampling by phenomenon relates to a specific linguistic feature, like a non-standard spelling. The meowlogism 'purrfect' is such a linguistic

Figure 8.3 Noodles being cute #AcademicsWithCats

feature. We would make a computer programme scrape 'purrfect' on the social media channels and would then analyse how and where 'purrfect' occurs.

The method of sampling by individuals or groups involves the selection of certain categories of users and user networks. When we use this method, we decide on particular users or groups and collect their data. With our cat-related research interest, we can decide to look at the posts and comments of, say, Simon's Cat, Felix the Huddersfield Station Cat, or Daily Black Cats.

The last sampling method is called sampling by convenience, which means that we take whatever data we can get. In some cases, a convenience sample is the only possible way to gather data, but we are not working systematically and our datasets may turn out to be unsuitable.

To collect user-based data, the second option in CMC data collection, we do our research with the users themselves. We contact the users directly and conduct interviews or group discussions, or use questionnaires to find out more about the linguistic practices. To identify participants, we observe our preselected group and find out who the core account holders are. We are free in choosing the channels in our communication with the research participants, and we can carry out the interviews orally via video calls or in writing via e-mail, message services, or online surveys.

It is best to collect both types of data in a cyclical process; after asking people for permission to use their posts, we focus on the screen data to get linguistic data before analysing that data. For the users' own insights into their linguistic practices and for background information, we contact the users for follow-up interviews. Based on what we find, we go back to collect more screen data to deepen our understanding.

How to ... Address the Issue of Socio-Demeowgraphic Information

Another issue to consider in research is that of social identity factors, which are central to sociolinguistics because linguistic features are often correlated with social variables. In the real world, we have certain cues about the socio-demographic background of our participants, but in digital spaces, users are anonymous and these cues are missing.

When sociolinguists select their sample in the real world, they usually take a location and consider the socio-demographic variables they have defined in their research question, such as gender, age, social class, social status, and ethnic background. To fill the sample, researchers use a diagram with boxes or cells for the chosen social variables and then indicate how many people they interview for their research. For linguistic research, large sample sizes are not necessary, and it is common to fill each cell for the chosen variables with five people, although smaller sample sizes with a minimum of two people in each cell are also acceptable.

In the real world, identifying the factors, like age, is straightforward, while in the digital spaces, determining these factors is not so easy. There are three ways we can address the issue of the missing social identity cues. The first is to contact the users and ask them about their socio-demographic background after we have collected our data. This method is impractical, especially with large quantities of data. The second is to look at the social identity cues that the users themselves have left online, like screen names, avatars, and member signatures. Alternatively, we could take online-specific identity categories of, say, admins and normal group members or new and older members.

Applied to the cat accounts in digital spaces, we have the online-specific categories of cat account holders and followers or subscribers on the various social media platforms. The third way is to interpret the discourse practices the participants use to construct their own and others' online identity. A difference between the first two ways and the third lies in how we can analyse our data. When we use variables, we can do a quantitative analysis with statistical methods. However, when we focus on the discourse practices, we use a qualitative analysis of describing and coding.

8.3 Pawtrol: Getting Purrmission

Hi there, 😺 would it be ok for you if I use your posts in my research on language in cat communities? Your privacy will be protected, of course, and I will use your name only if you explicitly allow me to do so. I would call you something like Rascal or Sweetie. You can find out more about my research project on my blog or you can contact me via email Thanks, Edith aka Murrli (Asking for permission in direct messages on Instagram before data collection)

Even though posts on social media are seen by many followers and are considered as in the public domain by some, researchers have to ask for permission to use people's data. When we collect our data, we need to think about privacy protection, not just for legal reasons but also for ethical ones. There are no general ethics rules for researchers as the available guidelines differ between countries and universities. One general precondition for research, however, is that as researchers, we should do everything possible to protect our participants' anonymity online and offline, and we should include nothing that can make others find out who the participants are in their real lives.

The question to address is which type of information we are allowed to collect, to analyse, and then to publish. Legal protections of individuals are in place concerning data protection and privacy. The GDPR came into effect in the European Union in 2018 as a legally binding framework regarding the data of EU citizens. Without going into the regulations, the essence is that, without the individuals' permission, we are not allowed to collect and store any personal data. Additionally – and this is of importance for researchers outside the EU – if our research plans include EU residents, we are bound by the GDPR.

Please be aware that the GDPR requires you to minimize the personal data collected to only what is absolutely necessary for the purpose you are pursuing. Please do not collect data you don't need just because you feel a need for completion.
(*Consent Form Wizard* by DARIAH ELDAH, 2020)

As researchers, we usually ask people for permission before we undertake a survey or data collection. Participants have to give their informed consent, which allows us to collect their data. In our informed consent form, we have to fulfil the regulations of the GDPR or other applicable legal frameworks. Otherwise, we violate the law. Associations and research institutions have published guidelines and other information helping researchers with the legal and ethical prerequisites for research. One such association is the Digital Research Infrastructure for the Arts and Humanities within the European Research Infrastructure Consortium (DARIAH-EU). Together with cat Filou (Figure 8.4), the Ethics and Legality in Digital Arts and Humanities (ELDAH) working group within DARIAH-EU has produced the *Consent Form Wizard*, which helps researchers to have a GDPR-compliant consent form.

The survey is completely anonymous, and I only ask for some demographic data for my research, like the country you live in or what your native language is. Apart from that I do not ask for personal data. I will delete your data from the server when the survey is finished.
(Introductory Text to the July 2019 Survey)

The Association of Internet Researchers (AoIR) has published ethical guidelines for researchers to follow, with the latest version published in 2019. The AoIR focusses on ethical decisions internet researchers should think about, such as how we acquire de-identify, securely store, aggregate, and publish the data. Data storage, aggregation, and publication are serious issues because we have to make sure that we protect our participants and their privacy.

As already mentioned in the previous section, Instaloader and Facepager scrape only publicly available data. The issue here is

Figure 8.4 Vigilant Filou working for ELDAH

whether and to what extent people are aware of the fact that more information about them can be downloaded than what is visible on screen. Timestamps, geolocations, and location ID are also available together with other social media account information.

If you are not happy with answering the questions, you can withdraw at any stage of the survey.
(Introductory Text to the July 2019 Survey)

The *Recommendations on Good Practice in Applied Linguistics* by the British Association for Applied Linguistics (BAAL), provide us with key questions we should ask ourselves with regard to our research. The questions relevant for the surveys done for this book are listed in the BAAL recommendations in the guidelines' sections on the type of research, on our responsibilities to and relationship with our participants, and on our responsibilities to our colleagues. While all of the questions listed in the BAAL guidelines are important and have been addressed prior to research, the focus here is on our relationships with the participants and our responsibilities to them. In particular, I am addressing the issues of taking into account their rights, interests, sensitivities, privacy, and autonomy, of obtaining informed consent, of making clear the participants' right to withdraw at any time, and of making every effort to protect the participants' confidentiality and anonymity.

(1) How are the rights, interests, sensitivities, privacy and autonomy of the informants taken into account?

Participants have been asked for permission to use their posts. In cases where quotations are used, participants have been shown the context in which these quotations are used. No identifying information has been collected in the surveys, and the data has been anonymised. All the names of the cat accounts from which the data has been scraped have been changed.

(2) Has informed consent been obtained (including from children and adults with impairments in understanding), where appropriate, and does it cover the full duration of the project?

Yes, participants have been asked for consent prior to the data collection.

(3) Have informants' rights not to participate been made explicit?

Yes. Participants were told that they could withdraw from the survey at any time.

(4) Has every effort been made, where appropriate, to protect informants' confidentiality and anonymity?

Yes, no identifying information has been collected. Names have been changed.

Additionally, literature on research ethics suggest that as researchers, we should continuously reflect on our own ethical behaviour, whether we use our data the best way possible, whether we treat our participants fairly and accurately in our research, and whether we harm or benefit our participants with our research. Even though we are dealing with cats and not humans in our research, there is a real human behind every cat account whose privacy and data have to be protected. Despite all this seriousness, I agree with Respondent 5's comment:

What a fun study to do. And how interesting to delve into our feelings about our pets.
(Respondent 5)

Sources Used in This Chapter

🐾 Androutsopoulos (2014a) for research methods
🐾 Hazen (2014) for research methods
🐾 Holmes and Wilson (2017) for research methods
🐾 Podhovnik (2018) for research methods
🐾 AoIR (2019) for ethics
🐾 BAAL (2021) for ethics
🐾 DARIAH ELDAH (2020) for ethics
🐾 GitHub (2021) for open-source software
🐾 Hammond (2020) for Python
🐾 Python Software Foundation (2021) for Python
🐾 R (2021) for R
🐾 Winter (2019) for R
🐾 Jünger (2021) for Facepager
🐾 Koch-Kramer and Graf (2021) for Instaloader
🐾 Mundigl (2015) for the 'split-text tool'
🐾 Provalis Research (2017) for QDA Miner Lite
🐾 Brown and Miller (2013) for linguistic terms in the glossary
🐾 Crystal (2008) for linguistic terms in the glossary

Examples and Quotes in This Chapter

🐾 Hazen (2014, p. 11)
🐾 DARIAH ELDAH (2020)
🐾 'API' (2021) for definition of API
🐾 Bednarik (2019) for the most popular cat names
🐾 freemurrli (2017) for research blog

Suggestions for PURRther Reading

🐾 BAAL (2021)
🐾 Androutsopoulos (2014a)

9

Linguistic Scratching Posts

Happy #Caturday.
Instagram post 9 July 2016
(Murrli)

In March 2021, a search for the hashtag #CatsOfInstagram came up with almost 160 million hits on Instagram. One of the millions of #CatsOfInstagram images is my cat Murrli posing and wishing her followers a Happy Caturday (Figure 9.1). Cats wishing others a lovely day, especially on Caturday, is a common practice for cat account holders on Instagram, often one of the first to be picked up by people new to cat-related digital spaces. Sending wishes out to followers is part of the feline purrspective as well as of the human perspective, and it is only one practice among others.

In this chapter, we look at how we can analyse the data collected in the cat-related digital spaces and describe the linguistic differences in how we talk about our cats online. Taking a dialectological approach with a list of keywords, we show the variation in the words, the word formations, and the spellings cat account holders use in the cat-related digital spaces. We also use the categories of the feline purrspective and the human perspective, the cat-related examples of which illustrate the variation in meaning.

There is also some general demographic information concerning users of social media platforms. To show the vastness of user numbers and posts we are dealing with, this chapter provides us with some statistics for the four social media platforms that make up the scratching posts of this chapter, namely Facebook, Instagram, Twitter, and YouTube.

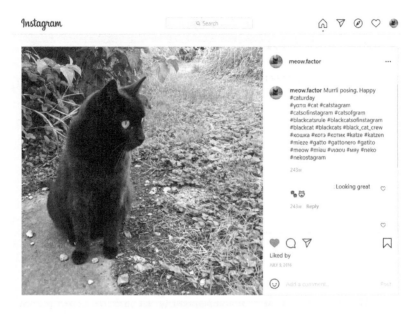

Figure 9.1 Instagram post of Murrli

Concepts Discussed in the Chapter

🐾 dialectology
🐾 language variation
🐾 lexical variation
🐾 morphology
🐾 orthography
🐾 semantic variation

Words from the Clawssary

🐾 * 🐾 blending 🐾 clipping 🐾 compounding 🐾 conversion 🐾 dialectology 🐾 lexicology 🐾 meowlogism 🐾 meowpheme 🐾 morphology 🐾 n 🐾 petfluencer 🐾 semantics 🐾 stories

9.1 Scratches in the Right Places

As we have already seen in Chapter 2, a way to mark off the feline territory is to take a list of keywords and see which words occur in the localities. This is a method used in dialectology, which looks at regional variation in the use of particular keywords. We are taking the same approach here. What made my method different from a traditional dialect questionnaire was that the list of keywords used was not available up front but was compiled after the data collection in the cat-related digital spaces. In the case of the language in cat-related digital spaces, the choice of keywords is based on my observation of the online spaces and on user-based data.

The result is a list of 80 keywords and concepts related to cats and cat-related online spaces. The asterisk is a wildcard operator to represent characters. For example, the expression '#*day' yields words that begin with the hashtag # and end in 'day', like #MondayNonday, #WhiskersWednesday, and #Caturday. Unlike a dialectological questionnaire, the keywords and concepts are listed from A to Z and are not grouped thematically. The full list of keywords is included in the keyword list in Appendix A.3.1. Here are some of the first items from the list as an example.

#* /HASHTAGS in general
#*DAY
CAT
AAH/AAW
BABY
BELLY
BIRD
BOX
BOY
BROTHER/BROFUR

This list allows us to systematically search for these keywords and cat-related concepts in the data and look for catspeak-specific expressions, meowphemes, emotional responses, and hashtags to compile a wordlist. We only have to list all the occurrences for each of the keywords.

In addition to presenting the data as a wordlist (Section 9.2: Cattolog ov Pussonyms), we can also group the words based on cat-related concepts and categories (Section 9.3: Cat-Related Categories), depending on which perspective we take and what has proved to be relevant in the data. For example, we can categorise the words based on which perspective is taken in the post. There is the typical feline purrspective, and there is the human perspective.

Feline Purrspective

referring to humans, like 'humans', 'dad', 'mum/mom', 'servant'
actions in real life, like 'eat', 'chase', 'scratch', 'jump', 'hunt',
'sleep', 'sit in a cardboard box'
actions on social media, like 'partying', 'celebrating', 'visiting other
cats', 'events', 'communicating', 'eating and drinking', 'having
fun', 'supporting others'

Human Perspective

referring to cats, like 'goddess', 'queen', 'prince', 'princess', 'royal',
'child', 'baby', 'companion'
cats as a species, like 'black', 'ginger', 'tortoise', 'tabby'
interactions with cats, like 'feed', 'snuggle', 'cuddle', 'play'
interactions with humans, like chatting and asking for advice
animal welfare, like talking about shelters and charities, animal
rights, animal abuse

The different ways of categorising the keywords highlight different
aspects of the data and complement each other to get a fuller picture
of what is going on in the cat-related digital spaces.

9.2 Scratches in the Cattolog ov Pussonyms

Itz da Cattolog ov Pussonyms Dokta Hediff
(Tweet by Olly)

The section heading here actually comes from user-based data. In
my tongue-in-cheek quest to 'get more cats into linguistics', I asked
for a purrieties version for 'wordlist'. Olly, who we met in Chapter 7
(Figure 7.6), provided the expression 'Cattolog ov Pussonyms' in his
purriety idiolect.

The wordlist – or our Cattolog ov Pussonyms – has been created
with the help of the software QDA Miner Lite and the split text tool
for Microsoft Excel. QDA Miner Lite is a qualitative data analysis tool
that allows us to create variables, like 'cat name', 'type of cat', 'name
of cat', and 'social media platform', when compiling a project. In
addition to the qualitative coding, these variables prove useful because
we can specify the variable we want to analyse when we retrieve text
or codes. The split text tool is a script used in Microsoft Excel that

Table 9.1 *Five most frequently occurring content words*

Instagram		Facebook		Twitter		YouTube	
cat	1133	cat	1135	cat	412	cat	633
happy	931	cats	675	happy	100	cats	257
love	816	love	648	new	84	love	256
thank	740	grumpy	271	cats	80	cute	196
cats	517	day	267	here	80	video	123

separates a text into individual words and lists them in alphabetical order ready for any search we want to conduct. Both tools together enable us to come to results with relative ease and speed.

For the wordlist, we select the variable 'platform' in Miner Lite because we are interested in the locality. QDA Miner Lite presents us with a table with individual columns for 'text' and 'social media platform'. The split text tool, into which we import the data, gives us two outputs, namely, on one Excel sheet, the alphabetical list of all words and, on the second sheet, the unique words and word count as a list from most frequent to least frequent.

While the Cattolog of Pussonyms does not take into account any frequency numbers, a look at the frequency of unique words is still interesting. Like in any corpus, the most frequent words are grammatical function words, such as articles, prepositions, and pronouns. Yet when we look past the function words, we find the content words. Unsurprisingly for cat-related digital spaces, the most frequent content word is 'cat', with the word 'cats' also being among the five most frequent on all platforms. The other entries differ slightly across the platforms. On a sidenote, Table 9.1 includes the number of occurrences only as additional information but not for statistical use. We go into statistics in Chapter 10.

Both tools, QDA Miner Lite and the split text tool, provide results for the keywords and concept (Table 9.1). For some cat-related concepts, there are more variants, while for others there are fewer. The following concepts have gone into the Cattolog ov Pussonyms: the meowphemes 'meow/mew', 'purr', 'fur', 'paw', 'claw', 'cat', 'kitten', 'puss', 'fluff/floof', and 'whisker'; the verbal responses 'aaw/aah', 'haha/hehe/heehee/kkkk', 'LOL/LMAO/OMG/WTF'; and the hashtags related to days and cats. As is done in dialectology, all the

Table 9.2 *Pivot table for 'amazing'*

Word Selected First	Platform Selected First
ameowsing	**Facebook**
Facebook	ameowsing
ameowzing	ameowzing
Facebook	**Instagram**
Instagram	ameowzing
Twitter	a-meowzing
a-meowzing	meowmazing
Instagram	meowzingly
meowmazing	**Twitter**
Instagram	ameowzing
meowzingly	
Instagram	

variations for a concept are shown in the list together with the locality they have occurred in – the respective social media platforms in our case.

Depending on the box ticked first (the variable 'platform' or the respective concept), the pivot table in Excel gives us either the words in alphabetical order together with the localities they occur in or the list of localities together with all the words used. Table 9.2 shows the two different ways of presenting the data for the catspeak equivalents of 'amazing' in 'meow/mew'. For the Cattolog ov Pussonyms, the second way, i.e. showing the platform first, consumes less space, which is the reason the data is presented that way.

The meowpheme 'cat' and the hashtags containing #*cat* include more variants than other meowphemes. 'Meow', 'purr', 'paw', and 'kitten' are also popular, and cat-related concepts and expressions occur on all platforms. The only exceptions are hashtags because there are hardly any hashtags on YouTube.

MEOW/MEW

The meowpheme 'meow/mew' occurs on Facebook, Instagram, Twitter, and YouTube. The meowlogisms refer to English 'amazing', 'awesome', 'beautiful', 'fabulous', 'family', 'fantastic', 'Fin Bec' (wine), 'mafia', 'magical', 'magnificent', 'majesty', 'mama', 'marshmallow', 'marvellous', 'massage', 'meditate', 'Merlot', 'model(s)', 'modelled', 'moment(s)', 'Mondays', 'more', 'Morticia', 'most', 'mouse', 'mousers', 'mummy(s)' or 'mommy(s)', 'museum', 'namaste', 'news', 'super-model', 'Valentine', 'yoga', and 'yogi'. The words 'meow' and 'mew' and their variations refer both to the cat sound 'meow' and to the personal pronouns 'I' and 'you'.

Facebook
  ameowsing, ameowzing, meow, meowdels, meowed, meowing, meow-language, meow-lentine, meowma, meowmeow, meowmeowmeow, meows, meow-tones, meowy, mewing, mews, the-godfather-of-the-meowfia
Instagram
  ameowzing, a-meowzing, bestmeow, cat-meow, fabmeowlous, fab-mewlous, fameowly, mameows, memeow, meow, meowback, meow-beautiful, meowbec, meowday, meowdel, meowdeled, meowdeling, meowdels, meowditate, meowed, meowellous, meowesome, meow-fine, meowga, meowgamonday, meowgi, meowgnificent, meowing, meowissed, meowjasty, meowjesty, meowjitos, meowless, meowlot, meowmaste, meowmazing, meowment, meowments, meowmeow, meowmie, meowmy, meowndays, meowness, meowr, meows, meow-shmellow, meowsie, meowssage, meowst, meowstest, meowtastic, meowticia, meowvalous, meowvelous, meoww, meowww, meowwww, meowwwwwww, meowy, meowzers, meowzingly, mew, mewo, mews, mew-seum, mewwww, supermeowdel
Twitter
  ameowzing, catsmeow, meow, meowbox, meowgical, meows, meowy, mew, mewbox, mews
YouTube
  meowed, meowing, meows, meowtastic, meoww, meowwww, mew

PURR

'Purr' as a meowpheme occurs on all four platforms. The meowlo-gisms refer to English 'approved', 'beautiful', 'big purr', 'birthday', 'burger', 'burrito', 'burritos', 'crazy parents', 'favourite', 'followers', 'harrumph', 'little purr', 'party', 'paw', 'per thousand', 'perfect', 'perfection', 'perfectly', 'performance', 'perhaps', 'person', 'personal', 'personality', 'perspective', 'please', 'pleasure', 'practising', 'prayers', 'praying', 'precious', 'predecessor', 'presents', 'Presley', 'privilege', 'probably', 'professional', 'professional fighters', 'protect', 'proud', 'purchase', 'purr', 'super', 'Targaryen' (from *House of Thrones*),

'terminators', 'terrific', and 'Thursday'. The character 'r' in the
meowpheme 'purr' is lengthened by including more 'r's in a number
of words – probably to indicate a stronger feline purr.

Facebook
apurroved, purr, purrayers, purrchase, purrecious, purred, purrfect,
purrfectly, purrformance, purring, purrito, purrlease, purrleasure,
purrminators, purrrfect, purrrfectly, purrrito, purr-rito, purrrivi-
lege, purrrrrfect, purrrrsday, purrrrtect, purrs, purrsonality, purrsonality, su-purr

Instagram
purr, purracticing, purraying, purrease, purred, purresents, purrfect, purr-fect, purrfection, purrfectly, purrfessional, purrfighters,
purrformance, purrger, purrhaps, purrific, purring, purrito, purri-
toes, purritos, purrlease, purrrday, purrrfect, purrr-fect, purrrr,
purrrrfect, purrrrfection, purrrrhitoh, purrrrrfect, purrrrrrrrrfict,
purrrrsday, purrrty, purrs, purrsday, purrsley, purrspective, purrth-
day, purrtiful, purrty

Twitter
crazy purrents, favpurrite, followpurrs, purr, purr-ecious, purre-
decessor, purrfect, purr-fect, purrfection, purrgaryen, purr-humph,
purring, purrito, purrlease, purrleasure, purrobably, purroud, purrrfect, purrrleaseeee, purrrrfect, purrs, purrsonal, purrty, supurr

YouTube
bigpurrr, familyofpurrrs, littlepurrr, purr, purrfect, purrfesional,
purring, purrr, purrrfect, purrrrs, purrrthousand, purrs, purr-son

FUR

As a meowpheme, 'fur' occurs on all four platforms. There are
meowlogisms referring to 'best friends', 'brother', 'cat for nature',
'everybody', 'everyone', 'first', 'fluffy Thursday', 'forever', 'Friday',
'friend', 'cat-feature', '(feline police) officer', 'panther(s)', 'prefer', 'sister', 'Thursday', and 'wonderful'. The expression 'fur-ternity (leave)'
indicates a leave taken on behalf of a pet similar to 'maternity/pater-
nity leave'. In the blended words 'brofur' and 'sisfur', 'fur' indicates
'cat brother' and 'cat sister' and is a reference to feline family relationships in the compound words 'furbaby' (and spelling varieties),
'furball', 'furbrother', 'furbuds', 'furfriends', 'furchild', and 'furkid(s)'.
The word 'friend(s)' occurs in a number of spelling variants.

Facebook

fur, furbabies, fur-babies, furbaby, fur-baby, furbabysitting, furball, furbrother, furbuds, furchild, furest, furever, furkid, furkids, furred, furriends, furrrever, furry, fursday, fur-ternity, prefurs

Instagram

brofur, catfurnature, fur, furbaby, fur-baby, furball, furballs, furever, furfeature, furfriend, furiday, furiend, furiends, furless, furr, furrbaby, furrday, furrend, furrends, furrever, furrfried, furriday, furriend, furriends, furring, furrrever, furrriend, furrriends, furry, furs, furst, panfur, panfurrs, sisfur, wonder-fur

Twitter

bestfuriends, everyfurries, evfurryone, fluffyfursday, fur, furend, furever, furkids, furme, furriends, furry, fursday, panfur, panfurs, sisfur

YouTube

fur, furrever, furries, pawcifur

PAW

The meowpheme 'paw' occurs on all platforms. The meowlogisms refer to 'adoption party', 'adorable', 'angry', 'anybody', 'Apollo', 'applaud', 'arrest (made by feline police officer)', 'assistant', 'autograph', 'awesome', 'birthday party', 'box party', 'cat patrol', 'everybody', 'fantastic', 'paw friend', 'handful', 'high five', 'important', 'kiss my paw', '(feline police) officer', 'paparazzi', 'parents', 'parties', 'party', 'partying', 'patrol', 'paw stamp', 'paw track', 'paws need claws', 'paws up' (hands up), 'pedi'(cure), 'pedicure', 'perfect', 'persistent', 'personal', 'police', 'portrait', 'positive(ly)', 'possibilities', 'power', 'preparing', 'programme', 'prosecco', and 'Secret Santa'. In line with the cat purrspective, 'paw' is used instead of 'hand' in expressions like 'a pawfull of dollars', 'paw five', 'paws up', and 'Santapaws' (Santa Claus)'. The meowlogism 'pawfficer' – created to indicate a police cat – appears in a number of spelling variants.

Facebook

catpawsitive, paw, pawcifer, pawdicure, pawesome, pawfficer, pawficer, pawfull, pawing, paw-prints, paws, pawsecco, pawsome, pawtasic, pawtograph, pawtrait

Instagram
adoptionpawty, anypawdy, apawllo, appawd, birthdaypawty, box-
pawty, everypawdy, impawtent, paw, pawdorable, pawdy, pawesome, pawfive, pawgramme, pawngry, pawparazzi, pawpedi,
pawrents, pawrrents, paws, pawsie, pawsies, pawsitive, pawsitively,
pawsneedclaws, pawsome, pawsomely, pawsup, pawtastic, pawties,
pawty, pawtying, pawtys, pawtyyy, prepawing
Twitter
catpawsitive, catpawsitivepro, catpawtrol, eberypawdy, epaw, impa-
want, impawtent, kissmypaw, paw, pawarrest, pawciffer, pawesome, pawfect, pawfficer, pawficer, pawproject, paws, pawsistant,
pawsitive, pawsitivity, pawsome, pawsonal, pawstamp, pawtrack,
pawtrol, pawz, santapaws
YouTube
paw, pawcifier, pawcifur, pawer, pawesome, pawfficer, pawficer,
pawicfer, pawing, pawlice, paws, paw-sibilities, pawsitive, pawsitively, pawsome, pawty

CLAW

The meowpheme 'claw' occurs on all platforms. The meowlogisms are
based on 'starship' (as in 'Clawship Enterprise'), 'claustrophobic', and
'closet'. In the word 'dewclaws', 'claw' has been modified with 'dew'.
The other occurrences of 'claw' refer to the cats' claws themselves.

Facebook
claw, clawed, clawing, clawless, claws, declaw, declawed, dewclaws,
stopbreedspecificlaws
Instagram
claw, claws, clawship, clawstrophobic
Twitter
claw, claws, clawsit
YouTube
claw, clawing, claws, declawed

CAT

The meowpheme 'cat' occurs on all four platforms. The meowlogisms are based on 'amazing', 'anaconda', 'aspiration', 'astronauts',
'attitude', 'attorney', 'avocados', 'Cabernet', 'cat ambassador', 'cat
cafe', 'catfights', 'Christmas', 'Cleopatra', 'congrats', 'congratulations', 'contemplating', 'democrat', 'Dracula', 'exactly', 'fabulous',

'fantastic', (weather) 'forecaster', 'furniture', 'gentlemen', 'Kavanaugh' (possibly), 'Nostradamus', 'satisfaction', 'Saturday', (feline) 'unicorn'. The meowpheme 'cat' also appears as a verb as 'to cat', which means 'to be/to behave/to live like a cat', in expressions like 'Good catting!' or 'Know how to cat'.

In compound words with 'cat' in initial position, like 'catdaddy' and 'catservants', 'cat' is used to indicate 'of the cat'. Another way of spelling these words includes a space or a hyphen between the two words, as in 'cat daddy' and 'cat-daddy'. There are also compound words with 'cat' in final position, with the initial word modifying the word 'cat'.

Facebook
    bobcat, bobcats, buttcat, castlecats, cat, catabulous, catbernet, catcafe, catcon, catconners, catdaddy, cat-daddys, cat-dragon, catemplating, caterday, catfights, catguy, catificaciones, catification, catified, catify, catio, catisfaction, catitude, catking, catlady, cat-less, cat-like, catlogic, catlover, catman, catmas, catnap, catnip, catpawsitive, catpeople, cats, catsday, catservants, catspiration, catted, cattery, catty, caturday, catvalentine, catwoman, cleocatra, commoner-cat, democat, forecatter, gentle-cat, gingercat, grumpy-cat, grumpy-cat, kingcat, king-cat, kitty-cat, kitty-cats, orangecat, pussycats, rocketcat, super-cat, teen-cat, tomcat, tomcats, wildcat

Instagram
    avocatos, businesscat, calicocats, cat, cataconda, catastic, catcula, catfurnature, cat-loving, catman, catmen, cat-meow, catnap, cat-napping, cat-napping, catnip, catniptimes, catnuzzling, catphoto, catpuns, cats, catscatscats, catscircus, catself, catselfie, catseye, catsitter, catsitting, catskills, catsnap, catsnet, catstradamus, catstronauts, catsuit, catswag, cat-tastic, cattitude, cattoasting, cattongue, caturday, caturdays, catwatcher, catwrangler, catyoga, cleocatra, cocat, communitycat, concats, concatulations, cupcats, firecat, firecats, ninjacat, studycat, sunningcat, supercat, tortiecat, tuxedocat

Twitter
    allotmentcat, ambassacats, cat, catamazing, catbeen, catconworldwide, catcuddles, catday, catfanatic, caticorn, catification, catifying, cat-iversary, catmando, catmas, catmom, catnap, catnerds, catnip, catniphollow, catparty, catpawsitive, catpawsitivepro, catpawtrol,

catpeople, catprotection, cats, catselfie, cattery, catting, cattorney, caturday, caturdays, catvanaugh, concatulations, cybercat, excatly, girlcat, guardcat, hmcabinetcat, homycat, laundrycat, linguisticats, momcat, multitaskingcat, neighborcat, palmerstonfocat, policecat, pro-cat, rescuecat, roguecats, shopcat, straycat

YouTube
cat, catdaddy, cat-family, catified, cat-loving, catman, catnip, cats, catss, cattastic, catttttttttt, catty, caturday, catwoman, cat-yep, grumpycat, keyboardcat, kitty-cat, lapcat, mama-cat, mycatfrom-hell, naincat, nyancat, petthedamncat, scaredy-cat, stuntcat

KITTEN

The meowpheme 'kitten' is used on all four platforms. The meowlogisms refer to 'kindergarten', '(elder) statesperson', and 'mojito'. In the variety 'kittehing', the word is used similar to 'catting' and means 'to be/to live/to behave like a kitten'. 'Kitten' meaning 'young cat' appears in a number of variants. The term 'kitty loaf' is the kitten variant of 'cat loaf', which is the position of a cat with paws and tail tucked in.

Facebook
insta-kitties, kitteh, kittehing, kitten, kittengarden, kittenhood, kitten-hood, kittenlady, kittenrescue, kittens, kitters, kittie, kitties, kitty, kitty-cat, kitty-cats, kitty-sitters, kittytherapy, permakitten, stateskitty

Instagram
kitt, kittay, kittea, kitteh, kitten, kittenish, kittens, kittie, kitties, kittors, kitttty, kitty, kittykat, kittylady, kittyloaf, kittymojito, kittypants, kittys, kittyssweet, kittyyyy

Twitter
kitt, kitte, kittehboi, kitten, kittengardrn, kittenlife, kittenrescue, kittens, kitties, kitty, kittykasa, kittyknowledge, kittylibfront, kittys, kittytherapy

YouTube
kitteh, kittehhhhh, kitten, kittenlady, kittens, kittensssss, kitties, kitty, kitty-cat, kittypet, kittys

PUSS

The meowpheme 'puss' occurs on all four platforms. The only meowlogism found in the data refers to 'Mussolini'. Otherwise, 'puss' is used for 'cat'.

Facebook
  puss, pussies, pussy, pussycats, pussys
Instagram
  puss, pusscat, pussolini, pussy, pussycat
Twitter
  puss
YouTube
  puss, pussies, pussy

FLUFF/FLOOF

'Fluff' and 'floof' are used as meowphemes on all four platforms and can be interchanged. Meowlogisms formed with 'fluff' and 'floof' relate to 'fabulous', 'fantastic', and 'Thursday'. 'Fluff' and 'floof' are used in compound words to indicate the characteristics of the fur of a longer-haired cat, like Ma'a, Purr Reviewer 1 (Figure 9.2), who I often call 'Bauscherl', an equivalent in German to 'floofkins'. The meowpheme appears as the verbs 'to fluff/to floof' as 'floofing' and 'fluffing', which means 'to be/behave/live like a floofy/fluffy cat'.

Facebook
  floof, floofday, floofed, flooffff, flooffiness, floofiest, floofin, floofiness, floofing, floofkin, floofkins, floofmeister, floofness, floofs, floofster, flooftabulous, flooftastic, flooftime, floofy, floofykins, floofyness, fluff, fluffball, fluffballs, fluffiest, fluffiness, fluffy, fluffycatcrew
Instagram
  floof, floofed, floofier, floofy, floofyface, fluff, fluffball, fluffbucketpaws, fluffed, fluffer, fluffin, fluffiness, fluffing, fluffs, fluffy, fluffyball, fluffybears, fluffycat, fluffycats, fluffyyyy, fluffyyyyy
Twitter
  dafluffarooniez, floof, floofed, floofy, fluff, fluffiest, fluffy, fluffyf, fluffyfuraday, fluffyfursday
YouTube
  floof, floofy, fluff, fluffay, fluffer, fluffy

Figure 9.2 Her Fluffy Floofiness Ma'a, aka Purr Reviewer 1

WHISKER

'Whisker' as a meowpheme occurs on all platforms, although it is not used very often in meowlogisms. The only meowlogism 'whiskerlicious' refers to 'delicious'. The expression 'box-and-whisker-plot' found on Twitter is a statistical term related to data visualisation. It occurs in the digital spaces of academics with cats and refers to the R software programming package CatterPlot, which we came across in Chapter 5. The name CatterPlot itself is a meowlogism using the meowpheme 'cat' to refer to the term 'scatterplot', which is another statistical tool for graphic data visualisation.

Facebook
well-whiskered, whiskas, whisker, whiskers, whiskerswednesday

Instagram
whiskerswednesday, workinwhiskers
Twitter
box-and-whisker-plot, whisker, whiskerlicious, whiskers, whisker-swednesday
YouTube
whiskerz

WRITTEN EMOTIONAL RESPONSES

In the cat-related digital spaces, there are some common reactions to images and captions expressed in writing, like finding something cute (AAW), being amazed or happy (AAH), and laughing (HAHA/HEHE/HEEHEE) and abbreviations expressing surprise and excitement (OMG), laughing (LMAO), and swearing (WTF). These written reactions occur on all platforms and show variation in spelling. The expressions 'OMC' and 'OMCat' are short for 'Oh my Cat!', and 'mol' is the purrified version of 'lol' and means 'meowing out loud'.

AAH

Facebook
aaaaah, ah, ahh, ahhh, ahhhh, ahhhhhh
Twitter
aah, ah, ahhh, ahhhh, ahhhhh, ahhhhhhhh, ahhhhhhhhhhhh
YouTube
aaa, aaaa, aaaaa, aaaaaaaa, aaaaaaaaaaaaaaaaaaaaaa, aah

AAW

Facebook
aw, aww, awww, awwww, awwwww, awwwwwe, awwwwww, awwwwwwxxxxx
Instagram
aahw, aaw, aawww, aw, awawawawaa, aweeee, awh, awhh, awnn-nn, aww, awweee, awwnn, awwpraying, awww, awwwbig, awwwe, awwwhappy, awwwhave, awwwso, awwww, awwwwbig, awwwwe, awwwwh, awwwww, awwwwww, awwwwwwone, awwwwwww, awwwwwwww, awwwwwwwww, awwwwwwwwwww
Twitter
aw, aww, awwdorable, awww, awwwcats, awwww, awwwww

YouTube
aaaaaaaaaaaaaaaaaaaaaaaaaaawwwwwwwwwwwww, aaaaaaaa-
ah, aaaaaw, aaaawwwwhhhh, aaaw, aaawww, aaw, aawwee, aw,
aww, aww-ing, awww, awwww, awwwww, awwwwww, awwwwwww, awwwwwwwwww, awwwwwwwwwwww, awwwwwwww-
wwwww, awwwwwwwwwwwwwww

HAHA/HEHE/HEEHEE

Facebook
bahahaha, bwahaha, haha, hahaa, hahaha, hahahahahahaha,
heehee, hehe
Instagram
ahaahaha, ahaha, ahahaaaaaaaaaa, ahahaahahahah, ahahah, aha-
haha, ahahahaha, ahahahahaha, ahahahahahahaaaaa, ahahaha-
hahahahah, ahahahgaaa, ahahhaha, ahahhahahahahahahaha, ahha-
haha, bahahaha, bahahahaha, buahahahaha, bwahahaha, ehe-
heehe, eheheh, ehehhehe, haha, hahaa, hahaaha, hahabest, hahah,
hahaha, hahahaa, hahahaaaaa, hahahaah, hahahah, hahahaha,
hahahahaa, hahahahaah, hahahahah, hahahahaha, hahahaha-
haa, hahahahahaaaa, hahahahahaha, hahahahahahah, hahahahahahahaha, hahahahahahahaha, hahahahahahahahahaha,
hahahahahahahahahahshahahahahahahahahahahahahahahaha,
hahahahahha, hahahahahhaah, hahahahahhahaah, hahahahh,
hahahahhh, hahahahsa, hahahh, hahahha, hahahhaha, hahah-
hahaha, hahahhahahah, hahahhahahahaha, hahahhahahahaha-
hahahahaahahaha, hahahhahahha, hahhaha, hahhahah, heehee,
hehe, hehehe, heheheheeh, hehehehehe, hehehhee, hhahahaha,
madhahaha, mwuahahaha, teeheehee, tehehe, whahah, whahaha
Twitter
haha
YouTube
aaahahahf, aahaahahahahahahahahahaha, ahahahahahah, ahahah-
haha, haha, hahah, hahaha, hahahaha, hahahahaha, hehe

LOL/LMAO/OMG/WTF

Facebook
lmao, lol, omg, omggg
Instagram
lmao, lmaooo, lmaoooo, lmaoooooo, lol, lolllll, lolol, lololol,
lols, omc, omcat, omg, omgdness, omggg, omgggg, omggggg,

omgggggggg, omgitsakitten, omgoodness, omgosh, omgoshhh,
omgsh, omgwtf, wtf
Twitter
  lol, mol, omg
Youtube
  lmao, lol, omg, omgg, omggg, omgggg, omggggg

HASHTAGS

Hashtags are used to categorise and highlight the content of a post.
While it is not necessary to use hashtags, they make easier for people
to follow certain topics and for algorithms to suggest related content.
Hashtags are common on Instagram, Twitter, and Facebook. On
YouTube, hashtags are not really used. The data provides material
for two groups of hashtags, namely weekdays and cats. Providing the
lists of hashtags would take up too much space, which is why just
a summary is given below. The full list of hashtags is provided in
Appendix A.3.2.

On social media in general, there are hashtags for every day of
the week and for special occasions. These hashtags mean that we
post a certain image and/or text on a specific day. On Thursdays,
for example, we can post something from our past with the hashtag
#ThrowbackThursday. In the cat-related digital spaces, the hashtags
are applied to the cats, which means that on #ThrowbackThursday
we see images of the cats as tiny kittens – the cats' past. The two hashtags consistently used across the platforms are #TongueOutTuesday
and #WhiskersWednesday.

Depending on the virtual community we are in, we use different
hashtags and structure our week for our cat images slightly differently.
A typical week of the virtual black cat community Murrli was part of
looks like this: Monday is #MeowgaMonday, with cats doing yoga
poses; Tuesday is #TongueOutTuesday and shows cats with their
tongues out; Wednesday as #WhiskersWednesday is reserved for cats'
whiskers; Thursday is #PantherThursday, dedicated to black cats;
Friday means parties in cardboard boxes with #FridayNightBox-
Pawty; Saturday is #Caturday, and all images are fine as long as
they show a cat; and Sunday is #SundayFunday, and images usually
show relaxed cats.

The second group of hashtags we are looking at refer to cats
themselves, like #BlackCat or #CatsOfInstagram. There are many

cat-related hashtags, and each cat species or type of cat creates hashtags related to their own group, like #SiberianCat, #GingerCat, and #TabbyCat. Famous cats have their very own hashtags, such as #GrumpyCat, #KeyboardCat, and #SimonsCat. On a sidenote, the reason the list includes so many hashtags referring to black cats is the fact that the sample is black cat biased.

9.3 Scratches in the Cat-Related Cat-egories

In cat-related digital spaces, communication happens on two levels: the feline level and the human level. Depending on the identity chosen, cat account holders and their followers post as their cats or as themselves. The roles are not fixed, though, and the feline purrspective may change to the human perspective and vice versa in the posts and comments. The interaction can be cat–cat, cat–human, human–human, and human–cat. We are choosing the feline and the human levels as our lexcial concepts, which we describe below.

The Feline Purrspective

Always know who is in charge, hooman!
(Comment on Facebook)

The feline purrspective is taken in cat–cat interaction and in cat–human interaction when the cat 'is writing' the post or comment. The general premise of the feline purrspective in the digital spaces is that cats are able to share their everyday lives on social media. For cat account holders and users alike, this is a given, and users accept that it is the cats talking and acting. While not all cat account holders go as far as to take up the cat purrsona with the personal pronoun 'I' or the variants 'ay', 'meow' or 'mew', the main focus of the post is on the cats and on what they do. The cat purrsona is fully accepted by the followers who directly address the cat in comments and replies.

A typical post by a cat is multimodal and consists of an image and the caption. In the caption, the cats describe what they are doing, thinking, wishing for, planning, remembering, and a lot more. The feline voice is signalled by linguistic means, and depending on the cat account, we find catspeak purrieties and meowlogisms to various extents. Some accounts have a broader feline accent than others by using catspeak and meowlogisms as much as possible, while others limit the cat accent to first-person pronouns, like 'I' and 'my', to indicate the feline purrspective.

As already mentioned, we can look at the data in terms of concepts. For the feline purrspective, there is the way cats refer to people, what cats do in real life, and how cats live their social media lives in the cat-related digital spaces. In the posts and comments, cats refer to people as their family, their humans, their parents, and their servants. Other cats are family members and their friends. In the data, the relevant words occur like this:

- catmom, hew-mom, hoomom, hoomums, humom, humoms, mom, momcat, momma, mommas, mommi, mommie, mommies, mommy, moms, momy, mum, mumcat, mumma, mummy, mums
- catdad, catdaddy, cat-daddys, dad, daddy, daddys, dads, granddad, grumpydad, hudad
- pawrents, pawrrents, purrents
- (human) servant, servants, catservants, slave, footman, human slave, huslave, minion, hew-man, hooman, hoomans, hoomen, hooooman, hooomans, hooooooman, hoooooooman, hoooooooooman, human, human-friend, human-friends
- bestfuriends, friend, friends, furend, furfriend, furiend, furiends, furrend, furrends, furriend, furriends, furrriend, furrriends

The feline actions include actions in real cat life, such as hunting ('chaysing mowseez'), purring, eating, and sleeping (in 'sunpuddles' for example), scratching, stretching, grooming, and sitting in a cardboard box, like Professor Mauz, the ginger tom in the Facebook video (Figure 6.6). Once again on a sidenote, the feline purrsona of Professor Mauz was transferred to real life when his owner was introduced as 'Professor Mauz' at an academic conference.

In addition to real-life behaviour, the feline actions include scenes from an imaginary life, like partying and celebrating, visiting other cats, participating in events, communicating, eating and drinking, having fun in general, and supporting others. A very big part of a cat's life, real or imaginary, is dedicated to food and drink. Words and hashtags related to eating occur in the data. Some mentions relate to real cat food and prey, such as 'bird' and 'mouse', while others are playful inventions, like 'tunatini' or 'meowjito'. A recurring food item is 'catnip' (or the clipped form 'nip'), which is jokingly regarded as a semi-illicit substance. The expression 'birderer' refers to 'bird murderer'.

catnip
  catnip, catniphollow, catniptimes, crazycatnippawty, kitnipbox, nip, nipclub
fish
  salmon, needthatsalmon, tuna, toona, tunatini, tunatinis, tunatuesday
treats
  dreamy, dreamies, getafewtreats, treat, treats, treattuesday, wantmoretreats, nom, nomnom, nomnomnom, noms
drinks
  pawsecco, catnip wine, meowgarita, tunatini, meowtini, furgundy, purrgundy, meowjito, milk, cream, catbernet, meowbec, meowlot
bird
  bird, birder, birderer, birdies, birdiiiiiiiiii, birds, bird-watching, birdy
mouse
  mice, micey, mouse, mouse-catching, mouser, mousers, mouses, mowseez

Not everything is light-hearted and fun in the feline view of life – there are also serious issues where cats offer their support to others. These support actions work on an individual as well as on a group basis: sending good wishes for sick cats, sharing the grief for cats who have died, and posting encouraging messages for owners whose cats have gone missing. In situations like these, it is common for cats to join 'pawcircles' in support.

Events, too, take place in cat-related digital spaces, usually indicated by hashtags. Virtual birthday parties (often referred to as 'pawties'), 'box hopping' visits to other cats and their cardboard boxes, and some regular events like 'Gladders Yoga Night', which is a yoga session run by the unofficial cat account of Gladstone, the Treasury Cat, on Wednesdays. Known by the hashtag #GladdersYoga, Gladders, as Gladstone is commonly known, calls out yoga poses for cats – illustrating them in a multimodal way with cat images of cats in various poses, such as stretching or grooming.

Another example is The Edible Cats Club, a virtual community on Twitter, which organises regular events for 'friends in food and fun'.

Figure 9.3 ECC barmen waiting for orders

There are the weekly #ECCEnrolment events, when new members are
welcomed and virtual sightseeing tours given with and for the cats.
Additionally, the ECC, as the virtual community is referred to, invites
its members to join in remembrance vigils, wakes, and #ACandleFor
events. The cats Olly, Nacho, and Buddy work at the ECC Bar to serve
drinks (Figure 9.3), and Marmite, who had the initial idea to form the
club, is the Head Honcho (Figure 9.4). We come across Gladders and
the Edible Cats Club in Chapter 10 in the social network analysis.

We reach out and offer emotional support to each other through the good
and difficult times.
(Marmite, Head Honcho)

The Human Perspective

In the cat-related digital spaces, there is also human–cat interaction
and human–human interaction. On the one hand, people who normally interact as their cat purrsona switch to their human identity
sometimes; on the other hand, others always interact as humans but
accept the other users' cat purrsonas. The common denominator is a
love for cats and for animals in general.

There are several ways in which we humans see the cats of
the cat-related digital spaces. First, we ascribe a high status to

Figure 9.4 ECC Head Honcho Marmite

the cats by adoring them as goddesses and royalty. In the posts and comments, we address and describe cats as 'empress', 'queen', 'queenie', 'king', 'prince', 'princess', 'goddess' and 'god', 'majesty', 'meowjasty', 'meowjesty', 'royal', and 'royalty'. Second, we refer to our cats as our children and to ourselves as their parents. We and our feline companions, like Jeebus, Sooty, and Betty (Figure 9.5) are one big family.

baby
  baby, baby-he, furbaby, fur-baby, furbabies, fur-babies, furrbaby, jelly babycakes
girl
  girl, babygirl
boy
  boi, boy, boys, boyyy, birthday boy, kittehboi, wonderboy
brother and sister
  fur-brother, brother, brofur, brofer
  'sister, sisters, sisfur

Third, we refer to the cats as predators by calling them 'lion' and 'living room lion', 'panther', and 'tiger' as well as 'hunters', 'natural

Figure 9.5 Jeebus, Sooty, and Betty are family

born killers' with their 'kill sheet', 'bunny slayers', and 'Tabbyraptor'. Wicht, Purr Reviewer 2, certainly feels like a proper tabbyraptor (Figure 9.6).

Fourth, we find cats beautiful and soft as well as cute (see also 'aaw' and variants in the Cattolog ov Pussonyms) and funny (see 'haha/hehe/heehee' and variants in the Cattolog ov Pussonyms). In general, we love our cats and express that love.

model
   meowdel, meowdeled, meowdeling, meowdels, nexttopmeowdel, supermeowdel, topmeowdels

darling
   darling, darlings, dah-ling

cute
   cutee, cuteee, cuteeee, cuteeeee, cuteeeeee, cuteeeeeee, cuteeeeeee-eee, cuteer, cuteness, cutenessssssssssssssssssss, cuter, cutes, cutest, cutie, cutieeee, cutie-pie, cutier, cuties, cutiesttttt

gorgeous
   gorgeous, gorgious, gorgeus

Figure 9.6 Tabbyraptor Wicht, aka Purr Reviewer 2

fluff/floof

floof, flooffff, flooffiness, floofier, floofiest, floofin, floofiness, floofing, floofkin, floofkins, floofmeister, floofness, floofs, floofster, flooftabulous, flooftastic, flooftime, floofy, floofyface, floofykins, floofyness, fluff, fluffay, fluffball, fluffballs, fluffed, fluffer, fluffiest, fluffin, fluffiness, fluffing, fluffs, fluffy, fluffyball, fluffycat, fluffycats, fluffyyyy, fluffyyyyy

love

lovely, love, loveable, lovebug, lovecat, lovecats, loved, loveee, loveeeee, loveeeeee, lovelies, loveliest, loverly, loves, loveses, lovey, loveys

sweet

sweet, sweeter, sweetest, sweetests, sweetheart, sweethearts, sweetie, sweetiecake, sweetieeeee, sweetie-pie, sweeties, sweetiest, sweetmaau, sweetness, sweets, sweety, sweetyyyyy

Fifth, we describe what we do for and with our cats, like feeding and as well as cuddling, snuggling, playing with toys, and taking care of them, which includes visits to the vet.

cuddle
catcuddles, cuddle, cuddlebug, cuddle-bug, cuddled, cuddlely, cud-
dler, cuddlers, cuddles, cuddliest, cuddliness, cuddling, cuddly,
cuddlycat, double-cuddle
snuggle
catsnuggles, snuggle, snuggled, snugglefest, snuggler, snugglers,
snuggles, snuggling, snuggly
toys
toy, toys, cattoys, fishtoy, toyforcats, funnytoy, everythingisacattoy
vet
supervet, takeyourcattothevetday, vet, veterinarian, veterinary, vets,
V. E. T.

Sixth, we use terms to indicate that our cats belong to a specific
group based on their fur colour or history. We assign hashtags
and words to black, ginger, tabby, tortoise, calico, stray, feral,
rescue, shelter, and other cats. Accordingly, we find 'tabbyraptors'
(Figure 9.6) and 'gingerninjas' (Figure 9.7). As mentioned previously,
my data is black cat biased, which explains the many expressions used
for black cats.

calico
calico, calicocats, calicocatsofinstagram
ginger
ginger, gingercat, gingerfurbabies, gingermenace, gingerninja, gin-
gers, kissagingerday
grey
gray, grey, greycatday, greycatsoftwitter, greys, grey-white
tabby
orangetabby, silvertabby, tabby, tabbycat, tabbycatsofinstagram,
tabbyface, tabbyraptor, tabbys, tabbysplace, tortie-tabby
tortoise
torti, tortie, tortiecat, torties, tortie-tabby, tortishell, tortitude,
tortoiseshell
black
baby-panther, blackpanther, housepanther, housepanthers, little-
pantherpride, lovemyminipanther, minipanther, mini-panther,
officialpanfur, panfur, panfurrs, panfurs, panfursquad, panther,

Figure 9.7 Leo the ginger ninja

pantherandpanda, panthercat, pantherdom, pantheress, panther-
ette, panthergirl, pantherific, panthering, pantherish, pantherlooks,
panthers, panthersrule, pantherthursday, peculiarpanther, white-
panther

Related to communication about their own cats in cat-related
digital spaces, people ask others for help and advice in cat health
related matters. Posts and comments include questions about cat
food, cat health, experiences with vet visits (sometimes spelled
V. E. T. in case the cat is reading), and conversations about topics
not related to cats.

Room in the digital spaces is also given to cat welfare and animal
welfare matters. People post and comment on shelter and rescue cats,
cats up for adoption, stray and feral cats, and cruelty towards animals
in general, often using the hashtag #AdoptDontShop. Cat shelters
and charities show cats in need of help and purrsonify the cats by
sharing their – often sad – stories.

Other cat accounts, too, raise awareness for cat welfare issues.
A famous example is the social media presence of Jackson Galaxy, a

thecatdaddy ✓ · Abonniert   ···

thecatdaddy ✓ Twofer Tuesday? Yep - our 6 month-old foster kitten, Faith, is modeling a pretty cute #TongueOutTuesday and throwing in a side of #ToebeanTuesday action just for added cuteness. We're working on socializing this little lady so she can become more comfortable with humans... And hint, hint - she'll be available for adoption (in the Los Angeles area) along with her littermate, Gracie, in just a couple weeks or so...

3 Wo.

Figure 9.8 Jackson Galaxy raising awareness for foster kitten

cat behaviour, and wellness expert and TV host of the series *My Cat from Hell*. Using the feline-related hashtags, like #AdoptDontShop, #TongueOutTuesday, and #ToebeanTuesday, Jackson Galaxy talks about cat behaviour, rescue and shelter cats, and animal charities (Figure 9.8). In the comments, people share photos of their cats and their experiences and ask for advice. In turn, photos of #TeamCat-Mojo – as Jackson Galaxy's followers are referred to – are reposted and get a special mention on the official channels.

Twofer Tuesday? Yep – our 6-month-old foster kitten, Faith, is modelling a pretty cute #TongueOutTuesday and throwing in a side of #ToebeanTuesday action just for added cuteness. We're working on socializing this little lady so she can become more comfortable with humans ... And hint, hint – she'll be available for adoption (in the Los Angeles area) along with her littermate, Gracie, in just a couple weeks or so ...
(thecatdaddy)

9.4 Scratches in Numbers

#CatsOfInstagram
157,113,998 posts on 01 March 2021
157,169,431 posts on 02 March 2021
157,194,555 posts on 03 March 2021

157,247,932 posts on 04 March 2021
157,439,262 posts on 06 March 2021
157,521,390 posts on 08 March 2021
(Observation during one week on Instagram)

In March 2021, I checked daily for a six-day period to see how many images had been posted with the hashtag #CatsOfInstagram, and as we can see from the cumulative figures in the quote above, more than 400,000 new Instagram posts were shared in one week. To get more idea of the vastness of social media, we can go to statistics portal www.statista.com. On the portal, we find statistics related to cats and to social media platforms. We need to treat those figures with caution, though, because they are somewhat out of date.

That said, if we had done our dialectological fieldwork in the offline world, we would have provided some background information on the respective localities of the language varieties we were examining. Therefore, we take to these statistics to get a general view of the social media platforms on which we find the cat-related digital spaces. We get an idea of the user numbers on the platforms, the overall age-group distribution, the overall gender distribution, and the top activities on the social media platforms.

One such set of statistics lists the countries with the most cat owners worldwide as of 2017 (Figure 9.9). According to the statistics, Russia is the number one country for cat ownership as almost 60% of all households have at least one cat. In the United States, Argentina, and Italy, 43%, 41%, and 40% of people, respectively, own a cat. The UK is ranked 9, with 32%, which means that almost a third of all households share their life with pet cats. A different set of statistics based on a survey by the Pet Food Manufacturing Association, though, says that an estimated 17% of UK households own cats – in other words, this survey gives a lower number of cat households in the UK than the other research.

Statista also provides dossiers with the most relevant statistics that are available for Instagram, Facebook, YouTube, and Twitter. In January 2021, Facebook was the most used social media platform with 2,740 million active users, followed closely by YouTube with 2,291 million. Instagram was ranked fifth with 1,221 million, and Twitter with 353 million users is at number 16. The dossiers also give figures for the activities done on social media platforms and lists figures for each platform for viewing photos, watching videos, sharing content

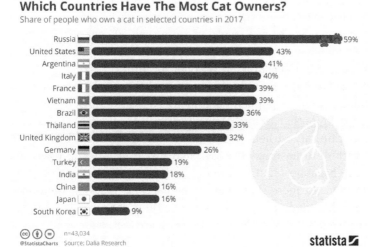

Which Countries Have The Most Cat Owners?

Share of people who own a cat in selected countries in 2017

Russia — 59%
United States — 43%
Argentina — 41%
Italy — 40%
France — 39%
Vietnam — 39%
Brazil — 36%
Thailand — 33%
United Kingdom — 32%
Germany — 26%
Turkey — 19%
India — 18%
China — 16%
Japan — 16%
South Korea — 9%

n=43,034
@StatistaCharts   Source: Dalia Research

statista

Figure 9.9 Countries with most cat owners

with everyone, sharing content one to one, networking, providing news, featuring products, and promoting businesses.

Instagram

Instagram is an online photo-sharing platform and is currently in the top five of the most-used social media platforms with more than one billion users worldwide. In January 2021, the 10 countries with the most users were the United States and India (both with 140 million users), Brazil (99 million), Indonesia (85 million), Russia (56 million), Turkey (46 million), Japan (38 million), Mexico (32 million), the United Kingdom (31 million), and Germany (26 million). The majority of Instagram users worldwide fall into the two age groups of 18–24 and 25–35. As for gender distribution, there are slightly more female users than male users worldwide.

In 2019, Instagram's top three activities were viewing photos, watching videos, and sharing content with everyone, and the top three reasons for using Instagram were given as 'to see what my family/friends are up to', 'to kill time when I'm bored', and 'to keep in touch with my friends/family'.

We also get some insight into the most popular types of posts and length of the captions on Instagram. Images are by far more popular than videos or carousels. The length of posts is given in characters, and it becomes obvious that users tend towards longer captions. Most commonly, posts have a length of more than 300 characters (35.8%), closely followed by posts of between 150–300 characters (30.8%), and posts with 50–150 characters account for 26.1%.

As for hashtags, fewer hashtags – one to three per post – or even no hashtags are more popular than many hashtags – four to 10 or more than 10. More than a third of posts are with 1–3 hashtags (35.2%), less than a third are without hashtags (28.7%), a little less than a quarter are with 4–10 hashtags (23.1%), and just over an eighth with more than 10 hashtags (12.9%). Emoji in captions are not that common on Instagram. In more than half of the captions (52.3%), there are no emoji, while slightly bit more than one third of the posts contain one to three emoji (38.2%). Four to 10 emoji are less common (8.7%), and 10 or more emoji are not used very often (0.8%).

In the United States, 17% of social media users follow animals on social media. In June 2020, four cats made it into the top 10 of the most followed pets on Instagram: the feline petfluencers with the most Instagram followers are Nala Cat, Grumpy Cat, Lil BUB, and Venus the Two Face Cat.

Facebook

Facebook is the most-used social media platform worldwide with 2,740 million users. The top 10 countries as far as users are concerned are India (320 million users), the United States (190 million), Indonesia (140 million), Brazil (130 million), Mexico (93 million), the Philippines (83 million), Vietnam (68 million), Thailand (51 million), Egypt (45 million), and Bangladesh (41 million).

As for gender, Facebook has more male users than female users. In January 2021, 44% were female and 56% were male. Facebook is most popular in the age groups of 18–24 and 25–34 worldwide, though in the United States the two most popular age groups are 25–34 and 35–44.

The top three activities on Facebook are viewing photos, sharing content with everyone, and watching videos. The top three reasons to use Facebook are to keep in contact with friends and family, to get entertainment, and to get news (in 2019 in the United States). The type of Facebook page posts are status posts, image/photo posts, video posts, and link posts. The dossier does not give information about the length of posts or the usage of hashtags and emoji.

YouTube

The video-sharing platform YouTube was estimated to have 1.86 billion users worldwide as of January 2021. In 2019, it had 2 billion logged-in users a month. In 2018, YouTube was the most popular video platform in the United States, even more popular for watching videos than Facebook, Instagram, and Twitter.

The dossier on YouTube gives some demographic information on age and gender. The statistics on age groups for 2020 shows that YouTube is used by Internet users of all ages. In the United States, more than 70% of users aged 15–55 and slightly fewer than 70% of users over 56 went onto YouTube in 2020. The statistical information on gender shows that YouTube is as popular for women as for men, with 72% of female and male internet users viewing videos on YouTube.

No data has been given for the top three activities on YouTube. The top three reasons for watching videos on YouTube are to get entertainment, to get news, and to follow brands. The dossier does not give information on comments, their length, or the use of emoji in the comments and does not feature a statistics on hashtags.

Twitter

Twitter had 353 million users worldwide as of January 2021. The top 10 countries for Twitter users are the United States (69.3 million users), Japan (50.9 million), India (17.5 million), the United Kingdom (16.45 million), Brazil (16.2 million), Indonesia (14.05 million), Turkey (13.6 million), Saudi Arabia (12.45 million), Mexico (11 million), and France (8 million). While Twitter has fewer users than the other platforms, it was ranked third in terms of market share in the US in January 2021.

The dossier gives information on the age profile and the gender of global audiences. Twitter is more popular in older age groups, and users tend to fall into the age groups of 35–49 (28.4%), 25–34 (26.6%), and 18–24 (25.2%). There are more male users than female users. More than two thirds of Twitter users are male (68.5%), and less than one third are female (31.5%).

Twitter's top three activities are getting news, viewing photos, and – tied in third place – sharing content with everyone and watching videos. The top three reasons for using the platform are given as to get news and to get entertainment – which are tied in first place – and to keep in contact with friends and family. The length of tweets is limited to 280 characters. The dossier does not give information on hashtags, emoji, or cat accounts.

#CatsOfInstagram
407,392 posts
(Week 1–8 May 2021)

Sources Used in This Chapter

- Mundigl (2015) for the 'split text tool'
- Provalis Research (2017) for Qualitative Data Analysis (QDA)
- Podhovnik (2018) for meowlogisms on Instagram
- Institute for Systems Biology (2017) for Catterplot
- Google (2021) for YouTube
- Twitter Inc. (2021a) for Twitter
- Facebook (2021) for Facebook
- Instagram (2021a, b) for Instagram
- Statista (2021a, b, c, d) for dossiers

Examples and Quotes in This Chapter

- '#CatsOfInstagram' (2021) for the hashtag #CatsOfInstagram
- 'kkkk' (2006) for the entry on 'kkkk'
- @EdibleCatsClub (2020) for the Edible Cats Club on Twitter
- PFMA (2020, 2021) for cat ownership
- McCarthy (2017) for cat ownership
- Armstrong (2018) for Figure 9.9
- Karl Stocker: personal communication

10

#StatsWithCats

Stats with Cats: The Domesticated Guide to Statistics, Models, Graphs, and
Other Breeds of Data Analysis
(Book title (Kufs, 2011))

In this chapter, the cats take us on a trip to statistical methods
so that we can interpret and visualise the cat-related online data. As
we have seen in the previous chapter, there are many different cat-
related and cat-inspired words and expressions in the cat accounts.
This chapter provides us with a quantitative add-on with a statistical
approach to how we talk about our cats online.

To approach the language variation in the data, we select the social
media platforms and the cat account types as sociolinguistic variables.
In our statistical approach, we take frequencies and crosstabs to
look at linguistic variation across four social media platforms and
four cat account types. We look at the choices of non-meowlogisms
and meowlogisms on Facebook, Instagram, Twitter, and Youtube
as well as in the collective, for-profit celebrity, working-for-cause,
and individual cat accounts. The linguistic variables we compare
are the non-meowlogism/meowlogism pairs 'awesome/pawsome', 'per-
fect/purrfect', 'friends/furiends', and 'panther/panfur'.

Additionally, we are taking a detour through big data and social
network analytics to find out more about how we form networks in cat-
related digital spaces. With a social network analysis, we can illustrate
the structure of a social network, which we do by using examples from
one cat-related virtual community and one cat-related affinity space.

Concepts Discussed in the Chapter

🐾 domains of language use

253

🐾 data sampling
🐾 statistical methods
🐾 quantitative methods
🐾 frequencies
🐾 crosstabs
🐾 linguistic variable
🐾 big data
🐾 social network analytics
🐾 nodes
🐾 edges
🐾 density
🐾 plexity
🐾 speech accommodation

Terms from the Clawssary
🐾 Atlas Force 2 🐾 degree 🐾 edge 🐾 modularity 🐾 network density
🐾 network plexity 🐾 node 🐾 speech accommodation

10.1 #Meow and Places

Before we go into the statistics, let us very briefly recall the domains of language use and online-specific categories for data sampling that we discussed in Chapters 7 and 8, respectively. The domains of language use shape our language choice because different settings and different topics make us decide which code or variety we use. For the data sampling, we have used the online-specific categories of 'social media platform as place' and 'type of cat account'.

The overall question is whether we can identify a connection between linguistic variables and non-linguistic variables. The linguistic variables we analyse are the meowphemes PAW, PURR, and FUR in four selected non-meowlogism/meowlogism pairings, while the non-linguistic variables are 'place' and 'type'. In our collected data, there are many occurrences of the words 'awesome', 'perfect', 'friends', and 'panther' and their variants, which is whey they are ideal for our analysis of the linguistic variables. Our linguistic variables are, thus, PAW in 'awesome/pawsome', PURR in 'perfect/purrfect', and FUR in 'friends/furiends' and 'panther/panfur'.

Table 10.1 *Absolute frequencies of words in the Purrieties corpus and its subcorpora (platform)*

Facebook	Instagram	Twitter	YouTube	Purrieties Corpus
103,732	114,254	43,129	34,365	295,480

We group the spelling variants of the respective meowlogisms together for our comparison across the social media platforms and the cat account types. For example, the different renderings of the meowpheme PURR in 'purrfect' have all been categorised as 'purrfect'. In this chapter, we are interested in whether the users have chosen the meowphemic form or not rather than which variants exist. The variants are all listed in the previous chapter.

To approach the #StatsWithCats, we consider our data as a corpus (the Purrieties corpus) and apply the descriptive statistical methods of frequency and crosstab (cross-tabulation) to the linguistic and non-linguistic variables. With that kind of description, we can give a good overview of our data, something we would not achieve without number crunching.

The first set of numbers we look at is the absolute frequency of the whole Purrieties corpus and then of the non-meowlogism/meowlogism variables for the subcorpora. First, we consider the social media platforms as the non-linguistic variable of 'place'. For the absolute frequency, we simply count all the occurrences of the words in the corpus and in the subcorpora.

In absolute numbers, the Purrieties corpus consists of 295,480 words and is made up of four subcorpora categorised as 'place'. Table 10.1 shows the figures for the subcopora Facebook, Instagram, Twitter, and YouTube. When we look at the figures in the table, two things become obvious straightaway: first, the corpus is on the small side with less than 300,000 words, and second, the subcorpora have different sizes. The largest subcorpus is Instagram, the smallest is YouTube. The subcorpora are different in size because the posts have attracted a different number of comments and the comments have been included in the corpus.

Because we have subcorpora of different sizes, we make the frequencies comparable in the second step. In descriptive statistics, we use relative frequencies. Relative frequencies are comparable because they have been normalised to account for corpus size differences. In the case of the Purrieties corpus, the number of total words varies between the four subcorpora, and we recalculate the absolute frequency as a relative frequency. The relative frequency is also called the normalised frequency.

In Chapter 9, the words 'cat', 'cats', 'cute', 'day', 'grumpy', 'happy', 'love', 'new', 'thank', and 'video' have been shown as the most frequently occurring content words in the Purrieties corpus. We now take the absolute frequencies of these words (given in Table 9.1 in Chapter 9) and recalculate them as relative frequencies. The relative frequencies offer us a first basis for comparison.

For the relatively small Purrieties corpus, the frequency has been normalised for 10,000 words. This means that the frequency indicates a hypothetical count of how often a specific word would occur in a 10,000 word corpus. For example, the relative frequency for 'cat' in the Purrieties corpus is 112.1, which means that we would find 112.1 occurrences of 'cat' within every 10,000 words. Other bases for normalisation, say 1,000,000 words, are used for larger corpora.

The relative frequency evens out any size differences between the subcorpora, which means that we can interpret the different relative frequencies for 'cat' (shown in Table 10.2) as indicators for differences between the platforms: there are hypothetically more than 180 occurrences per 10,000 words on YouTube, 109 words on Facebook, just under 100 on Instagram, and 95 words per 10,000 on Twitter. The word 'cat' is, thus, hypothetically twice as popular on YouTube as on Twitter.

Table 10.2 *Relative frequencies (RF) of most frequently used content words on the social media platforms (per 10,000 words)*

Facebook		Instagram		Twitter		YouTube	
Word	RF	Word	RF	Word	RF	Word	RF
cat	109.4	cat	99.2	cat	95.5	cat	184.2
cats	65.1	happy	81.5	happy	23.2	cats	74.8
love	62.5	love	71.4	new	19.5	love	74.5
grumpy	26.1	thank	64.8	cats	18.5	cute	57.0
day	25.7	cats	45.3	here	18.5	video	35.8

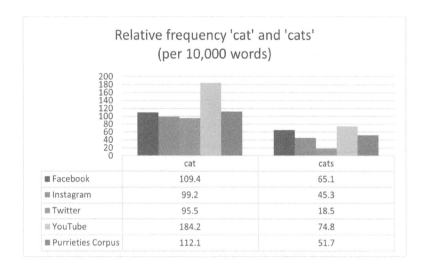

Relative frequency 'cat' and 'cats' (per 10,000 words)		
	cat	cats
■ Facebook	109.4	65.1
■ Instagram	99.2	45.3
■ Twitter	95.5	18.5
■ YouTube	184.2	74.8
■ Purrieties Corpus	112.1	51.7

Figure 10.1 Relative frequencies for 'cat' and 'cats' (per 10,000 words)

The visualisation of the figures as a chart makes the relative frequencies more tangible for those among us who find numbers a bit wobbly (like me). With Microsoft Excel, for example, we can easily visualise the differences across the platforms between 'cat' and 'cats' as a bar chart (Figure 10.1). Even without looking too closely, we can see that when we draw a curve along the highest points of the bars, the shape of the curves for 'cat' and 'cats' are very similar. This indicates for us that the hypothetical occurrences of both 'cat' and 'cats' is highest on YouTube followed by Facebook, then Instagram, and is the lowest on Twitter in our Purrieties corpus.

We apply the same method to the four linguistic variables and recalculate the absolute frequencies as relative frequencies for the pairings 'awesome/pawsome', 'friends/furiends', 'perfect/purrfect', and 'panther/panfur' (Table 10.3). Again, we interpret the figures as hypothetical occurrences per 10,000 words, which means that, for example, 'awesome' hypothetically occurs 4.6 times per 10,000 words in cat-related digital spaces on Facebook, 10.1 times on Instagram, 1.9 times on Twitter, and 4.4 times on YouTube. The frequency of the word 'awesome' in the whole Purrieties corpus is 6.3 words per 10,000.

The different relative frequencies mean that the four variables have occurred to a different extent in the cat-related digital spaces on the

Table 10.3 *Absolute and relative frequencies of non-meowlogisms and meowlogisms (platform)*

Absolute Frequencies	AWEsome	PAWsome	FRIEND	FURiend	PERfect	PURRfect	panTHER	panFUR
Facebook	48	8	124	1	21	12	26	0
Instagram	115	156	177	145	42	62	192	8
Twitter	8	13	64	2	11	18	15	40
YouTube	15	3	15	0	13	5	2	0
Purrieties Corpus	186	180	380	148	87	97	235	48

Relative Frequencies	AWEsome	PAWsome	FRIEND	FURiend	PERfect	PURRfect	panTHER	panFUR
Facebook	4.6	0.8	12	0.1	2	1.2	2.5	0
Instagram	10.1	13.7	15.5	12.7	3.7	5.4	16.8	0.7
Twitter	1.9	3	14.8	0.5	2.6	4.2	3.5	9.3
YouTube	4.4	0.9	0.5	0	3.8	1.5	0.5	0
Purrieties Corpus	6.3	6.1	12.9	5	2.9	3.3	8	1.6

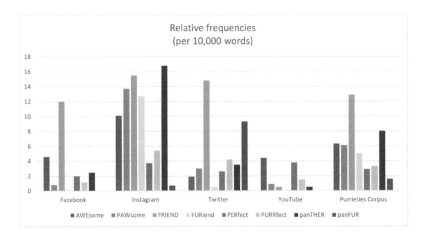

Figure 10.2 Relative frequencies by place

four social media platforms. The bar chart in Figure 10.2 visualises these differences in the subcorpora, and we see the 'interesting' bits straightaway. When we draw a curve along the heights of the bars, we receive a different shape for each platform, which indicates that we are on to something here that we should look at more closely.

In addition to describing the subcorpora with the relative frequency of the words, we are using crosstabs. With a crosstab, we can go further into the differences between the platforms when we compare the linguistic variables.

Conventionally, the linguistic variables are the column heads and the context variables are the row heads in the crosstabs. Accordingly, we list the variants 'awesome' and 'pawsome', friend' and 'furiend', perfect' and 'purrfect' as well as 'panther' and 'panfur' as the respective column heads and the social media platforms as the rows in Table 10.4. The numbers in the columns show in absolute numbers how often each variant has occurred.

With the crosstab, we can calculate the totals in three ways, namely as row totals, column totals, and grand totals. Each way indicates a different probability. We use the row totals to look at the likelihood of a linguistic variant within a context, the column totals to compare the contexts, and the grand totals to describe the corpus as a whole.

In the cells, we have the absolute number of occurrences, say for 'awsome' and 'pawsome', with which we calculate the percentages. We

Table 10.4 *Crosstabs for non-meowlogisms/*
meowlogisms and social media platforms

Platform	Non-Meowlogism	Meowlogism	Total
	AWEsome	PAWsome	Total
Facebook	48	8	56
Instagram	115	156	271
Twitter	8	13	21
YouTube	15	3	18
Total	186	180	366
	FRIENDS	FURIENDS	Total
Facebook	124	1	125
Instagram	177	145	322
Twitter	64	2	66
YouTube	15	0	15
Total	380	148	528
	PERfect	PURRfect	Total
Facebook	21	12	33
Instagram	42	62	104
Twitter	11	18	29
YouTube	13	5	18
Total	87	97	184
	panTHER	panFUR	Total
Facebook	26	0	26
Instagram	192	8	200
Twitter	15	40	55
YouTube	2	0	2
Total	235	48	283

obtain the probabilities when we divide the cell value by the respective total and then multiply it by 100, thus generating a percentage. For the likelihoods of 'awesome' versus 'pawsome' on, say, Instagram, we look at the row: there are 115 occurrences of 'awesome' and 156 occurrences of 'pawsome', which totals 271. The result for 'awesome' is 42.4% and for 'pawsome' 57.6%.

These percentages tells us whether 'awesome' or 'pawsome' is more likely on Instagram. In very general terms, a probability over 50% indicates a preference and under 50% a dispreference for a given variant of the linguistic variable in a specific context. With

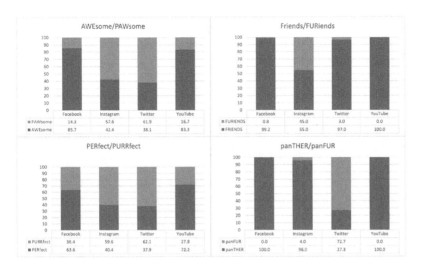

Figure 10.3 Likelihood of non-meowlogism/meowlogism on platform (row totals)

57.7%, 'pawsome' is, thus, the preferred choice on Instagram in the 'awesome/pawsome' pairing.

Based on the crosstab calculations, we can create charts to visualise the probabilities and, in turn, the language variation. Figure 10.3 shows the percentages calculated in the row totals and illustrates the meowlogism likelihood in the non-meowlogism/meowlogism pairings for each of the platforms.

The results from the row totals (Figure 10.3) show us that there are indeed differences between the platforms. On the whole, the cat-related digital spaces on Instagram and Twitter prefer the meowlogisms, while the spaces on Facebook and YouTube prefer the non-meowlogisms. With the figures from the row totals, we can now describe the preferences and dispreferences for non-meowlogisms and meowlogisms on the platforms.

For Facebook, there is a rather strong preference for non-meowlogisms, and cat-related digital spaces on Facebook clearly prefer 'awesome', friends', and 'panther'. The case of the pairing 'perfect/purrfect' is closer. While 'perfect' is the preferred form with 63.6%, the cat spaces on Facebook are still likely to use 'purrfect' with a probability of 36.4%.

On Instagram, cat-related digital spaces prefer meowlogisms. With a probability of more than 50%, 'pawsome' and 'purrfect' are more likely than 'awesome' and 'perfect', yet, 'friends' and 'panther' are more likely than 'furiends' and 'panfur'. That said, the case of 'friends/furiends' is close: both variants have the same distance from the 50% mark, namely ±5%, and although the likelihood of 55% for 'friends' makes the non-meowlogism the preferred variant, the likelihood of 'furiends' is not much smaller at 45%. Despite the tie of two non-meowlogisms and two meowlogisms as the preferred forms, meowlogisms are very much present on Instagram, which is why my judgement call is for meowlogisms.

On Twitter, the cat-related spaces show a preference for meowlogisms. The forms 'pawsome', 'purrfect', and 'panfur' are more likely than 'awesome', 'perfect', and 'panther'. In fact, 'panfur' is the strongly preferred variant on Twitter with a likelihood of more than 70%. In the pairing 'friend/furiend', the cat-related spaces clearly prefer 'friend'.

On YouTube, the cat-related spaces clearly prefer the non-meowlogisms. YouTube is different to the other three platforms as the cat-related spaces use a meowlogism form for only two of the four linguistic variables. We only have the meowlogism forms in the pairings 'awesome/pawsome' and 'perfect/purrfect', and for those, the non-meowlogism 'awesome' and 'perfect' are much more likely. For 'friend/furiend' and 'panther/panfur', the meowlogism form does not occur and we only find 'friend' and 'panther'.

We are changing the direction now in our look at the crosstab. Instead of rows, we choose the columns for our calculations. With the column totals (Figure 10.4), the perspective is now on the contexts in which the individual variants occur. We again take 'pawsome' as an example. The likelihood of 'pawsome' on Instagram is at almost 90%, which leaves only some 10% for YouTube, Facebook, and Twitter. This means that we are most likely to come across 'pawsome' on Instagram.

The bar charts shown in Figure 10.4 visualise the contextual differences for 'pawsome', 'purrfect', 'furiends', and 'panfur'. In the case of 'pawsome', we have already discovered that while it is present on all platforms, it occurs most often on Instagram. Similarly, the variant 'furiends' is almost an Instagram exclusive as its likelihood on Twitter and Facebook is close to 1% and is even 0% on YouTube.

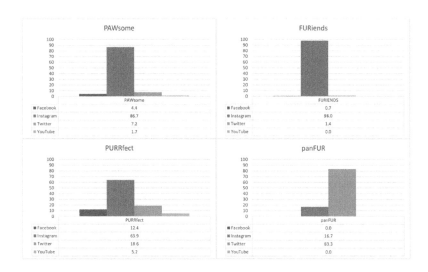

Figure 10.4 Probability of meowlogisms by context (column totals)

Connecting these findings with the notion of indexicality, we can say that cat account holders' use of 'pawsome' and 'furiends' conveys a membership in cat-related digital spaces on Instagram.

'Purrfect', too, clearly indicates Instagram. Yet when we compare the bar chart of 'purrfect' with those of the other variables, we notice that 'purrfect' is distributed across all platforms to a greater extent, which means that 'purrfect' has been adopted on all platforms.

'Panfur' is different. First, it only occurs on Twitter and Instagram, and second, it is clear indicator for Twitter rather than for Instagram. 'Panfur' is completely unlikely in cat-related spaces on Facebook and YouTube.

In general, both ways of tackling the crosstab (row total and column total) show that meowlogisms are very likely on Instagram, less likely on Twitter, and even less likely on Facebook and YouTube. Put differently, the more we belong to cat-related digital spaces on Instagram and Twitter, we more we use meowlogisms.

10.2 #Meow and Purrestige

The second non-linguistic variable we consider are the types of cat accounts. In Chapter 5, we categorised the types of cat account based

Table 10.5 *Absolute frequencies of words in the*
Purrieties corpus and subcorpora by type

Collective	For-Profit	Individual	Working	Purrieties Corpus
104,150	87,422	35,378	68,530	295,480

on the main (small) stories they tell and the main aims they pursue. In the cat-related digital spaces, there are collective cat accounts, for-profit celebrity cats, individual cat accounts, and working-for-cause cat accounts.

Very briefly, collective cat accounts feature different cats in their posts. For-profit celebrity cats are microcelebrities on social media, monetise their accounts, and have a clear marketing strategy. Individual cat accounts present the cats as family members in their everyday lives and are used to have fun. Working-for-cause cats are those cats who support charitable causes with their social media presence. Below, we refer to them simply as 'collective', 'for-profit', 'individual', and 'working' as the non-linguistic variable of 'type'.

Before we go into the variation of PURR, PAW, and FUR in our four pairings in connection with type as the non-linguistic variable, we again take a look at the overall corpus statistics. As we can see in Table 10.5, the subcorpora based on types of cat accounts have different sizes. The size differs because different numbers of comments were attracted by the various posts of the sampled cat accounts. The subcorpus 'collective' is the largest, followed by the 'for-profit' and 'working' subcorpora, and 'individual' is the smallest subcorpus.

As we have done with the platforms, we recalculate the absolute frequencies as relative frequencies to make the subcorpora comparable. Likewise, we normalise the relative frequencies of the non-meowlogisms and meowlogisms in 'collective', 'for-profit', 'individual', and 'working' for 10,000 words (Table 10.6).

Figure 10.5 offers us the visualisation of the relative frequencies in connection with the non-linguistic variable of type. When we draw a line joining the top of each bar, we have a different curve shape for each of the subcorpora, which indicates that there are differences between the types as far as the non-meowlogism/meowlogism use of PAW, PURR, and FUR is concerned.

Table 10.6 *Absolute and relative frequencies of non-meowlogisms and meowlogisms by type*

Absolute Frequencies

	AWEsome	PAWsome	Friends	FURiends	PERfect	PURRfect	panTHER	panFUR
Collective	60	92	101	54	34	22	104	30
For-Profit	34	15	94	1	26	29	35	1
Individual	21	51	58	85	10	19	95	17
Working	71	22	127	8	17	27	1	0
Purrieties Corpus	186	180	380	148	87	97	235	48

Relative Frequencies

	AWEsome	PAWsome	Friends	FURiends	PERfect	PURRfect	panTHER	panFUR
Collective	5.8	8.8	9.7	5.2	3.3	2.1	10.0	2.9
For-Profit	3.9	1.7	10.8	0.1	3.0	3.3	4.0	0.1
Individual	5.9	14.4	16.4	24.0	2.8	5.4	26.9	4.8
Working	10.4	3.2	18.5	1.2	2.5	3.9	0.1	0.0
Purrieties Corpus	6.3	6.1	12.9	5.0	2.9	3.3	8.0	1.6

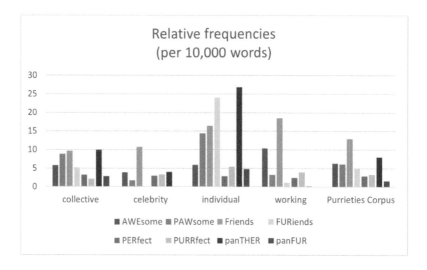

Figure 10.5 Relative frequency by type

The example of 'awesome/pawsome' shows us how to approach the relative frequency based on the type of cat account. In our description, we list the results. The non-meowlogism 'awesome' hypothetically occurs 5.8 times per 10,000 words in the 'collective' subcorpus, 3.9 times per 10,000 words in the 'for-profit' subcorpus, 5.9 times per 10,000 words in the 'individual' subcorpus, and 10.4 times per 10,000 words in the 'working' subcorpus. For the Purrieties corpus in total, the mean relative frequency for 'awesome' is 6.3 times per 10,000 words.

The figures for 'pawsome' are as follows: 'pawsome' occurs 8.8 times per 10,000 words in the 'collective' subcorpus, 1.7 times per 10.000 words in the 'for-profit' subcorpus, 14.4 times per 10,000 words in the 'individual' subcorpus, and 3.2 times per 10,000 words in the 'working' subcorpus. In the Purrieties corpus, 'pawsome' hypothetically occurs 6.1 times per 10,000 words.

The relative frequencies point us to a difference in the linguistic variable 'awesome/pawsome': the meowlogism form 'pawsome' has a higher relative frequency than the non-meowlogism 'awesome' in the 'collective' and 'individual' subcorpora. The crosstabs give us more insight.

For the types of cat accounts, too, we use crosstabs to see how the linguistic variables are distributed and how likely the meowlogism

Table 10.7 *Crosstabs for non-meowlogisms/*
meowlogisms and type of cat account

Type	Non-Meowlogism	Meowlogism	Total
	AWEsome	PAWsome	Total
Collective	60	92	152
For-Profit	34	15	49
Individual	21	51	72
Working	71	22	93
Total	186	180	366
	FRIEND	FURIEND	Total
Collective	101	54	155
For-Profit	94	1	95
Individual	58	85	143
Working	127	8	135
Total	380	148	528
	PERfect	PURRfect	Total
Collective	34	22	56
For-Profit	26	29	55
Individual	10	19	29
Working	17	27	44
Total	87	97	184
	panTHER	panFUR	Total
Collective	104	30	134
For-Profit	35	1	36
Individual	95	17	112
Working	1	0	1
Total	235	48	283

forms are. We calculate the percentages as row totals first to find out about which form – non-meowlogism or meowlogism – is preferred in each cat account type. Then we look at the column totals to describe the contexts (Table 10.7).

The row totals give us the meowlogism/non-meowlogism likelihood in each type of cat account. Figure 10.6 uses bar charts to visualise the row totals for 'awesome/pawsome', 'friends/furiends', 'perfect/purr-fect', and 'panther/panfur' for each of the cat account types.

As already mentioned in Section 10.1, a percentage of more than 50% means that a given variant of a variable is the preferred form. The figures for the collective cat accounts indicate that the

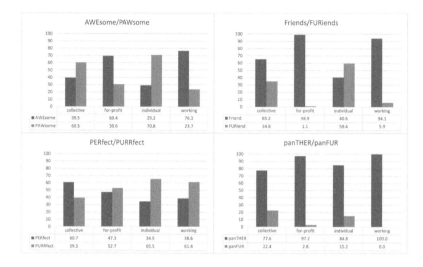

Figure 10.6 Likelihood of meowlogisms/non-meowlogisms in types of cat accounts (row totals)

non-meowlogisms are the preferred forms. The collective cat accounts prefer the variants 'friends', 'perfect', and 'panther'. However, in the pairing 'awesome/pawsome', the meowlogism 'pawsome' is the preferred form.

For-profit cat accounts, too, prefer the non-meowlogism forms. 'Awesome', 'friends', and 'panther' are more likely than 'pawsome', 'furiends', and 'panfur'. Here, the exception is the pairing 'perfect/purrfect' as 'purrfect' is preferable to 'perfect'.

Working cat accounts are similar to the for-profit cat accounts and prefer the non-meowlogisms 'awesome', friends', and 'panther' to the meowlogisms 'pawsome', 'furiends', and 'panfur'. Again 'perfect/purrfect' is a notable exception as it is the meowlogism 'purrfect' that is more likely.

Individual cat accounts are different from the other three types because the figures show us a clear preference for meowlogisms. The variants 'pawsome', 'furiends', and 'purrfect' are more likely than 'awesome', 'friends', and 'perfect'. Only in 'panther/panfur' is the non-meowlogism 'panther' the preferred form.

The column totals show us the distribution of the individual variants across the contexts. In Figure 10.7, the charts visualise for us the probabilities of the linguistic variants 'pawsome', 'furiends',

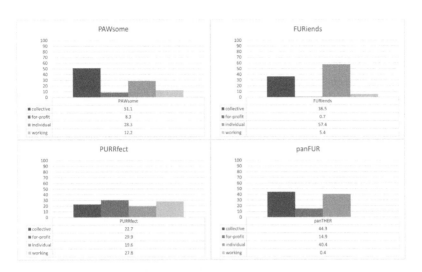

Figure 10.7 Probability of meowlogisms by cat account type (column totals)

'purrfect', and 'panfur' across the cat account types, and we can see that there are differences between the meowlogism likelihood for each of the variants. Simply by looking at the visualisation, we can already say that the likelihood of a particular cat account type using meowlogisms depends on the specific meowlogism.

We are most likely to encounter 'pawsome' in the collective cat accounts. The probability of 'pawsome' in the other cat account types is lower. Thus, an occurrence of 'pawsome' indicates for us collective cat accounts and, to a lesser extent, individual cat accounts.

When we come across the variant 'furiend', it most likely comes from the digital spaces of individual cat accounts and less likely from the collective cat accounts. We hardly find 'furiends' in the spaces of working cat accounts and for-profit cat accounts because the probability of 'furiends' is very low. Therefore, the use of 'furiend' points us mainly to individual cat accounts and somewhat less to collective cat accounts.

The variant 'purrfect' is different from 'pawsome', 'furiends', and 'panfur' because we cannot tie the use of the meowlogism 'purrfect' to one specific type of cat account. 'Purrfect' is likely to occur in all cat account types, with the percentages ranging from 30% to less than 20%. 'Purrfect' is most probable in the for-profit accounts, slightly less probable in the working cat accounts, less again in the spaces of collective cat accounts, and least likely in the spaces of individual cat accounts.

The variant 'panfur' has the highest probability of occurrence in the spaces of collective and individual cat accounts. The probability of 'panfur' in the spaces of for-profit cat accounts is much less and is close to zero in the spaces of working cat accounts. The use of the meowlogism 'panfur' is, thus, an indicator for collective and individual cat accounts.

Number crunching gives us insights we might miss otherwise. In linguistic research, descriptive statistics is just a first step. For the Purrieties corpus, we use absolute and relative frequencies as well as crosstabs to find out more about the connection between linguistic and non-linguistic variables. Nevertheless, with descriptive statistics, we have to keep in mind that the results are valid for our corpus only. If we were to establish a generalisability of our results beyond the Purrieties corpus, we would have to incorporate inferential statistical methods like *Mission Impawssible?* has done for the dog-related spaces on Reddit. For inferential statistics, however, we need a different research setup and more knowledge of statistical methods.

That said, we have already laid the ground work for further research, and we can point to areas that we could go into in more detail. When we compare our findings concerning 'place' and 'type', we discover that the non-linguistic variables have a different effect on the use of meowlogisms: the figures for 'place' show us that the use of meowlogisms is platform-dependent, while the type of cat account does not really affect the choice between non-meowlogism and meowlogism in our pairings. This is an assumption we could test with a research design that specifically addresses the question of 'place' versus 'type' or – even better – various combinations of 'place' and 'type'.

10.3 #Meow and Social Network Analysis

#Caturday: 59,713 tweets between 7 May 2021 and 18 May 2021 (Tweets collected with TAGS)

In terms of numbers and statistics, we can get a bigger picture of the activities in cat-related digital spaces by applying big data tools.

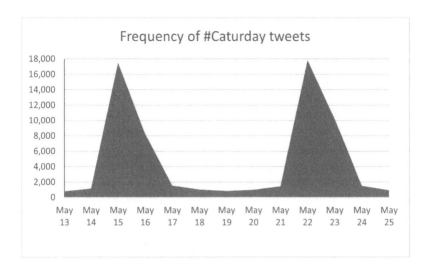

Figure 10.8 Frequency of #Caturday tweets

Figure 10.8, for example, is based on almost 60,000 tweets gained with the tool TAGS in one week of May 2021. The figure visualises the daily frequency of the hashtag #Caturday on Twitter, and it does not really come as a surprise that the spikes in frequency – which incidentally look like cat ears – occur each Saturday. In cat-related digital spaces, #Caturday is the most common hashtag on Saturdays.

Big data tools, like TAGS or the open-source programme Gephi, help us to illustrate digital networks. TAGS is available as a spreadsheet on Google and harvests tweets based on keywords. The outcome is called an archive, which can be explored with Google Sheets or downloaded to be used in Microsoft Excel. Gephi shows how people are linked with each other online and visualises social networks by applying algorithms to the data. The programme displays the online interaction with node and edges. Nodes are the users on social media platforms, and edges are the posts, reposts, links, and more. The terms 'nodes' and 'edges' are not only applied by Gephi but are used in social network analysis to indicate people and the relationships between them.

#GladdersYoga and #ECCHappyHour

In connection with social networks, sociolinguistics also refers to 'density' and 'plexity' to describe different types of networks. Network density refers to how much and whether the members of a person's network know and interact with each other without that person present. If our network is dense, members interact with each other without us present. Network plexity indicates on how many levels members are linked with each other – whether they interact on one or on more levels, in one or more contexts. Relations can be uniplex and multiplex. In a uniplex network, people communicate in one context only, whereas in a multiplex network, people meet in more contexts.

In cat-related digital spaces, there are different types of networks. The cat-related networks vary in both density and plexity. Some cat-related spaces, like the @EdibleCatsClub, are dense and multiplex: members communicate with each other on many topics and meet each other online, not only on Twitter but also in other less public online environments. Other cat-related networks are looser and/or uniplex, for example, #GladdersYoga, where the connecting node is the cat account of Treasury Mog.

Social networks and language are connected. As our networks shape our language, our speech indicates the types of networks we belong to. We tend to use the same language as others in groups we belong to, especially when we like the people we regularly interact with. In this context, sociolinguistics talks about speech accommodation. Speech accommodation means that people make their language similar to the language of their addressees when they like each other or want to please others or put them at ease. Simply put, the closer we are, the more alike is our language.

Speech accommodation happens in the cat-related digital spaces. The specific cat-related space we are in shapes the type of catspeak we use, if we use catspeak at all. If and to what extent we use meowlogisms or the more individual types of purrieties (the cat-inspired idiolects) in our posts, like Hambspeak, Cheddarspeak, Pinkyspeak, Ollyspeak, or Nachospeak, depends on the cat-related digital space we are in and on its plexity and density. The more closely we feel connected to the other cat account holders and followers in the network, the more likely we are to use the same type of language.

Coming back to the big data tools, Gephi visualises a social network as graphs and offers the Twitter Streaming Importer as one of its plug-ins. With this plug-in, we can create a social network graph based on certain words, hashtags, and/or users. Gephi also gives us context information, such as the number of nodes and edges, and offers statistical tools, like modularity, which identifies the number of sub-communities.

The visualisation with Gephi shows the varying density of the individual cat-related digital spaces. When we look at two regular events on Twitter, we can see the differences. The two events chosen are #GladdersYoga, which happens each Wednesday on Twitter for everyone who follows #GladdersYoga, and #ECCHappyHour, a regularly occurring event run by the @EdibleCatsClub for club members and non-members on Twitter.

For #GladdersYoga, the Twitter Streaming Tool on Gephi has imported 109 nodes and 180 edges, and the Gephi statistics indicate 10 sub-communities. For #ECCHappyHour, there are 146 nodes and 4,395 edges with five sub-communities. For each of the events, the Twitter Streaming Tool was running for about three hours. These figures already tell us how dense the two different communities are.

Gephi provides us with a list of algorithms with which we can create a layout and with tools to visualise the graph the way we like best. Here, the layout of the graphs has been done with the algorithm Atlas Force 2. The nodes are the dots, and the edges are indicated by the lines. Each dot represents a user and each line an interaction between the users. The bigger the size of the nodes, the more relevant they are in their respective networks.

Judging from the graphs, #GladdersYoga (Figure 10.9) is not a dense network, with the user interaction spread across several digital spaces and a low level of connection among the users, while #ECCHappyHour (Figure 10.10) involves a very dense community with a lot of interaction between users. In the layout, I had to decrease the size of the edges for #ECCHappyHour, otherwise the only visible item would have been a flurry of edges.

In general, the graphs help us to identify networks on Twitter as we can see which nodes are connected to which and how strongly. When we observe the Twitter Streaming Tool in real time, we see how the network is computed, and we can expand those nodes and edges where a lot is happening. We can see the individual tweets on a different subscreen (called 'data laboratory view') in Gephi.

Figure 10.9 Visualisation of #GladdersYoga

#Caturday

Big data also offers us information on user locations. In addition to the user ID, tweets, retweets, and timestamp, the tool TAGS also retrieves the location from the users' Twitter profiles. As I wanted to examine in which locations worldwide the hashtag #Caturday is used, I ran the tool and ended up with approximately 100,000 tweets featuring that hashtag. From the timestamps in the data, Microsoft Excel created the cat-eared chart showing the frequency of tweets on the various days (Figure 10.8).

For my analysis concerning the locations, I decided to look at the tweets from Saturday 8 May 2021 and ended up with roughly 19,000 tweets. Before an analysis is possible, unnecessary information needs

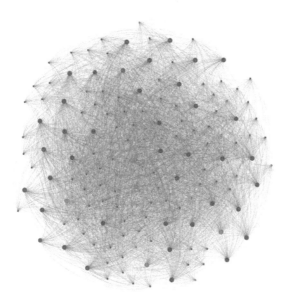

Figure 10.10 Visualisation of #ECCHappyHour

to be removed from the data. In line with research ethics and with GDPR ('only save the data needed'), all usernames and the tweets themselves were deleted from the data straightaway.

The next step is data cleaning. The TAGS tool collects the text as it is, which means that the information is too diverse for Microsoft to work with. The spelling of locations and the languages differ (e.g. English 'Munich' and German 'München'), some locations are given in non-Latin alphabets (मुंबई for Mumbai), and other locations are along the lines of 'if it fits I sits' or 'in my box' or are made-up places. After unifying the spelling, rewriting names in the Latin alphabet, and deleting fake places, around 9,000 tweets were left to be put onto a map. The Microsoft Excel pivot table came up with a list of 100 countries, which are given here from A to Z:

🐾 Algeria, Argentina, Australia, Austria

🐾 Bahamas, Bangladesh, Belarus, Belgium, Belize, Bolivia, Bosnia Herzegovina, Brazil, Bulgaria

🐾 Canada, Canary Islands, Chile, China, Colombia, Costa Rica, Cyprus, Czech Republic

🐾 Denmark, Dominican Republic

🐾 Ecuador, Egypt, El Salvador, Ethiopia

🐾 Finland, France

🐾 Georgia, Germany, Ghana, Greece, Guadeloupe, Guatemala

🐾 Honduras, Hungary

🐾 India, Indonesia, Iran, Iraq, Ireland, Israel, Italy

🐾 Japan

🐾 Kazakhstan, Kenya, Korea, Kuwait

🐾 Latvia, Lebanon, Lesser Antilles, Libya, Liechtenstein, Lithuania, Luxembourg

🐾 Macedonia, Madagascar, Malaysia, Malta, Mexico, Morocco

🐾 Nepal, Netherlands, New Zealand, Nigeria, Norway

🐾 Pakistan, Panama, Paraguay, Peru, Philippines, Poland, Portugal, Puerto Rico

🐾 Romania, Russia

🐾 Saudi Arabia, Senegal, Serbia, Singapore, Slovenia, South Africa, Spain, Sri Lanka, Sweden, Switzerland

🐾 Taiwan, Tanzania, Thailand, Turkey

🐾 Uganda, United Kingdom, Ukraine, United Arab Emirates, Uruguay, United States

🐾 Vanuatu, Vatican, Venezuela

In addition to the countries, cities and regions where the hashtag was used can be displayed on a map. The hashtag #Caturday was tweeted from 1,238 locations on 8 May 2021. Google's My Maps application uses a spreadsheet file to automatically put the locations on the map (Figure 10.11). What all the information immediately shows us is that #Caturday is a hashtag used worldwide, not limited to English-language regions.

The third and final step is to visualise #Caturday in Gephi (Figure 10.12) and take a look at the languages identified by the tool. On the weekend of 5 June 2021, I ran the Twitter Streaming Tool using the hashtag #Caturday as the keyword on Gephi and stopped the tool when it had imported almost 10,000 edges and 20,000 nodes.

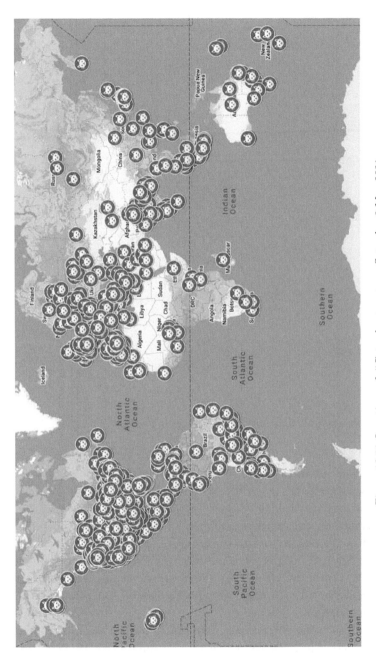

Figure 10.11 Locations of #Caturday tweets on Saturday 8 May 2021

Figure 10.12 #Caturday tweet network of Saturday 5 June 2021

The 20,000 interactions are similar in number to the 19,000 tweets collected with TAGS on a different Saturday.

Gephi displays the nodes based on certain attributes. The attributes important for our purpose are 'modularity' for partition, which computes the number of sub-communities, and 'degree' for ranking, which shows the degree of connection of nodes with edges in the network. The higher the degree, the closer the connection. With the 9,568 nodes and 19,757 edges, Gephi's modularity tool computed 167 sub-communities.

Language is one of the types of information the Twitter Streaming Tool gathers. Any API, like the Twitter Streaming Tool, that connects to Twitter's Streaming API can set the language attribute, which

Table 10.8 *Languages identified in #Caturday tweets on 5 June 2021*

ISO Code	Language
ar	Arabic
ca	Catalan
cs	Czech
cy	Welsh
da	Danish
de	German
en	English
es	Spanish
et	Estonian
fi	Finnish
fr	French
ht	Haitian
in	Indonesian
it	Italian
ja	Japanese
nl	Dutch
no	Norwegian
pl	Polish
pt	Portuguese
ro	Romanian
sv	Swedish
tl	Tagalog
tr	Turkish
uk	Ukrainian

relies on machine-readable language identifiers. Additionally, users have set an interface language and can specify additional languages for Twitter to select suitable content.

The language column in Gephi's data laboratory view lists all the languages identified in the collected tweets as ISO 639 language codes. In total, there are 26 labels, 24 of which refer to languages (Table 10.8). Of the other two, the category 'und' for 'undetermined' refers to tweets for which the language could not be identified, and the category 'null' means that there is no entry in the language column. A quick look at some of the nodes labelled 'undetermined' has shown that the tweets involved do not contain text.

Although Gephi provides figures for each identified language, they may not be that meaningful because for 63.53% of nodes, there is no entry, and 3.9% are undefined. English has been identified in 30.87% of cases and is the language used most. All other languages range between 0.3% and 0.01%. That aside, the number of identified languages shows that #Caturday is a worldwide phenomenon.

Statistics and big data alike offer another way of looking at cat-related data and car-related digital spaces. The crosstabs provide a broad description of the non-meowlogism/meowlogism variation in the cat-related digital spaces but do not interpret it. To draw conclusions for all cat-related digital spaces on social media platforms, a different research design and inferential statistical methods would have to be used.

Sources Used in This Chapter

🐾 Austin and Irvine (2020) for vernacular cat photos
🐾 Brezina (2018) for statistical methods in corpus linguistics
🐾 gephi.org (2017) for Gephi
🐾 Hawksey (2021) for TAGS
🐾 Holmes and Wilson (2017) for social network and speech accommodation
🐾 ISO (2021) for language codes
🐾 Totet (2020) for Twitter Streaming Importer
🐾 Twitter Inc. (2021b) for Twitter streaming parameters
🐾 Chiara Zuanni, personal communication, for social network analysis

Examples and Quotes Used in This Chapter

🐾 Kufs (2011)

Suggestions for PURRther Reading

🐾 Brezina (2018)

11

Cattitude and Purrception

I am glad you are researching us and our language
(Respondent 40 on *What would you like to add*)

So far in the book, we have looked at how we talk about our cats online from various sides in linguistics. In this chapter, we are now switching from the perspective of the linguist to that of the cat account holders and their followers in the cat-related digital spaces. In the surveys of 2019 and 2021, the respondents shared their views on purrieties and on cat-related digital spaces.

We go once more into the setup of the surveys and set them in the context of sociolinguistic attitude and perception studies. The two surveys were designed to find out the reasons why people participate in the cat-related digital spaces and what they think about the linguistic variations they encounter there. The interest here lies in how the answers of the respondents are analysed, categorised, and interpreted.

Then we delve into the findings of the two surveys in the sociolinguistic context of identity, attitude, and perception. The cat identity plays an important role in the cat-related digital spaces. Switching from the human identity to the cat identity online brings with it a switch in language variety, with the purrieties working as a recognisable indicator of identity. We are also looking at what the respondents said about their views on having and following accounts, and on how people talk about their cats online. While the cat-related digital spaces are generally seen as positive, people have different feelings about purrieties, ranging from positive to negative.

The term 'incidental material', which is the subheading of the final section (Section 11.6), has been borrowed from the *Survey of English Dialects* and refers to information that has not been directly asked for in the survey. Both surveys invited the respondents to share any additional comments if they wished to do so. The intention of such a question is to give people the opportunity to share their thoughts after they have filled in the survey.

Concepts Discussed in the Chapter

🐾 user-based data
🐾 survey
🐾 identity
🐾 attitude
🐾 perception

Terms from the Clawssary

🐾 covert prestige 🐾 matched-guise technique 🐾 Net Promoter Score
🐾 overt prestige 🐾 prestige 🐾 vernacular

11.1 Cats and Data from the Surveys

I would like to find out more about why your cat *talks the way he/she does*. I also want to test my existing theories and to see if I need to change my findings or not.
(Introduction to January 2021 Survey)

To research the users' perspective, two surveys, mentioned already in Chapter 8, were done online. In July 2019, when this book was in its initial stages, I wanted to find out more about the people in the cat-related digital spaces and their reasons for using purrieties for their cats. In January 2021, when this book was being written, I went back to some users for more user-based data. The July 2019 survey addressed the reasons for having and/or following cat accounts, attitudes towards purrieties, attitudes towards specific words and phrases, and some demographic information. The January 2021 survey searched for clarifications and more insight information from cat account holders who are very active in their cat-related digital spaces.

While Chapter 8 set the surveys in the wider research context, this section goes into more detail about sociolinguistic language and perception studies. In sociolinguistics, there are different ways to find out about attitudes to language, namely direct observation, direct questioning, and indirect measures. In a direct observation, we study language resources in the public sphere, like official documents, books, and newspapers and magazines, to search for any reference to language attitudes. While purrieties are used in the public sphere, I have not come across anything explicitly related to attitudes towards purrieties. Meowlogisms are used in books, newspapers, and magazines, with the intention of indicating that the content is cat-related.

In the direct questioning approach, researchers ask the participants directly about their views on language variations. The direct questioning approach can be done in writing or in person. Because I wanted to reach as many users as possible and in as many geographic places as possible, I decided on the written form for both surveys. An example of in-person interviews in the cat-related digital spaces is the marketing-based research on 'cat influencers' that we came across in Chapter 5.

To counteract the possibility that people do not share their true feelings in a survey, the matched-guise technique can be used. This is an indirect measures approach. An example of the matched-guise technique is a perception survey done in Greater Manchester, in which participants listened to audio stimuli of specific linguistic features and rated what they heard on scales. The study looked at the potential meanings of intervocalic [t] and t-glottaling in Greater Manchester. Based on their perception of t in 'kitty', the survey participants assigned social meaning to [t] or [ʔ], from which we find possible indexical fields for [t] and [ʔ] (Table 11.1).

For the purrieties in cat-related digital spaces, such a matched-guise approach is difficult to take. A perception survey with audio stimuli is impossible because the language varieties in cat-related digital spaces are written. While we could use written stimuli and ask participants to rate the written examples instead, the scales will prove more problematic. The questions to resolve here are, first, how to define a very clear research question that measures the 'catness' of the purrieties and, second, which scale to use – one ranging from 'very cat-like' to 'other animal-like', 'very cat-like' to 'human', or something else entirely?

All in all, 195 cat lovers have given me insights in a written direct questioning survey into why or why not they follow cat accounts and why or why not they use purrieties. Before we go into the survey responses in detail, there are some general remarks concerning the validity of the results: first, the sampling and the

Table 11.1 *Indexical fields for [t] and [ʔ] in kitty
in Greater Manchester*

intervocalic [t] in kitty	t-glottaling [ʔ] in kitty
more hard-working	less hard-working
more intelligent	less intelligent
more snob-like	less snob-like
more reliable	less reliable
more correct	less correct
more educated	less educated
more articulate	less articulate
more teacher-like	less teacher-like
less common	more common
less student-like	more student-like
less blunt	more blunt
less sincere	more sincere
less casual	more casual
richer	less rich
older	younger
less down to earth	more down to earth
less urban	more urban
less Northern	more Northern
less laid-back	more laid-back
Chorlton	less Chorlton
less outgoing	more outgoing
less confident	more confident
less working class	more working class
less Moss Side	more Moss Side
less Salford	more Salford
less Manchester	more Manchester

surveys were designed to elicit user-based data. That indicates an
a priori bias towards members of cat-related digital spaces and an
initial assumption of a positive attitude towards cat-related digital
spaces and their language varieties. With that in mind, the results
are valid – just not for the whole of the population.

Second, the analysis of the surveys is based on a qualitative content
analysis, which attempts to systematically and objectively analyse
the data with coding but essentially is subjective and interpretative.
Coding means to assign specific labels to words, sentences, and/or
paragraphs to interpret the text and to find connections between the
answers. To ensure consistency, the coding of the answers was done
in several cycles and with ample time in between. The codebook

(Table A.3) in Appendix A.4 lists the categories, the codes, the definitions of the codes, and examples of phrases. With the list of codes, it is just a matter of categorising the answers accordingly, as is done in the quote below, and then looking at the big picture.

I speaks lolcat too. I doin it rong?
(Respondent 47)
coded as 'LOLspeak/Catspeak'

11.2 Cats and Identity

cat and non-cats
(online specific user categories of Respondent 173)

In Chapter 7, we looked at how language choices reflect our identity creation and at style-shifting and code-switching. In the July 2019 survey, the participants talked about their online identities, and for them the cat-related digital spaces are an ideal place for online identity creation. When we open accounts for our cats (often in addition to our own personal accounts), we take on the identity of our cats in these accounts and post from the cats' point of view.

The possibility of having an online identity that is different to one's offline identity is a reason to have a cat account. As some respondents said in the survey, they have a cat account because they want to be a different person, to have fun, and to be silly. A cat account makes it possible for the respondents to express their views anonymously without giving away their real identity.

This different identity is that of a cat, and the change of identities from human to cat (from personal account to cat account) is usually accompanied with a shift in style and sometimes with a code switch. Style-shifting happens when the cat account holders switch from English to purrieties, and code-switching means that the cat account holders use English and purrieties instead of – or in addition to – the language(s) of their human accounts.

The use of purrieties identifies the posts as cat posts. Cats are given their own voice and write in their various purrieties to indicate their feline and not their owners' points of view. The switch to the purrieties indicates either 'It's the cat speaking now' or 'I am addressing the cat now'. For some respondents, purrieties are the language variety expected by the followers of their cat accounts. As the survey indicates, cat account holders are aware of the change in their use of language and what this change effects. The switch in style immediately signals 'Cat!' to others and helps to differentiate a cat-related post from a personal one.

For the cat account holders, the choice to use purrieties to show the cat identity is a conscious one. What is more, the cat account holders think about how their cats would sound if they could speak and make the language reflect the cats' personalities. The language develops over time into the purriety typical for the respective cat and becomes part of that cat account's identity. Using purrieties gives cats their unique online personalities, and respondents create different voices for their cats.

There are as many styles as there are cat staff to type them.
(Respondent 76)

You can develop a cats character virtually and also add some of your own characteristics to it (or project it on the cat)
(Respondent 195)

The January 2021 survey asked the cat account holders specifically for a description of their respective cat's language variety. The answers show the thoughts that go into creating the purrieties that best reflect the cats' different personalities and identities. In addition to mixing and mashing meowlogisms and catspeak, cat account holders add specific characteristics for their cats, like a lisp, the letter 'l' becoming a 'w', as in 'wike' for 'like', or inventing new words. Respondent A9 described the process of finding the right purriety for their cat:

As a young kitten, he was slowly learning about the world around him, and I needed to convey his infancy and innocence in an effective manner. Using regular English didn't fit, but I also had trouble writing in "improper" English. His language started off as simple and his posts were short. But as he grew, his vocabulary grew, and his own unique style developed.
(Respondent A9)

The followers with their own cat accounts accept the cat identity and address the cats rather than their human companions in their responses and comments. Human users without a cat account, too, generally shift to purrieties when they speak to the cat. In other (linguistic) words, this is the accommodation theory at work, where people adapt their language styles to the participants in the conversation.

Many of my friends are cats so I do use the language
(Respondent 109)

When speaking as my cat to other cats, I have to use the language of his
people.
(Respondent 117)

Yet our online identities are fluid, and there are situations and topics for which we switch back to our human identity. While we use purrieties in our cat identity for cat-related issues and feline points of view, we revert to our human identity if and when we see it as necessary. When the situation or the seriousness of the topic demands the human touch and a cat answer would not fit, we are our human selves. Serious topics, like cat-related issues of sheltering, rescuing, fostering, and adoption, as well as human-related concerns, like ill health, make the cat account holders use 'real language' (Respondent 89).

One respondent plays on the positive connotations of purrieties. In order to prevent negative situations from escalating, the respondent addresses humans with cat-inspired language:

To a cat it can be for encouragement, bonding, appreciation. To non-cats I've sometimes used it as a way of diffusing anger or try to calm someone, help them untangle from a situation, etc. It can be a gentle way to ease someone out of negative emotion. (Yes it does sometimes backfire but most times it works)
(Respondent 173)

In general, purrieties are a sign of group membership, and cat account holders want to show that they are part of the cat-related digital spaces. Depending on which digital space they belong to, cat account holders use the respective language variety. Respondents use purrieties because they want to belong to the community and show that they have the necessary code to do so. The purrieties signal that there is a bond between cat account holders and followers with in their respective cat-related digital spaces. Purrieties are part of the social media culture of cats.

I think it also defines groups of friends. Almost like their secret language. It can either be inclusive or make you stand out for being different. Example: With some people or groups I will use a meowlogism because they do and it is that groups preferred way of speaking. Not mine. A few I think are cute like the word pawsecco for Proseco. I also think the longer that you interact with the kitties of S[ocial] M[edia] the more prone that you are to adapt your ways of speech.
(Respondent A9)

Many cat account holders and their followers are multilingual in the global cat-related digital spaces. All over the world, cats have accounts in their names, and their owners generally use English as well as purrieties as the lingua franca. Users – and their cats – with native languages other than English switch between English, purrieties, and other languages in their interaction. The multilingual nature of cat-related spaces is also reflected in the survey. From the 195 survey participants, 42 are non-native speakers of English. Just like the native speakers, the non-native speakers use purrieties in their accounts to indicate the cat identity.

Not only English but also other languages have purrieties to show that it is the cats talking. In the survey, examples of purrieties in Spanish, Portuguese, and German were shared: in Mexico a 'candigato' (feline candidate) was running for mayoral office; in Brazil, an 'advogato' (feline lawyer) was officially hired by a law firm; and in Germany, a product was labelled as 'miausgezeichnet' (excellent). What the multilingual accounts have in common is their use of meowlogisms in English. Regardless of their native language, cat account holders use English meowlogisms to show their cat identity.

There are many examples of multilingual cat accounts. In addition to Horst the Hero (English, meowlogisms, and German) and Henry (English, meowlogisms, and Russian), who featured in Chapter 7, there are Flowerchild, on whose Instagram account posts and answers are in English, meowlogisms, and Finnish, there is Dolce, whose languages include English, meowlogisms, and Italian, as well as Phoebe and Jilly, with English, meowlogisms, and Dutch.

And there is Respondent 77, whose native language is 'Cat':

Is English your native language? (Question in July 2019 Survey)
No.
What is your native language?
Cat.
(Respondent 77)

11.3 Cats and Cattitude

The direct question 'What do you think about the way cats communicate with each other online?' in the 2019 survey attracted comments along the lines of 'Do they?' (Respondent 17), 'Erm, they can't?' (Respondent 93), '?' (Respondent 123), 'They don't, it's their owners'

· (Respondent 138), 'They don't, their owners do' (Respondent 183), and 'I'm not sure since it's actually the people communicating with each other, not the actual cats' (Respondent 189). These respondents are perfectly right in saying that cats cannot and do not communicate online because cats cannot and do not communicate with each other online. Yet, when we go along with the premise of the cat-related digital spaces that it is the cats themselves posting, commenting, and replying, the question makes sense. It made sense for the majority of respondents, who shared their attitudes towards the purrieties they had come across.

Before looking at what the respondents said, we consider how sociolinguistics connects languages and attitudes. Language attitudes reflect the attitudes towards the users and uses of a language and are formed by people's associations with its speakers, its contexts, and its functions. When we like the people and contexts associated with a language variety, we usually feel positively towards that variety. There is nothing language-inherent that makes one variety more beautiful than another. Language in itself is neither beautiful nor ugly; it is what we associate with it that shapes our view of it. Whether we think a language (variety) is beautiful or not depends on social and political factors as well as on the attitudes we have formed towards that language or language variety. Our attitudes may be shaped by the prestige of a language or language variety.

The prestige of a language variety may be overt or covert. Overt prestige refers to the associations we usually have with the standard language variety because we connect it with the more influential people in society. Covert prestige, however, is less noticeable at first glance (hence covert) and relates to the positive connotations we have with features of the vernacular language variety.

The question here is how the concepts of language and attitude apply to the online language varieties of the cat-related digital spaces. While the respondents shared their associations with the cat-related digital spaces and purrieties, they never referred to anything related to prestige, which indicates that prestige does not play a role in the digital communities. However, prestige may be attached to purrieties in the offline world. In cat-related stories, features of purrieties regularly occur in the news media to make the cat connection stronger. Thus, we are dealing with covert rather than overt prestige because purrieties are the vernacular of cat-related digital spaces.

Weez luvz da catspeek. Itz ower owun langwijj.
[We love catspeak. It is our own language.]
(Respondent A2)

The factors influencing the language attitudes in the cat-related digital spaces are related to the generally very positive atmosphere in those spaces. As the survey responses show, the positive connotations people have range from the differences between cat-related and other digital spaces, the effect of cats on humans, friendships and community spirit, and, of course, fun and entertainment. All of these factors make people have or follow cat accounts.

The positivity of cat-related digital spaces stands in contrast to the perceived negativity of human social media spaces. For the survey respondents, the atmosphere in cat-related digital spaces is positive and kind, with light-hearted and friendly commentary. Cat accounts are very inclusive and relatable. They are wittier, more supportive, and more thoughtful than human accounts. On the whole, they are non-political and offer content free of hate and unpleasantness. Cat-related digital spaces provide a 'friendly corner of the Internet' (Respondent 8) for the users to escape to. Based on their love of cats, people look past their differences and see that they have a lot in common. For the respondents, turning to cat-related digital spaces is often a relief from the unpleasant aspects of social media.

It provides total escapism from the stresses of daily life and allows me to enter a world where anything is possible. #CatsOfTwitter are kind and caring towards each other, humans and other animals – it's good for the soul. (Respondent 137)

It counters the glaring negativity that dominates social media (Respondent 68)

A relief from political insanity. Even the 'political' cat pages are better than what the humans are up to (Respondent 108)

Another positive factor is the cat's role as a companion. The answer 'I love cats', which has been used by many respondents, is typical for people in cat-related digital spaces. The respondents talk about their mutual love of cats (and animals in general), their beauty and cuteness, and the beneficial effects cats have on humans. Like Rocket and Nebula, cats are regarded as extended family and good friends

Figure 11.1 Rocket and Nebula – extended family and good friends

(Figure 11.1), and cat owners like to exchange stories and advice with others. Online and offline, cats make people happy, take away stress, and provide emotional support.

In a – at times – increasingly toxic world, cat accounts – like actual cats – calm me and rebalance me.
(Respondent 173)

I have cats as pets, so I enjoy comparing their actions to others. I love cats in general because they mirror my own personality.
(Respondent 6)

I love that these cats bring out the best in people and engender a sense of community. They are also great p.r for cats as many people don't realise how sociable they are. They often highlight good causes.
(Respondent 56)

It's fascinating to see how wrapped up with Cats our lives are and how the cats have such an impact on the world around them and beyond. They get me through crazy difficult days until I can come home to my fur kids
(Respondent 130)

Some respondents have mentioned specific cat accounts they follow. Mostly these specific cat accounts are accounts of working-for-cause cats.

Felix the Huddersfield Station cat, Cole and Marmalade, BenBen CatCat, Ernesto Sanctuary, Simons Cat, Robert the Allotment Cat, Larry the No. 10 cat and other govt. cats
(Respondent 171)

My favourite 'cat' accounts are ones where the cat has interaction with lots of people i.e Rolf, Cilla and Robert the allotment cat. Robert's account is my favourite as I love hearing about the seven cats that live there. This account also saved the allotment which is amazing.
(Respondent 86)

I must mention the Cat Reviewer which always makes me smile.
(Respondent 56)

The relationship factor, too, contributes to the positive attitude towards the cat-related digital spaces. In their answers, the respondents have compared the digital spaces with a friendly neighbourhood. The community spirit is very strong and caring. In feeling easily connected to other cat lovers around the world, people find common ground by sharing the stories and helping each other. Cat-related digital spaces become support networks for people in need of emotional as well as financial help. Out of the online activities around the cats, friendships have developed that are carried over into the real world.

When I first went on Twitter, I couldn't believe how many "cat accounts" were there. I found it charming and often humorous. I have been on Twitter since Nov 2016 and have made a core group of really good friends.
(Respondent A1)

And that is another reason I wanted to participate in catsoftwitter. It was the genuine kindness, generosity and caring that I saw time and time again
(Respondent A6)

... for some great social interaction between the owners. Many of these cats and their owners have become my friends.
(Respondent 144)

I didn't start out to give my cats an account on S[ocial] M[edia]. They just ended up being the nicest people so I gravitated there
(Respondent A9)

The fun factor creates a positive feeling in the cat-related digital spaces, and people go there for the entertainment and the humour the cat accounts provide. The respondents enjoy the pictures and videos of cats and the fun stories the cat account holders share. In the survey, some words came up repeatedly in the answers: 'cute', 'fun', 'witty', 'amusing', and 'adorable' were among the recurrent adjectives the respondents used.

It's always entertaining to read what the "cat" is saying.
(Respondent 136)

it's fun and I can be silly
(Respondent A5)

After holding back and simply reading the tweets I decided that it would be fun to put my cat out there and see if I could build up a following. I was lucky enough to have a really popular cat that was kind enough to introduce me and retweet me or I'm sure I could never have gotten to 500 followers.
(Respondent A6)

11.4 Cats and Purrception

Why are you likely/not likely to use cat-inspired language in your posts?
(Question in July 2019 Survey)
[It] would be pretentious since I do not have [a] cat to review my draft
(Respondent 56)

Perception studies in sociolinguistics usually survey spoken language in an indirect manner. The Purrieties study is different in two respects. First, purrieties are written varieties, and second, they have been surveyed in a direct manner with direct questions. Here we define perception as liking or not liking a language variety as well as being likely or not likely to use it, and we see the likelihood or non-likelihood of using purrieties as an indicator of how people perceive them.

To get the respondents into the right mind-frame for the question 'Why are you (not) likely to use cat-inspired language in your posts?', the survey included the so-called Net Promoter Score question 'How likely are you to use cat-inspired word play in your social media posts?'. Net promoter scores are used in marketing to rate customer experience, and we have to be careful in interpreting the quantitative results in terms of perception of a language variety.

In the July 2019 survey, the score for this question was -55, which only indicates that there is no active promotion for the use of purrieties. That score does not reflect the actual perception, which is not surprising given that purrieties are language varieties and not a business. There is also a difference between actively using and liking/not liking purrieties. The only aim of this question was to make the respondents reflect on their language use and, thus, give more insightful answers to the subsequent questions. As such, the Net Promoter Score question proved successful.

I love them.
(Respondent 69)

At first I found it annoying, but have now got used to it
(Respondent 55)

So so, can take or leave tbh.
(Respondent 151)

Dreadful
(Respondent 162)

As the four responses above show, people perceived the purrieties differently, and their associations with purrieties were positive, neutral, negative, or had changed over time. The questions on what respondents think about purrieties triggered mild and strong reactions, and a neutral stance occurred only rarely.

Positive Purrception
It's just pawsome and ameowzing ! Sounds just purrfect !
(Respondent 116)

The positive perceptions related to purrieties include words like 'sweet', 'nice', 'funny', 'fitting', 'appropriate', 'cute', '(pretty) creative', 'fun', '(very) cool', 'humorous', 'amusing', 'nice play on words', 'bring joy', 'imaginative', 'inventive', 'hilarious', 'amusing', 'fascinating', 'completely adorable', 'ingenious', and 'charming'. Some respondents have pointed out that, despite their positive associations with purrieties, they would not use them in their own posts.

The use of purrieties is also seen as connected to language proficiency as well as to language variation. For non-native speakers of English, they are like another language they want to learn. For native speakers of English, purrieties are a new language variety used by people who are very familiar with the rules to be followed or broken. On the one hand, purrieties have their own rules to be followed and, on the other hand, the standard language has rules to be violated. With their rules, purrieties add a new dimension to language.

As a speaker of English as a second language, I like striving to get some of them. It's engaging.
(Respondent 16)

It's a further language to learn
(Respondent 42)

Different groups of humans speak with their own grammar and spelling so why not Cats
(Respondent 109)

I think it is interesting that us cats all talk in different ways, but we all understand each other.
(Respondent 111)

It's an interesting new form of language. To be able to break the rules you must have a very firm grasp of them to begin with so I do not see this as a dumbing down of language.
(Respondent 24)

As an editor I think it's great fun and adds a whole new dimension to language
(Respondent 109)

Nevertheless, people have to use the purrieties correctly, cleverly, and well in their posts so as not to put off or detract other users of the cat-related digital spaces. Cat account holders and followers recognise and react with annoyance to an incorrect or unimaginative use of purrieties.

I become unreasonably enraged when people use lolspeak, l33t or haxxor incorrectly.
(Respondent 53)

I think it can be funny, but sometimes it's not used well or detracts from the tone of voice I would expect the cat to have.
(Respondent 81)

It can often be cute and funny when done well, but a lot of people don't use it creatively or cleverly.
(Respondent 80)

Needs to be done very well to be acceptable. If it is done well, it can be very funny.
(Respondent 186)

It's fine, but can be irritating in high doses. It's probably the all caps that irritate me about it, as I automatically translate all caps as shouting
(Respondent 105)

Things like MOL, PMSL (purring) I can live with but I find the badly spelled wording as in the sentence in capitals above a bit irritating. It makes me massively disinclined to follow an account that speaks like that. If I do follow I sometimes put them on mute straight away. I think it's because it's a bit childish (ikr) and lacks the nuance and cat-specificities of other words e.g. panfur
(Respondent 173)

In the survey, the respondents were also asked to list their favourite cat-inspired words or phrases. Some words occurred repeatedly, like 'Caturday', 'pawsome', 'purrfect', and 'furrends'. The numbers in brackets refer to how often the word was mentioned. The different spellings of 'furrends' and 'purrfect' have been subsumed under the most common spelling (unlike in Chapter 10, where the meowphemes FUR and PURR represent the variants). The respondents' favourite cat-inspired words are listed from A to Z:

adoptaversary
ambassacat
Ameowadeus
a-paw-lled
birdie day (4 times)
brofur
bum bum
cat box Sunday
catitude (twice)
catting
Caturday (14 times)
Clawdia
concatulations
Curiosity killed the cat
everypawdy
fank mew
furbulous
furever home
furfamily
furkid
furpals
furrends (7 times)
furrever
furry hugs and nose bumps
Gladders yoga

healing purrs
high tails
hissed off
hoomans (twice)
hoomum
house panfur
hugs and hisses
If I fits
I sits
kitten
kitty loaf Monday
LOL spak
Margaret Catcher the Iron Kitty
Meeeeooooowww
meow (twice)
meowga
meowmy
mew
mewsical
Nope
OMC (Oh my Cat!)
over the rainbow bridge
panfur (9 times)
paw work
paw circle
paw hugs (twice)
pawpawrazzi
paws for tea
pawsecco
pawsome (28 times)
pawtrol (3 times)
pawty (3 times)
paw-waves
purrecious
purrents
purrfect (24 times)
purrple
purrs and licks
Purrsday
purrsenal
purrsome
sending purrs and pawhugs
sqkwirruls
suppurvise
supurrvisor (twice)
thank mew
Tongue out Tuesday (twice)

tootsie tuesday
tuna Tuesday
whiskers Wednesday
wonderpurr

Changing Purrception

Some respondents had changed their perception over time. Usually, their view had turned from negative to positive, but there were also others who no longer liked purrieties.

At first I found it annoying, but have now got used to it
(Respondent 55)

My feelings have evolved over time. At first it confused me, then it annoyed me a bit (it's slow to read until you get used to it), but now I enjoy it.
(Respondent 117)

Took me a while to get used to but it's OK.
(Respondent 84)

I was initially very annoyed by it. I still tend to skip over and/or give less credence to what they say.
(Respondent 165)

Funny at first but then it gets a bit childish and repetitive
(Respondent 188)

Sometimes over kill and continually used becomes tedi[o]us.
(Respondent 134)

Negative Purrception

To describe their negative perceptions of purrieties, the respondents have used expressions like 'not so funny', 'not too fond', 'not so fussed about that', 'it's stupid', 'it's a bit silly', 'too hard to think about', 'tedious', 'childish', 'try to avoid', 'hard to read', 'annoying', 'slightly annoying', 'somewhat annoying', 'very annoying', 'repetitive', 'irritating', 'somewhat irritating', 'not a fan', 'hate them', 'detest it', 'not keen', 'confusing', 'horrible', 'stupid', 'makes my brain hurt', 'wrong', 'overdone', and 'unreadable'.

Some respondents dislike the purrieties because the posts are hard to read and difficult to understand. Other respondents object to the baby voice in the account and stop following the accounts.

It is a bit complicated to understand ... (maybe because my native language
is not English)
(Respondent 73)

It makes it hard to tell what people are saying a lot of the time
(Respondent 78)

I can't bear them, I have unfollowed several accounts that use this language
(Respondent 56)

I do not like lol speak. It comes across as baby talk and to me does not
mesh with the personality of cats.
(Respondent 102)

I find it too similar to baby speak which some parents do and I find it cringe
worthy.
(Respondent 90)

Some respondents took issue with the non-standard grammar and
spelling of purrieties – or, as one respondent put it, 'that sort of
language' (Respondent 19) – or 'cats whose spelling and grammar
could be improved upon' (Respondent 154). Those respondents said
they preferred the standard language variety, which they referred to as
'traditional', 'correct', 'proper', 'good', and 'right'. In connection with
standard and non-standard language use, the reason for the apparent
association of cat accounts with non-standard grammar and spelling
was not clear to the respondents, and they asked themselves why cats
would use non-standard features in their posts, given the feline love
for tidiness. It is as if it offended their perception that it is against
the nature of cats to be untidy.

I think if cats learned to speak/type, they'd learn to do it right. Because they
are way too tidy to allow mess like grammar mistakes in their accounts.
(Respondent 5)

Cats have impeccable grammar. Efurryone knows that.
(Respondent 99)

Silly, why would cats be unable to spell?
(Respondent 158)

Why do we assume cats can't spell
(Respondent 66)

Cats are smart and speak with good grammar and eloquence!
(Respondent 82)

I know how daft this sounds but also so uncat – cats are poised, deliberate
and aloof (why I like them!) – as If they would spell like an idiot.
(Respondent 93)

Some respondents felt that purrieties did not do justice to the
intelligence of the cats. Purrieties were perceived as being demeaning
to cats, infantilising them and making them appear silly. Respondents
expressed that cats are intelligent fellow creatures and should be
treated with respect when users impersonate them online.

Silly and insulting to cats.
(Respondent 169)

If my cats would talk they would curse. Reduces cats to infants.
(Respondent 174)

Cats should be impersonated with respect, as odd as that sounds, and not
as if they are unable to express themselves correctly. They're very intelligent
animals.
(Respondent 140)

This is a difficult question to answer – while it gives the cats their own voice,
it could also infantilise them and prescribe a social role for them entirely on
our terms. It could also encourage others to think of cats as intellectually
inferior.
(Respondent 1)

I also feel it lessens the dignity of those cats, portraying them as ignorant
and juvenile.
(Respondent 24)

It's just not how I think or want to write in relation to my cats. They have
great personalities and that's enough
(Respondent 101)

11.5 Cats and Incidental Material

What would you like to add? (Question in July 2021 Survey)

More cats please
(Respondent 71)

A question, such as 'What would you like to add?' at the end of a survey is a very useful tool because we get additional input from the respondents. It gives people the opportunity to add more of their thoughts if they want to. In the July 2019 survey, some respondents used purrieties in the answers, like 'commewnity', 'pawsome survey', 'furiend', and 'Purrs and hugs', and others left additional information that they thought was of interest.

I like that cats have their own commewnity and love that some like Larry the #10 cat and Islamicat use theirs to satirise or criticise political situations, etc.
(Respondent 97)

British political cats are brilliant. As are campaigning cats such as Robert the Allotment cat. And I want to go to Warwick Uni to meet Rolf!
(Respondent 44)

Aside from the fun aspects 1 think cats of twitter performs a useful role in helping locate lost animals, offering support to humans who are bereaved or having a difficult time for whatever reason. #CatsOfTwitter also raises money for charity – Aleppo cat man is a recent example. We also help out when people are in dire need – unfortunately that is too often these days. Good luck with your research.
(Respondent 119)

I also speak to some Japanese people in Japanese. They have their own wordplay around cats, which I haven't quite figured out yet.
(Respondent 138)

Some respondents also appreciated the research being done on cat-related digital spaces. The research on purrieties was meaningful for them because it was about their online spaces and their linguistic habits, and the respondents were interested in the results and would like to see them.

I am glad you are researching us and our language!
(Respondent 110)

Am very curious about the results of what you're doing.
(Respondents 108)

What a fun study to do. And how interesting to delve into our feelings about our pets. Are they animals? are they children? Are they even ours? or, really, do we belong to them? Thanks so much for allowing me to add my opinions to this study.
(Respondent A6)

Figure 11.2 Simba, king of our lives

11.6 Cats and Their Final Words

Just pointing out that this sort of thing is not just cats (or even mammals).
There are dogs, pigs, fish, birds, goats, rabbits, guinea pigs, rats, horses,
llamas, and more in animal social media.
(Respondent 104)

Language variation, or 'this sort of thing' as Respondent 104 called
it, also occurs in other social media. Wherever people meet and form
communities, they develop their own linguistic practices. This is all
true, and we could have chosen to describe how we talk about dogs
or llamas online. Yet, it is the cats like Simba (Figure 11.2) that rule
the Internet and our real world, so cats are the obvious choice for a
book about online language variation.

So where should we place this book in terms of linguistics? *Purrieties of Language* is essentially about regional and social language variation, which means it falls into the field of sociolinguistics where we try to find out which people are using which language varieties in which region and why. In our case, we have the cat account holders and their followers, who use various purrieties on different social media platforms.

In order to fully describe a language variety, we have focussed on the question of 'what', namely what happens in terms of language and what we notice. In this book we have noticed different sounds, different meanings, different word structures, different grammatical constructions, different ways of holding a conversation, and more. We have then described the patterns we have discovered, systematically focussing on the areas of phonetics and phonology, semantics, morphology, syntax, and pragmatics, to use the linguistic terminology. As we have seen in (and with) this book, the purrieties offer us so much linguistic material to study.

The question of 'why' is perhaps less visible at first glance because we have had to turn away from the sounds and words to non-linguistic factors, like the types of stories people tell, the types of cat accounts they manage, the types of places they use for posting, the types of images they share, and the types of technology they have available. As we have seen, these factors have affected the language that cat account holders and their followers use.

Cats are the underlying unifying theme in this book. In addition to the 'purely' linguistic topics, they have guided us through the methodological issues of designing our research studies, sampling, and analysing the data, all of which are important for any scientific study regardless of the discipline. Finding the cat examples used here has turned out to be an easy task because, with the affinity spaces of academics and their cats, we have a worldwide academic network across disciplines and fields.

For many of us, cats play a meaningful role in our lives, which makes the cat examples and, in turn, the linguistics behind them very relatable and fun (I hope). *Purrieties of Language* closes with the same message that was used at the end of the January 2021 Survey:

If you have questions about this survey or my research, please contact me
Thank you – thank mew – fanks
(End of January 2021 Survey)

Sources Used in This Chapter

🐾 Holmes and Wilson (2017) for language attitudes and research methodology

🐾 Podhovnik (2018) for meowlogisms in the news media

🐾 Reichheld (2003) for Net Promoter Score

🐾 Shamayleh (2019) and Shamayleh and Arsel (2020) for cats as petfluencers and strategies for visual and textual content creation

🐾 Drummond and Schleef (2016) for perception survey

🐾 Brown and Miller (2013) for linguistic terms in the glossary

Examples and Quotes in This Chapter

🐾 Drummond and Schleef (2016, figures 3.1 and 3.2) for Table 11.1

Suggestions for PURRther Reading

🐾 Holmes and Wilson (2017)

🐾 Drummond and Schleef (2016)

Appendix

Meowscellaneous

A.1 Words for Cats

Table A.1 Words for cats

Cat Word	Localities
baby	Austria, Canada, United Kingdom
Bloody Cat!	United Kingdom
bub	United Kingdom
cat	Australia, Austria, Canada, France, Germany, Ireland, Montenegro, Netherlands, United Kingdom, United States
catloaf	United States
catpuss	United Kingdom, United States
catso	United States
chonk	United States
chonkster	United States
Fat Cat	United Kingdom
feline	Australia, United States
fleabag	United Kingdom
furry	Australia, United Kingdom, United States
in charge cat	United Kingdom
kit	Austria, United Kingdom
kitteh	Austria, Canada, Germany, United Kingdom, United States

– continued on next page

Table A.1 (continued)

Cat Words	Localities
kitten	Austria, Canada, Germany, Ireland, United Kingdom, United States
kitter	Netherlands, United States
kittie	United States
kitty	Australia, Austria, Canada, Germany, Ireland, Netherlands, United Kingdom, United States
kittycat	Austria, United Kingdom, United States
meower	Netherlands
mog	United Kingdom
moggy	United Kingdom
panfur	Turkey
panther	Austria
pootchycat	United Kingdom
puddycat	United Kingdom
puppy	United States
puss	United Kingdom, United States
pusscat	United Kingdom
pusslet	United Kingdom
pussycat	United Kingdom
station cat	United Kingdom
tat	United Kingdom
tattie	United Kingdom

A.2 Endearments for Cats

Table A.2 Endearments for cats

Endearments	Localities
angel baby	United States
asshole	United States
baby	Austria, Canada, Ireland, Switzerland, United Kingdom, United States

– continued on next page

Table A.2 (continued)

Endearments	Localities
baby boy	United Kingdom
baby girl	United States
babycat	United States
beautiful	Germany, Ireland
beauty	Germany
best	United Kingdom
big boy	Ireland
boy	United Kingdom
bub	United Kingdom
bubba	United Kingdom
bubba baloo	United States
cat	Austria, United Kingdom, United States
Cat the boss	United Kingdom
Catcakes	United Kingdom
cat-cat	United Kingdom
catkin	United Kingdom
catlet	United Kingdom
catpuss	United Kingdom
catsy	United Kingdom
chap	United Kingdom
children	Germany
chubby	Australia
criminal	United Kingdom
cute little murderer	United States
cute stuff	United States
cutie	Austria, Germany
darling	United Kingdom, United States
dear,	United Kingdom
doofus	United Kingdom
dork	United Kingdom, United States
fat one	Austria
fatty-puss	United Kingdom
feline overlord	United Kingdom
floof	(no location given), United Kingdom
floofer	Netherlands

– continued on next page

Table A.2 (continued)

Endearments	Localities
fluff	Germany
fluff nugget	United States
fluffball	United Kingdom, United States
fluffpants	United Kingdom
fluffycat	United Kingdom
fluffynoo	United Kingdom
furball	Germany, United Kingdom, United States
furry friend	United Kingdom
furry thing	United Kingdom
furrypurry	United States
fuzzy	United Kingdom
fuzzy tracksuit man	United Kingdom
goblin	United Kingdom
good bean	Ireland
gremlin	United Kingdom
handsome	Ireland, United States
honey bunches of oats	Canada
housebear	United Kingdom
hunny bunny	Canada
idiot	Austria, United Kingdom
jerk	United States
kitcat	United Kingdom
kitten	Germany, United Kingdom
kittentail	United States
kitter	United States
kittie	United States
kitty	Austria, Montenegro, Netherlands, United Kingdom, United States
kittycat	(no location given), United Kingdom, United States
kittypuss	United States
lil guy	United States
little asshole	Germany
little fuzz	United Kingdom
little love	United Kingdom

– continued on next page

Table A.2 (continued)

Endearments	Localities
little monster	Germany
little mouse	Ireland
little one	United Kingdom, United States
little shit	Austria
little tat	United Kingdom
little thing	United States
love	United Kingdom, United States
lovebird	United States
lovely	United Kingdom
m'dear	United Kingdom
Mamma's baby	United States
meat bag	United Kingdom
meowcat	United Kingdom
mittenpaw	United States
mittentail	United States
moggins	United Kingdom
moglet	United Kingdom
monster/monstie	United Kingdom
moo	United Kingdom
moron	Austria
mucker	United Kingdom
my babies	(no location given)
my Dark Angel	Germany
my huntress	Germany
my Prince of Darkness	Germany
my princess	Germany
nasty beast	United Kingdom
nerd	United Kingdom
old bean	United Kingdom
old man	United Kingdom
old stick	United Kingdom
perfect baby	United Kingdom
pretty kitty	United States
pretty lady	Ireland
princess	United Kingdom, United States

– continued on next page

Table A.2 (continued)

Endearments	Localities
puddy	United Kingdom
puddy-tat	Germany
punkin'	United States
purball	United States
puss	United Kingdom
puss puss	United Kingdom
pusscat	United Kingdom
pusskin	United Kingdom
pusslet	United States
pussum	United Kingdom
pussycat	United Kingdom
sausage	United Kingdom
scooter	United States
shit butt	United Kingdom
silly	United States
smushie	Canada
snuggle bug	United Kingdom
snuggles	United Kingdom
squeaky	United States
squishy	Australia
stanky man	United Kingdom
stinkerooni	United States
strange horse	United Kingdom
sweet	United Kingdom
sweet boy	Ireland
sweet kitty	United States
sweet thing	Germany
sweetheart	United Kingdom
sweetie	Canada, Germany, United Kingdom, United States
sweetie-pie	Canada, United Kingdom
sweetpea	Canada, United States
sweetpuss	United States
tattie-puss	United Kingdom
The Kid(s)	Germany

– continued on next page

Table A.2 (continued)

Endearments	Localities
vile creature	United Kingdom
weirdo	United States

A.3 Wordlists

A.3.1 Keywords from A to Z

#* /HASHTAGS in general
#*DAY
CAT
CLAW
DAY
FUR
HISS
KITT
MEOW/*MEW*
*NIP
PAW
PURR
PUSS
WHISKER
AAH/AAW
BABY
BELLY
BIRD
BOX
BOY
BROTHER/BROFUR
CALICO
CONGRAT*
CREAM
CUDDLE
CUTE
DAD
EVERYBODY

EVERYONE
FLOOF/FLUFF
FOLLOW
FRIENDS/FURIENDS
GINGER
GOD
GORGEOUS
GRAY/GREY
HAHA
HAIR
HAVE/HAZ
HEHE
HOME
HUG
IIUMAN
JELLY
KISS
KKK (equivalent to LOL in Brazilian Portuguese and Korean)
LADY
LEG
LION
LITTER
LOL
LOVE
MOM/MUM
MOUSE/MICE
NAUGHTY
NOM
OH
OMG/OMC
PANTHER
PERFECT/PURRFECT
POOR
PRETTY
QUEEN
RAINBOW
RAT
ROYAL
SALMON

SWEET
TABBY
THANK
TIGER
TOE/BEANS
TOILET
TORT*
TREATS
TUNA
WEEKEND
WTF/LMAO
ZOOM*

A.3.2 Hashtags

Hashtag–Days

Monday

Facebook
#EasyMonday#Monday, #MondayMood, #MondayMorning, #MondayMotivation

Instagram
#ByeMondayPawty, #CatsAgainstMondays, #EasyMonday, #MeowgaMonday, #Monday, #MondayBringItOn, #Monday-Mood, #MondayMorning, #MondayMotivation, #MoodOfThe-Day, #MousieMonday, #Nonday

Twitter
#MondayMood, #MondayMorning, #MondayMotivation

Tuesday

Facebook
#Tuesday, #TuesdayMotivation

Instagram
#TissuePaperTuesday, #TongueOutTuesday, #tot, #Tounge-OutTuesday, #TreatTuesday, #Tuesday, #TuesdayMotivation, #TunaTuesday

Twitter
#GiveBackTuesday, #GivingTuesday, #ToebeanTuesday, #TongueOutTuesday, #TuesdayTaco

Wednesday

Facebook
#WaybackWednesday, #Wednesday, #WednesdayMood, #WednesdayWisdom, #WhiskersWednesday, #Humpday

Instagram
#WaybackWednesday, #Wednesday, #WednesdayMood, #WednesdayWisdom, #WhiskersWednesday, #WhiskerWednesday, #WickedCatWednesday, #WickedDogWednesday, #WickedHumanWednesday, #WickedWednesday, #Humpday

Twitter
#WellnessWednesday,   #WeskerWednesday,   #Humpday, #HumpdayMood, #HumpdayMotivation

Thursday

Facebook
#ThrowbackThursday, #Thursday, #ThursdayThoughts, #tbt

Instagram
#CatBalletThursday, #PantherThursday, #ThrowbackThursday, #Thursday, #ThursdayScratchPawty, #ThursdayThoughts, #tbt

Twitter
#FluffyFursday, #Fursday, #RememberMeThursday, #ThankfulThursday, #ThrowbackThursday, #ThrowbackThursdays, #tbt

Friday

Facebook
#FlashbackFriday, #Friday, #FridayParty

Instagram
#FlashbackFriday, #Friday, #FridayFace, #FridayFeeling, #FridayFeelings, #FridayNightBoxPawty, #FridayNightTentPawty, #FridayParty, #Friyay, #HawaiianShirtFriday, #tgif

Twitter
#FridayFeeling, #FridayMood, #FridayMotivation, #Friyay, #HappyFriday, #JellyBellyFriday, #tgif

Saturday

Facebook
#Caturday

Instagram
#Caturday, #CaturdayCuties, #CaturdayNightDerpOff
Twitter
#Caturday, #Caturdays, #SaturdayLive

Sunday

Facebook
#FundaySunday, #SundayFunday
Instagram
#FundaySunday, #Sunday, #SundayFunday
Twitter
#CatBoxSunday, #LazySunday, #SundayFunday, #SundayMo-
tivation, #SundaySnooze, #UberSunday

Special Days

Facebook
#BlackCatAppreciationDay, #InternationalCatDay
Instagram
#BlackCatAppreciationDay, #BlackCatDay, #CatsOfTheDay,
#InternationalBlackCatDay, #InternationalCatDay, #National-
BlackCatDay, #TakeYourCatToTheVetDay, #WorldCatDay
Twitter
#BlackCatAppreciationDay, #GreyCatDay, #InternationalCat-
day, #BlackCatMojoMonth

Hashtags–Cats

Facebook
#BigCatrescue, #CastleCats, #Cat, #CatCafe, #CatCon, #Cat-
Daddy, #CatGuy, #Catification, #CatLogic, #CatLover, #Cat-
LoversClub, #CatPeople, #Cats, #CatServants, #CatsOfInsta-
gram, #Catspiration, #CatsWatchingMcfh, #CatToys, #Catur-
day, #CatValentine, #CatWoman, #FluffyCatCrew, #GingerCat,
#GrumpyCat, #ILoveMyCat, #ILoveMyCats, #LapCatpower,
#LittleCatsHelpingBigCats, #LoveCat, #LoveCats, #MyCatFrom-
Heaven, #MyCatFromHell, #OrangeCat, #RealMenLoveCats,
#SiberianCat, #ToyForCats, #YourCatPhoto
Instagram
#AdoptBlackCat, #AdoptBlackCats, #AdventureCat, #Adven-
tureCats, #AstroCat, #AstroCats, #BeKindToCats, #BigCatRes-
cue, #BlackCat, #BlackCatAwareness, #BlackCatClub,

#BlackCatDay, #BlackCatFeatures, #BlackCats, #BlackCatsAre-
GoodLuck, #BlackCatsAreLucky, #BlackCatsAreMagic, #Black-
CatsAreTheBest, #BlackCatsAssemble, #BlackCatsClub, #Black-
CatsMatter, #BlackCatsOfIg, #BlackCatsOfInstagram, #Black-
CatsRock, #BlackCatsRule, #BlackCatsTellAll, #BlackCatsUnite,
#BuzzfeedCats, #CalicoCats, #CalicoCatsOfInstagram, #Castle-
Cats, #Cat, #CatasticWorld, #CatCafe, #CatCartoon, #CatCEO,
#CatCollage, #CatCon, #CatDad, #CatDaddy, #CatDadsWorld-
Wide, #CatFan, #CatFeatures, #CatFlirting, #CatGrass, #Cat-
Guy, #CatHair, #Catification, #CatLife, #CatLoaf, #CatLogic,
#CatLove, #CatLover, #CatLovers, #CatLoversClub, #Catnap,
#Catnip, #CatnipTimes, #CatOfIg, #CatOfInstagram, #Cat-
People, #CatPhoto, #Cats, #Cats, #BlackCats, #Black, #Cat-
sAgainstMondays, #Catsagram, #CatsAndBabies, #CatsAndYoga,
#CatsAreLovee, #CatsAreTakingOver, #CatsAtWork, #CatsDaily,
#CatServants, #CatsInBoxes, #CatsLady, #CatsLove, #CatsLover,
#CatsOfDay, #CatsOfIg, #CatsOfInsta, #CatsOfOnstagram,
#CatsOfWorld, #CatsOnInstagram, #Catspiration, #CatsRule-
TheWorld, #Catstagram, #CatsWatchingMcfh, #CatsWithTheir-
TonguesOut, #Cattitude, #CatToys, #Caturday, #CaturdayCut-
ies, #CaturdayNightDerpOff, #CatValentine, #CatWoman, #Cat-
WorldDomination, #CatYoga, #CheekyCat, #CrazyCatlady,
#CrazyCatnipPawty, #CrazyForBlackCats, #CuteCat, #Cute-
Cats, #CuteCatsOnInstagram, #ExcellentCats, #FluffyCat,
#FluffyCatCrew, #FluffyCats, #FluffyCatsOfInstagram, #Fun-
nyCat, #FunnyCats, #GiftsForCatLovers, #GingerCat, #Grumpy-
Cat, #GrumpyCats, #HappyCat, #HappyCatsOnline, #HotDudes-
WithCats, #HungryCat, #IgCat, #ILoveBlackCats, #ILoveMy-
Cat, #ILoveMyCats, #InstaBlackCats, #InstaCat, #LapCatPower,
#LazyCat, #LeagueOfExtraordinaryBlackCats, #LittleCatsHelp-
ingBigCats, #LoveBlackCat, #LoveBlackCats, #LoveCat, #Love-
Cats, #LoveMyBlackCat, #LuckyBlackCat, #MyCatFromHeaven,
#MyCatFromHell, #NaughtyCat, #NorwegianForestCat, #Office-
Cat, #OmCat, #OrangeCat, #PoliceCat, #RealMenLoveCats,
#RescueCat, #ScienceWithMyCat, #SiberianCat, #SiberianCats,
#SiberianCatsOfInstagram, #SillyCats, #SimonsCat, #Simons-
CatAsks, #SimonsCatOfficial, #SimonsRealCats, #SpaceCat,
#StopBullyingCats, #TabbyCat, #TabbyCatsOfInstagram,

#TeamCatMojo, #ToyForCats, #UltimateFightingCat, #Wicked-Cat, #WickedCats, #YourCatPhoto

Twitter

#AcademicsWithCats, #AmbassaCats, #BestCat, #BigCatnap, #BlackCat, #BlackCatMojoMonth, #BlackCats, #BlackCatsa, #BlackCatsOfTwitter, #BlackCatsRock, #BlackCatsRule, #blackCatsRuleTheWorld, #Cat, #CatAmazing, #CatAmazingToy, #CatCampers, #CatBuysRock, #Catification, #CatLife, #CatLogic, #CatLover, #CatLovers, #CatMojo, #CatMom, #Catnap, #CatNerds, #Catnip, #CatPawsitive, #CatPawsitivePro, #CatPeople, #CatproofChristmasTree, #Cats, #CatSelfie, #CatsHelpSaveLives, #CatsInBoxes, #CatsOf, #CatsOfInstagram, #CatsOfLinguists, #CatsOfTwitter, #CatsRule, #CatVideos, #ChristmasWithCats, #CommunityCats, #CraftyCatMom, #CrazyCatGuy, #CrazyCatPeople, #CroydonCatKiller, #EverythingIsACatToy, #GreyCatsOfTwitter, #GuardCat, #IAmTheStationCat, #LittleCatsHelpingBigCats, #MyCatFro, #MyCatFromHeaven, #MyCatFromHell, #PoliceCat, #SimonsRealCats, #TeamCatMojo, #TotalCatMojo, #WorkingCats,

YouTube

#CatDaddy, #GrumpyCat, #KeyboardCat, #MyCatFromHell

A.4 Codebook

Table A.3 Codebook

Category	Code	Definition	Example Phrase
Attitude	Positive	Statements indicating a positive attitude towards cat-related digital spaces	They're sociable and entertaining
	Negative	Statements indicating a negative attitude towards cat-related digital spaces	A step too far for me right now

– continued on next page

Table A.3 (continued)

Category	Code	Definition	Example Phrase
	Neither	Statements indicating an attitude neither positive nor negative	No opinion
	Likely to use	Statements referring to the use of purrieties	Because it's fun, and thinking like a cat is a good (and effective) way to relieve stress
	Not likely to use	Statements referring to the non-use of purrieties	It's a bit silly for me
	Like	Statements indicating the like of purrieties (reading, but not using)	Enjoy them
	Do not like	Statements indicating that the respondent does not like purrieties (reading)	Annoying
Factors	Fun and entertain-ment	Statements indicating fun	Hilarious!
	Love of cats	Statements referring to the love of cats (and of animals in general)	I like cats
	Effects of cats	Statements referring to the effect cats have on human beings (health, stress-related, etc.)	They often brighten my day when stressed
	Specific cats	Statements mentioning specific cat accounts	Cole and Marmalade

– continued on next page

Table A.3 (continued)

Category	Code	Definition	Example Phrase
	Issues (shelter, health, other)	Statements related to animal issues (shelter, rescue, health, ownership)	I follow groups who save cats and share on social media to help them get adopted
	Friendships	Statements referring to friendships between humans	We understand each other and have a similar sense of humour
	Atmosphere	Statements referring to the atmosphere in the cat-related digital spaces	I think they are warm and a fine place to visit
	Not following	Statements indicating that the respondent does not follow cat accounts/does not know about cat-related digital spaces	I don't follow cat accounts
Language	Language (*normal, proper*)	Statements about respondent's own language use in cat-related digital spaces (referring to English)	My cat speaks normal English with a few things thrown in
	Meowlogisms	Statements referring to meowlogisms	I'm a big fan of meowlogisms

– continued on next page

Table A.3 (continued)

Category	Code	Definition	Example Phrase
	LOLs-peak/Cats-peak	Statements referring to LOLspeak/Catspeak	Things like MOL, PMSL (purring) I can live with
	Words and phrases	Statements containing purrieties	just a bit of fun – but don't purrrticularly use it myself ... sorry I had to !
Identity	Cat identity	Statements referring to the cat identity	It reinforces the idea that this is my cat's account
	Human identity	Statements referring to the human identity	The people behind the cats are nice and supportive

References

Aberconway, Christabel. 1949. *A Dictionary of Cat Lovers*. London: Michael Joseph.

Adger, David. 2019. *Language Unlimited: The Science Behind Our Most Creative Power*. Oxford: Oxford University Press.

Androutsopoulos, Jannis. 2006. Introduction: Sociolinguistics and computer-mediated communication. *Journal of Sociolinguistics*, **10**(4), 419–438.

Androutsopoulos, Jannis. 2007. Bilingualism in the mass media and on the Internet. In Monica Heller (ed), *Bilingualism: A Social Approach*. London: Palgrave Macmillan UK, pp. 207–230.

Androutsopoulos, Jannis. 2014a. Computer-mediated communication and linguistic landscapes. In Janet Holmes and Kirk Hazen (eds), *Research Methods in Sociolinguistics: A Practical Guide*. Chichester, West Sussex: John Wiley & Sons, pp. 75–90.

Androutsopoulos, Jannis. 2014b. Moments of sharing: Entextualization and linguistic repertoires in social networking. *Journal of Pragmatics*, **73**, 4–18.

Androutsopoulos, Jannis. 2015. Networked multilingualism: Some language practices on Facebook and their implications. *International Journal of Bilingualism*, **19**(2), 185–205.

AoIR. 2019. *Ethics*. https://aoir.org/ethics/.

API. 2021. *Cambridge English Dictionary*. https://dictionary.cambridge .org/dictionary/english/api.

Armstrong, Martin. 2018. *Infographic: Reigning cats and dogs*. www.statista.com/chart/13299/reigning-cats-and-dogs/.

Austin, Jessica, and Irvine, Leslie. 2020. 'A very photogenic cat': Personhood, social status, and online cat photo sharing. *Anthrozoös*, **33**(3), 441–450.

BAAL. 2021. *Recommendations on Good Practice in Applied Linguistics*. 4th ed. British Association for Applied Linguistics. www.baal.org.uk.

Bartram, Naomi. 2019. *Obsessed cat owners take 7 photos of their pets every day*. www.heart.co.uk/lifestyle/cat-owners-7-photos-pets-everyday/.

BBC. 2014. *voices*. www.bbc.co.uk/voices/.

Bednarik, Kara. 2019. *Cool cats: Most popular cat names and claims.* www .embracepetinsurance.com/waterbowl/article/popular-cat-names.

Blommaert, Jan, and Varis, Piia. 2015. Enoughness, accent and light communities: Essays on contemporary identities. *Tilburg Papers in Culture Studies,* **139**. Tilburg University.

Boberg, Charles, Nerbonne, John A., and Watt, Dominic James Landon. 2018a. *The Handbook of Dialectology.* 1st ed. Hoboken, NJ: Wiley-Blackwell.

Boberg, Charles, Nerbonne, John A., and Watt, Dominic James Landon. 2018b. Introduction. In Charles Boberg, John A. Nerbonne, and Dominic James Landon Watt (eds), *The Handbook of Dialectology.* Blackwell Handbooks in Linguistics. Hoboken, NJ: Blackwell Publishing, pp. 1–15.

Bobis, Laurence. 2001. *Die Katze. Geschichte und Legenden.* Leipzig: Gustav Kiepenheuer Verlag GmbH.

Boersma, Paul, and Wennink, David. 2021. *Praat: Doing phonetics by computer.* Version6.1.51. www.praat.org. www.fon.hum.uva.nl/praat/.

Bradshaw, John. 2014. *Cat Sense: The Feline Enigma Revealed.* London: Penguin Books.

Braunegger, Jessica. 2016. *Expurrliarmus – Cats and their role in contemporary British pop culture.* https://britcats.wordpress.com.

Brezina, Vaclav. 2018. *Statistics in Corpus Linguistics: A Practical Guide.* Cambridge; New York, NY: Cambridge University Press.

British Library. 2021. *BBC voices.* https://sounds.bl.uk/Accents-and-dialects/BBC-Voices.

Brown, Keith, and Miller, Jim. 2013. *The Cambridge Dictionary of Linguistics.* Cambridge: Cambridge University Press.

Brubaker, Jed R. 2008. Wants moar: Visual media's use of text in LOLcats and silent film. *Gnovis Journal,* **8**(2), 117–124.

Brügger, Niels. 2016. Digital humanities in the 21st century: Digital material as a driving force. *Digital Humanities Quarterly,* **10**(2). www.digitalhumanities.org/dhq/vol/10/3/000256/000256.html.

Bucholtz, Mary, and Hall, Kira. 2004. Language and identity. In Allesandro Duranti (ed), *A Companion to Linguistic Anthropology.* Oxford: Blackwell Publishing, pp. 369–394.

Bucholtz, Mary, and Hall, Kira. 2005. Identity and interaction: A sociocultural linguistic approach. *Discourse Studies,* **7**(4–5), 585–614.

Burgess, Jean, Mitchell, Peta, and Münch, Felix Victor. 2019. Social media rituals: The uses of celebrity death in digital culture. In Zizi Papacharissi (ed), *A Networked Self and Birth, Life, Death.* New York: Routledge, pp. 224–239.

'cat'. 2021. *Urban Dictionary.* www.urbandictionary.com/define.php?term= Cats.

'cat' n. 2021. *OED Online.* Oxford University Press. www.oed.com/view/ Entry/28649?rskey=qPueHU&result=2&isAdvanced=false#eid.

Cats Protection. 2020. *About CP/Who are cats protection?* www.cats.org.uk/ about-cp.

#CatsOfInstagram. 2021. *Hashtag on Instagram.* www.instagram.com/ explore/tags/catsofinstagram/?hl=en.

@_chrysalism_. 2019. *The Comprehensive Unabridged Meowrihamb Blepster's Dictionary of Hambspeak (2019 Edition).* www.docdroid.net/ 1NS6UVD/the-comprehensive-unabridged-meowrihamb-blepster-s-dictionary-of-hambspeak-2019-edition-pdf.

Crystal, David. 2008. *A Dictionary of Linguistics and Phonetics.* 6th ed. Malden; Oxford; Victoria: Blackwell Publishing.

Crystal, David. 2010. *The Cambridge Encyclopedia of Language.* 3rd ed. Cambridge: Cambride University Press.

Crystal, David. 2018. *The Cambridge Encyclopedia of the English Language.* 3rd ed. Cambridge; New York, NY; Port Melbourne; New Delhi; Singapore: Cambridge University Press.

Curious Zelda and Taghioff, Matt. 2019. *The Adventures of Curious Zelda.* London: Sphere.

Dailey-O'Cain, Jennifer. 2017. *Trans-National English in Social Media Communities.* London: Palgrave Macmillan.

DARIAH ELDAH. 2020. *Welcome to the DARIAH ELDAH Consent Form Wizard (CFW)!/CFW.* Digital Research Infrastructure for the Arts and Humanities DARIAH-EU. Ethics and Legality in Digital Arts and Humanities. https://consent.dariah.eu/.

Darvin, Ron. 2016. Language and identity in the digital age. In Sian Preece (ed), *The Routledge Handbook of Language and Identity.* New York: Routledge, pp. 523–540.

Dash, Anil. 2007. *Cats can has grammar.* https://anildash.com/2007/04/23/ cats_can_has_gr/.

Davies, Mark. 2013. *Corpus of global web-based English: 1.9 billion words from speakers in 20 countries (GloWbE).* www.english-corpora.org/glowbe/.

Davies, Mark. 2018. *The 14 billion word iWeb corpus.* www.english-corpora .org/iWeb/.

Deportes 13/AFP. 2018. *Bayern elige al gato como su figura en triunfo sobre Besiktas* www.t13.cl/noticia/deportes13/futbol-internacional/bayern-elige-al-gato-invadio-cancha-como-su-figura-triunfo-besiktas.

Dingemanse, Mark, and Thompson, Bill. 2020. Playful iconicity: Structural markedness underlies the relation between funniness and iconicity. *Language and Cognition*, **12**(1), 203–224.

Dingemanse, Mark, Perlman, Marcus, and Perniss, Pamela. 2020. Construals of iconicity: Experimental approaches to form-meaning resemblances in language. *Language and Cognition*, **12**(1), 1–14.

Drummond, Rob, and Schleef, Erik. 2016. Identity in variationist sociolinguistics. In Sian Preece (ed), *The Routledge Handbook of Language and Identity.* London, New York: Routledge, pp. 50–65.

@EdibleCatsClub. 2020. *Profile.* https://twitter.com/EdibleCatsClub

Eisenstein, Jacob. 2018. Identifying regional dialects in on-line social media. In Charles Boberg, John A. Nerbonne, and Dominic James Landon

Watt (eds), *The Handbook of Dialectology*. London, New York: Wiley-Blackwell, pp. 368–383.

Emojipedia.org. 2020a. *Emoji version 1.0*. https://emojipedia.org/emoji-1.0/.

Emojipedia.org. 2020b. 🐈 *Cat emoji*. https://emojipedia.org/cat/.

Emojipedia.org. 2020c. 😺 *Cat face emoji*. https://emojipedia.org/cat-face/.

Engelthaler, Tomas. 2017. *Dataset – Humor norms*. Github. https://github.com/tomasengelthaler/HumorNorms.

Engelthaler, Tomas, and Hills, Thomas T. 2018. Humor norms for 4,997 English words. *Behavior Research Methods*, **50**(3), 1116–1124.

Eppink, Jason. 2015. *How cats took over the Internet. An exhibition at Museum of the Moving Image, on view August 7, 2015-February 21, 2016*. Museum of the Moving Image, New York.

Eurostat. 2018. *Language Day 2018 – Eurostat*. https://ec.europa.eu/eurostat/en/web/products-eurostat-news/-/edn-20200925-1.

Facebook. 2021. *Facebook Help Center*. www.facebook.com/help/?helpref=hc_global_nav.

FC Bayern US. 2018. *Who is your player of the match vs. @BesiktasEnglish? #BJKFCB*. https://twitter.com/FCBayernUS/status/973998766914236416.

Fiorentini, Ilaria. 2013. 'ZOMG! Dis iz a new language': The case of Lolspeak. *Newcastle Working Papers in Linguistics*, **19**(1), 90–108.

Foucart-Walter, Elisabeth, and Rosenberg, Pierre. 1988. *The Painted Cat: The Cat in Western Painting from the Fifteenth to the Twentieth Century*. New York: Rizzoli.

freemurrli. 2017. *The meow factor. Cats in digital spaces/research blog*. https://meowfactor.hypotheses.org/about-2.

Gall Myrick, Jessica. 2015. Emotion regulation, procrastination, and watching cat videos online: Who watches Internet cats, why, and to what effect? *Computers in Human Behavior*, **52**, 168–176.

Galtung, Johan, and Ruge, Mari Holmboe. 1965. The structure of foreign news: The presentation of the Congo, Cuba and Cyprus crises in four Norwegian newspapers. *Journal of Peace Research*, **2**(1), 64–90.

Gawne, Lauren, and Vaughan, Jill. 2012. I can haz language play: The construction of language and identity in LOLspeak. In Maïa Ponsonnet, Loan Dao, and Margit Bowler (eds), *Proceedings of the 42nd Australian Linguistic Society Conference 2011*. Canberra: Australian Linguistic Society, pp. 97–122. http://hdl.handle.net/1885/9404.

Gee, James Paul. 2005. Semiotic social spaces and affinity spaces: From the age of mythology to today's schools. In David Barton and Karin Tusting (eds), *Beyond Communities of Practice: Language, Power and Social Context*. Cambridge: Cambridge University Press, pp. 214–232.

Georgakopoulou, Alex. 2021. Small stories as curated formats on social media: The intersection of affordances, values & practices. *System*. DOI: 10.1016/j.system.2021.102620

Gephi.org. 2017. *Gephi – The open graph viz platform*. https://gephi.org/.

GitHub. 2021. *GitHub: Where the world builds software.* https://github.com/.

Google. 2020. *Manage super chat & super stickers.* https://support
.google.com/youtube/answer/7288782

Google. 2021. *Review and reply to comments – YouTube Help.* https://support
.google.com/youtube/answer/9482367?hl=en&ref_topic=9257890#
zippy=%2Care-viewers-told-when-i-heart-like-dislike-pin-or-reply-to-
their-comment%2Cwhat-happens-when-i-mark-a-comment-as-spam%2
Chow-do-i-unpin-a-comment.

Grieve, Jack. 2013. A statistical comparison of regional phonetic and lexical
variation in American English. *Literary and Linguistic Computing,*
28(1), 82–107.

Grieve, Jack, Nini, Andrea, and Guo, Diansheng. 2017. Analyzing lexical
emergence in Modern American English online. *English Language and
Linguistics,* **21**(1), 99–127.

Hammond, Michael. 2020. *Python for Linguists.* 1st ed. Cambridge, New
York: Cambridge University Press.

Hawksey, Martin. 2021. *TAGS.* https://tags.hawksey.info/.

Hazen, Kirk. 2014. A historical assessment of research questions in sociolinguistics. In Janet Holmes and Kirk Hazen (eds), *Research Methods
in Sociolinguistics. A Practical Guide.* Malden, MA; Chichester, West
Sussex: Wiley Blackwell, pp. 7–22.

Herring, Susan, and Dainas, Ashley. 2017. 'Nice picture comment!'
Graphicons in Facebook comment threads. *Proceedings of the 50th
Hawaii International Conference on System Sciences.* http://hdl.handle
.net/10125/41419, pp. 1–10.

Herring, Susan C. 2012. Linguistic creativity online: A cross-cultural study
of special internet language varieties. *Pragmatics Festival 20,* Aug.

Herring, Susan C. 2019. The coevolution of computer-mediated communication and computer-mediated discourse analysis. In Patricia Bou-Franch
and Pilar Garcés-Conejos Blitvich (eds), *Analyzing Digital Discourse.*
Cham: Springer International Publishing, pp. 25–67.

Hickey, Raymond. 2018. Dialectology, philology, and historical linguistics.
In Charles Boberg, John A. Nerbonne, and Dominic James Landon
Watt (eds), *The Handbook of Dialectology.* Blackwell Handbooks in
Linguistics. Hoboken, NJ: Blackwell Publishing, pp. 23–38.

Holmes, Janet, and Wilson, Nick. 2017. *An Introduction to Sociolinguistics.*
5th ed. Learning about Language. London; New York, NY: Routledge.

Ilbury, Christian. 2020. 'Sassy queens': Stylistic orthographic variation in
Twitter and the enregisterment of AAVE. *Journal of Sociolinguistics*
24(2), 245–264. https://doi.org/10.1111/josl.12366

Instagram. 2021a. *Features.* https://about.instagram.com/features.

Instagram. 2021b. *Instagram Help Center.* www.facebook.com/help/insta-
gram/1986234648360433.

Institute for Systems Biology. 2017. *ISB Q&A: David Gibbs, research scientist.*
https://isbscience.org/news/2017/03/20/isb-qa-david-gibbs-research-
scientist/.

ISO. 2021. *ISO 639 – language codes.* www.iso.org/iso-639-language-codes .html.

Jünger, Jakob. 2021. *strohne/Facepager.* https://github.com/strohne/ Facepager

'kitteh'. 2007. *Urban Dictionary.* www.urbandictionary.com/define.php? term=kitteh.'

'kkkk'. 2006. *Urban Dictionary.* www.urbandictionary.com/define.php? term=kkkk.'

KnowYourMeme.com. 2007. *Cats.* https://knowyourmeme.com/memes/ subcultures/cats.

Koch-Kramer, André, and Graf, Alexander. 2021. *instaloader. v4.8.1.* https:// instaloader.github.io/.

Konrad, Artie, Herring, Susan C., and Choi, David. 2020. Sticker and emoji use in Facebook Messenger: Implications for graphicon change. *Journal of Computer-Mediated Communication,* **25**(3). DOI: https://doi.org/10.1093/jcmc/zmaa003.

Kooser, Amanda. 2019. *This cat is chonky: The fat-cat online shrine lifting humans from despair – CNET.* www.cnet.com/news/this-cat-is-chonky-the-fat-cat-online-shrine-lifting-humans-from-despair/.

Kufs, Charles. 2011. *Stats with Cats: The Domesticated Guide to Statistics, Models, Graphs, and Other Breeds of Data Analysis.* Tucson, AZ: Wheatmark.

Larry Number 10. 2020. *#CatNamesWorldCup.* https://twitter.com/Number 10cat/status/1241758649485271041.

Leaver, Tama, Highfield, Tim, and Abidin, Crystal. 2020. *Instagram. Visual Social Media Cultures.* Cambridge, UK; Medford, MA: Polity Press.

Leemann, Adrian, Kolly, Marie-José, and Britain, David. 2018. The English Dialects App: The creation of a crowdsourced dialect corpus. *Ampersand,* **5**, 1–17.

Lock, Helen. 2015. Paws for a moment and vote for your favourite academic cat. *The Guardian.* www.theguardian.com/higher-education-network/2015/dec/17/paws-for-a-moment-and-vote-for-your-favourite-academic-cat.

'LOLcat'. 2007. *Urban Dictionary.* www.urbandictionary.com/define.php? term=lolcat.

LOLCatBible. 2008. *How to speak LOLcat.* LOLCat Bible Translation Project. Web Archive. Library of Congress. www.loc.gov/item/lcwaN0010498/.

LOLCatBible. 2017. *Ceiling Cat Prayer.* LOLCat Bible Translation Project. https://web.archive.org/web/20170505035638/http://www.lolcatbible .com/index.php?title=Ceiling_Cat_Prayer.

'LOLspeak'. 2010. *Urban Dictionary.* www.urbandictionary.com/define.php? term=LolSpeak.

Mahler, Hanna. 2020. *'Mission impawssible?' An analysis of community-specific orthographic variation and lexical creativity online.* M.Phil. thesis, Albert-Ludwigs-Universität, Freiburg im Breisgau.

Markus, Manfred. 2019. *Innsbruck EDD online 3.0.* http://eddonline-proj.uibk.ac.at/edd/index.jsp.

McCarthy, Niall. 2017. *Infographic: Which countries have the most cat owners?* www.statista.com/chart/10267/which-countries-have-the-most-cat-owners/.

McCulloch, Gretchen. 2019. *Because Internet: Understanding the New Rules of Language.* New York, NY: Riverhead Books.

Miltner, Kate. 2012. *Srsly Phenomenal: An Investigation into the Appeal of LOLCats.* MSc dissertation, London School of Economics.

Miltner, Kate M. 2014. 'There's no place for lulz on LOLCats': The role of genre, gender, and group identity in the interpretation and enjoyment of an internet meme. *First Monday,* **19**(8).

Mundigl, Robert. 2015. *The implementation of word clouds with Excel.* www.clearlyandsimply.com/clearly_and_simply/2015/03/the-implementation-of-word-clouds-with-excel.html.

Nikolajeva, Maria. 2014. Devils, demons, familiars, friends: Toward a semiotics of literary cats. *Marvels & Tales,* **23**(2), 248–267.

O'Meara, Radha. 2014. Do cats know they rule YouTube? Surveillance and the pleasures of cat videos. *M/C Journal,* **17**(2).

Owen, Patrick J., and Lamon, Severine. 2021. *Are cats good? An important study.* DOI: 10.17605/OSF.IO/V48D7, https://osf.io/v48d7/

Page, Ruth. 2018. *Narratives Online. Shared Stories in Social Media.* New York: Cambridge University Press.

Parry, David. 1977. *The Survey of Anglo-Welsh Dialects. The South-East,* vol. 1. Swansea: David Parry, University College Swansea.

Penhallurick, Robert J. 2018. *Studying Dialect.* Perspectives on the English language. London: Palgrave Macmillan International.

PFMA. 2020. *Cat ownership in the UK 2010–2019.* www.statista.com/statistics/515339/cats-ownership-in-the-united-kingdom-uk/.

PFMA. 2021. *Historical pet population.* www.pfma.org.uk/historical-pet-population.

Podhovnik, Edith. 2008. *The phonology of Neath English: A socio-dialectological survey.* Ph.D. thesis, Swansea University, Swansea. http://ethos.bl.uk/OrderDetails.do?uin=uk.bl.ethos.587852.

Podhovnik, Edith. 2016. The meow factor – An investigation of cat content in today's media. In *Proceedings of Arts & Humanities Conferences.* International Institute of Social and Economic Sciences, pp. 127–139.

Podhovnik, Edith. 2018. The purrification of English: Meowlogisms in online communities. *English Today,* **34**(03), 2–16.

Provalis Research. 2017. *QDA Miner Lite – Free qualitative data analysis software.* https://provalisresearch.com/products/qualitative-data-analysis-software/freeware/.

Python Software Foundation. 2021. *Welcome to Python.org.* www.python.org/.

QGIS. 2021. *Welcome to the QGIS project!* https://qgis.org/en/site/.

R. 2021. *R: The R Project for Statistical Computing.* www.r-project.org/.

Reichheld, Frederick F. 2003. The one number you need to grow. *Harvard Business Review* 12. https://hbr.org/2003/12/the-one-number-you-need-to-grow

Sacquin, Michele. 2010. *The Well-Read Cat*. Paris: Bibliotheque nationale de France.

Schötz, Susanne. 2016. *Cat vocalisation types*. Meowsic. http://vr.humlab.lu.se/projects/meowsic/catvoc.html.

Schötz, Susanne. 2018. *The Secret Language of Cats*. London: HQ.

Schötz, Susanne. 2019. Paralinguistic information and biological codes in intra- and interspecific vocal communication: A pilot study of humans and domestic cats. In *Proceedings from FONETIK 2019 Stockholm, 10–12 June 2019 Paralinguistic*, pp. 67–72, https://zenodo.org/record/3246003#.Yx-CHLTP1GA

Schötz, Susanne. 2020. Phonetic variation in cat-human communication. In M. Ramiro Pastorinho and Ana Catarina A. Sousa (eds), *Pets as Sentinels, Forecasters and Promoters of Human Health*. Cham: Springer Nature Switzerland, pp. 319–347.

Schötz, Susanne, Eklund, Robert, and van de Wejer, Joost. 2016. Melody in human-cat communication (Meowsic): Origins, past, present and future. *Proceedings of FONETIK 2016, TMH-QPSR* **57**(1), 19–24. www.ida.liu.se/~robek28/pdf/Schotz_Eklund_VanDeWeijer_2016_Meowsic_Fonetik2016.pdf

Schötz, Susanne, van de Weijer, Joost, and Eklund, Robert. 2019. Phonetic methods in cat vocalisation studies: A report from the Meowsic project. *Paper presented at FONETIK 2019, 10–12 June 2019, Stockholm*. https://zenodo.org/record/3245999.

Seargeant, Philip. 2019. *The Emoji Revolution: How Technology Is Shaping the Future of Communication*. Cambridge; New York: Cambridge University Press.

Shafer, Leah. 2012. I can haz an internet aesthetic?!? LOLcats and the digital marketplace. In *Northeast Popular/American Culture Association Conference*, St John Fisher College, Rochester, NY, October 26–27.

Shafer, Leah. 2016. Cat videos and the superflat cinema of attractions. *Film Criticism*, **40**(2), https://doi.org/10.3998/fc.13761232.0040.208.

Shamayleh, Ghalia. 2019. *Engagement and monetization on Instagram pet influencer communities*. M.Phil. thesis, John Molson School Of Business. Concordia University, Montreal.

Shamayleh, Ghalia, and Arsel, Zeynep. 2020. Orchestrating pet influencers: Rhetorical and visual strategies in creating mediated platform content. In Jennifer Argo, Tina M. Lowrey, and Hope Jensen Schau (eds), *NA – Advances in Consumer Research*, vol. 48. Duluth, MN: Association for Consumer Research, pp. 874–879.

Simon's Cat. 2021. *About*. www.youtube.com/c/SimonsCat/about.

Spitzberg, Brian H. 2006. Preliminary development of a model and measure of computer-mediated communication (CMC) competence. *Journal of Computer-Mediated Communication* **11**(2), 629–666.

Statista. 2021a. *Facebook Statista dossier.* www.statista.com/study/9711/facebook-statista-dossier/.

Statista. 2021b. Instagram *Statista dossier.* www.statista.com/study/21392/instagram-statista-dossier/.

Statista. 2021c. *Twitter Statista dossier.* www.statista.com/study/9920/twitter-statista-dossier/.

Statista. 2021d. *YouTube Statista dossier.* www.statista.com/study/15475/youtube-statista-dossier/.

Thibault, Mattia, and Marino, Gabriele. 2018. Who run the world? Cats: Cat lovers, cat memes, and cat languages across the Web. *International Journal for the Semiotics of Law – Revue internationale de Sémiotique juridique*, **31**(3), 473–490.

Totet, Matthieu. 2020. *TwitterStreamingImporter.* https://gephi.org/plug-ins/#/plugin/twitter-streaming-importer.

Truan, Naomi. 2022. 'I am a real cat': French-speaking cats on Twitter as an enregistered variety and community of practice. *Internet Pragmatics*, https://doi.org/10.1075/ip.00083.tru

Turner, Dennis C. 1995. *Die Mensch-Katze-Beziehung: Ethologische und Psychologische Aspekte.* Jena, Stuttgart: Gustav Fischer.

Turner, Dennis C. 2000. The human–cat relationship. In Dennis C. Turner and Patrick Bateson (eds), *The Domestic Cat: The Biology of Its Behaviour.* Cambridge: Cambridge University Press, pp. 193–206.

Turner, Dennis C., and Bateson, Patrick. 2014. *Domestic Cat: The Biology of Its Behaviour.* 3rd ed. Cambridge: Cambridge University Press.

Tweetolectology. 2021. *Investigating the diffusion of morphosyntactic innovations using social media.* http://tweetolectology.com.

Twitter Inc. 2021a. *Help Center.* https://help.twitter.com/en.

Twitter Inc. 2021b. *Standard stream parameters.* Twitter Developer Platform. https://developer.twitter.com/en/docs/twitter-api/v1/tweets/filter-realtime/guides/basic-stream-parameters.

Unicode Consortium. 2007. *L2/UTC document search by number: Results.* www.unicode.org/cgi-bin/GetMatchingDocs.pl?L2/07-257.

Unicode Consortium. 2009. *Unicode proposals.* www.unicode.org/cgi-bin/GetMatchingDocs.pl?L2/09-026.

Unicode Consortium. 2019. *The most frequent emoji.* https://home.unicode.org/emoji/emoji-frequency/.

University of Leeds. 2014. *Impact case study. The BBC 'Voices' projects: Transforming the public and professional understanding of the nation's speech.* https://impact.ref.ac.uk/casestudies/CaseStudy.aspx?Id=6383.

Upton, Clive, Parry, David, and Widdowson, J. D. A. 1994. *Survey of English Dialects: The Dictionary and Grammar.* London; New York: Routledge.

Van Keymeulen, Jacques. 2018. The Dialect Dictionary. In Charles Boberg, John A. Nerbonne, and Dominic James Landon Watt (eds), *The Handbook of Dialectology.* Hoboken, NJ: John Wiley & Sons, Inc, pp. 39–56.

Van Mensel, Luk, Vandenbroucke, Mieke, and Blackwood, Robert. 2016. Linguistic landscapes. In Ofelia García, Nelson Flores, and Massimiliano Spotti (eds), *Oxford Handbook of Language and Society*. Oxford: Oxford University Press, pp. 423–449.

Wells, J. C. 1982. *Accents of English*, vol. 2. Cambridge: Cambridge University Press.

Westbury, Chris, and Hollis, Geoff. 2019. Wriggly, squiffy, lummox, and boobs: What makes some words funny? *Journal of Experimental Psychology: General*, **148**(1), 97–123.

White, E. J. 2020. *A Unified Theory of Cats on the Internet*. Stanford: Stanford University Press.

wikiHow. 2020. *How to make a cat using your keyboard*. www.wikihow.com/Make-a-Cat-Using-Your-Keyboard.

Winter, Bodo. 2016. *iconicity_senses*. Collaboration with Lynn Perry, Marcus Perlman and Gary Lupyan on sensory iconicity. https://github.com/bodowinter/iconicity_senses.

Winter, Bodo. 2019. *Statistics for Linguists: An Introduction Using R*. New York, NY: Routledge.

Winter, Bodo, Perlman, Marcus, Perry, Lynn K., and Lupyan, Gary. 2017. Which words are most iconic? Iconicity in English sensory words. *Interaction Studies*, **18**(3), 443–464.

Wright, Glen. 2015. Cats and academia: A short history. *Times Higher Education*. www.timeshighereducation.com/blog/short-history-cats-and-academia.

Wright, Glen. 2017. *Academia Obscura. The Hidden Silly Side of Higher Education*. Unbound.

Zuckerman, Ethan. 2008. *The cute cat theory talk at ETech*. https://ethanzuckerman.com/2008/03/08/the-cute-cat-theory-talk-at-etech/.

Zuckerman, Ethan. 2014. Cute Cats to the Rescue? Participatory media and political expression. In Danielle Allen and Jennifer Light (eds), *Youth, New Media and Political Participation*. MIT Libraries, Cambridge, MA: MIT Press, pp. 131–154.

Clawssary

.

* placeholder to indicate additional characters.

accent features of pronunciation that identify where a person is from, regionally or socially; a speech variety differing in its pronunciation from other varieties.

acoustic phonetics the study of the acoustic properties of sounds produced in speech; deals with the physical properties of speech sounds; is based on the principles of acoustics, the branch of physics devoted to the study of sound.

acronym a word that is made up of the initial letters of a phrase, e.g. #tot for #TongueOutTuesday.

affix a form attached to a word to make it more complex (e.g. 'de – panther – ise'), see also **prefix** and **suffix**.

API application programming interface; allows two applications to talk to each other.

articulatory phonetics the study of the way speech sounds are made – articulated – by the speech organs; the descriptive terminology is taken from anatomy and physiology and from observation and listening.

Atlas Force 2 an algorithm used for the layout in Gephi.

blending the fusion of two elements to form a new word (e.g. 'Caturday' from cat and Saturday).

cardinal vowel system an arbitrary set of fixed reference points to classify vowel sounds; are not the vowels of a particular language; the vowels of a particular language are plotted with reference to the cardinal vowels, usually represented in the vowel quadrilateral; the cardinal vowel system is based on a combination of articulatory and auditory judgements; the cardinal vowels are not real vowels but are invariable reference points.

channel the mediating technology transmitting multimodal communication, (e.g. mobile device, keyboard).

clipping forming a new word by shortening (e.g. *nip* from *catnip*).

CMC mode socio-technical constructs combining online messaging protocols with social and cultural practices, like email, messaging, or video conferences.

code a language or a variety of a language; different accents, different linguistic styles, different dialects, and even different languages that contrast with each other for social reasons.

code-mixing rapid switching from one language to another within a conversation.

code-switching use of more than one language during a conversation; switching between two languages or dialects in the same conversation, usually dependent on social or other contextual factors; switching can occur within a sentence (intra-sentential switching) or at a sentence or clause boundary (inter-sentential code switching).

community of practice a group participating in communication tasks together, sharing particular aims and assumptions about communication and often using specialised code; a group interacting regularly who have common attitudes and values and a shared repertoire.

compounding two separate words become one (e.g. *pawcircle* from *paw* and *circle*).

consonant one of the two general categories used for the classification of speech sounds – the other being vowels; formed by a closure or narrowing of the vocal tract so that the airflow is either completely blocked or restricted, thus producing audible friction; usually described in terms of place and manner of articulation.

conversion a word formation process in which the word changes its word class without attaching another affix (e.g. *cat – to cat*).

covert prestige favourable associations with the use of vernacular forms.

creole originally a pidgin language that over time has acquired a number of native speakers and has become a native language.

critical discourse analysis analysis of texts in relation to social and political structures and power.

data scraping gathering data from online sources.

degree one of the metrics the Gephi algorithms work with, based on the number of edges connected to a node.

dialect a regionally or socially distinctive variety of language.

dialectology the systematic study of dialects, originally the study of rural dialects and particularly their phonology, morphology, and lexicon, and also of their distribution; more recently, the study of urban dialects, including their syntax.

digital humanities interdisciplinary field of studies combining various disciplines of humanities with digital technologies.

discourse 1. in writing or speech, any coherent sequence of sentences with a structure, typically marked by various cohesive devices; 2. a style of language.

discourse analysis the analysis of discourse from any perspective – the connections between sentences, information structure, ideology and choice of grammar and vocabulary etc.; the study of patterns of linguistic organisation in discourse.

edge type of interaction, like tweet, re-tweet, post, etc.

ethology the study of human and animal behaviour.

F0 (f nought) the fundamental; is relevant for intonation as it displays a reasonably close resemblance to pitch movements.

faceted classification tool a classification that uses categories that can be combined as needed to describe a concept.

feature any typical or noticeable property of spoken or written language.

formant a concentration of acoustic energy in a particular frequency band; show up as thick dark bars on a sound spectograph.

fundamental frequency a term from physics; refers to the lowest frequency component in a complex frequency; in speech, it is the lowest frequency at with which the vocal cords vibrate.

Github a repository of codes used by developers and companies for open-source development; founded in 2008 and now owned by Microsoft.

glossary a wordlist (e.g. of a text) in alphabetical order with explanations of the words' meanings.

graphicon a blend of *graphical* and *icon*; an umbrella term for graphical devices found on social media, like emoji, emoticons, stickers, GIFs, images, and videos.

Hambspeak a cat-inspired language variety which is used, for instance, in the Facebook group *This Cat is Chonky*.

iconic sign a sign whose form has some connection with its meaning.

iconicity refers to signs whose physical form corresponds to characteristics of the situations; the property of natural language – semantic and pragmatic properties are paralleled in grammar and in sound.

ideophone a class of words in a language; a vivid representation of meaning in sound.

idiolect the linguistic habits of an individual speaker.

IMP interactive multimodal platforms; social media sites with two or more semiotic modes, usually text plus audio, video, and/or graphics to support human to human communication.

inter-sentential switching changing codes between sentences.

International Phonetic Alphabet a system of phonetic transcription with the aim of providing a transcription system for all known languages, devised by the International Phonetic Association in 1888 and modified since then; the most widely used system for transcribing the sounds of a language.

intra-sentential switching changing codes within sentences.

IPA International Phonetics Association; also International Phonetic Alphabet.

lexeme the smallest contrasting unit in a semantic system, also called a lexical item.

lexicography the art and science of dictionary-making.

lexicology the overall study of a language's vocabulary (including its history).

linguistic landscape the linguistic objects found in public spaces (e.g. signage, advertising, etc.).

LOLspeak is related to the images of LOLcats (funny cat memes) and is characterised by features such as baby voice and specific orthographic, grammatical, and lexical features; also called 'kitteh-speak'.

ludling a language game characterised by distinctive structure, especially in morphology and phonology.

matched-guise technique used in research on language attitudes; speakers adopt guises by convincingly switching language varieties and producing the same utterances in the various guises. Listeners are not aware that the stimuli are produced by the same speaker.

media coactivity interaction by using different modes on one and the same platform.

media studies study of the media, including mass media, from the angle of sociology, history, psychology, semiotics, and critical discourse analysis.

meowlogism a cat-related neologism; refers to a word formation that, in a cat-inspired word play, has been given a 'purrified' or 'catified', twist.

meowpheme a cat-related word used to make a word into a meowlogism.

metrolingualism how people in big cities manipulate their linguistic resources across languages and ethnicities.

mode a specific communication type; there are CMC modes and semiotic modes.

mode of discourse the medium in which a text is realised (e.g. speech or writing).

modularity one of the metrics the Gephi algorithms work with; used to identify the internal structures of a network.

monolingualism knowledge of only one language.

morph the smallest chunks into which spoken or written words can be divided; morphs can carry grammatical meaning.

morpheme abstract units of meanings; the meanings can be grammatical and lexical; the minimal unit of grammar.

morphology the branch of grammar that studies the structure or forms of words; the structure of words and of grammatical categories realised by morphs.

multilingualism knowledge of more than one language; the use of multiple languages by an individual speaker or by a community; is more common than monolingualism.

n number of survey respondents.

neologism a word newly introduced into a language, either by being borrowed or invented.

Net Promoter Score a marketing tool to measure customer experience, usually consisting of a single question along the lines of *How likely are you to recommend a business to a colleague?* For the rating, a scale from 0 to 10 is used, with 0 meaning *not at all likely*, 5 *neutral* and 10 *extremely likely*. Ratings of 9 and 10 indicate *promoters*, of 7 and 8 *passively satisfied*, and of 0 to 6 *detractors*.

network density the degree to which members of a person's network are in touch with each other.

network plexity the range of different types of interactions people are involved in with other people.

node social media account user.

onomatopoeia words imitating or echoing the sound produced by some process or creature.

overt prestige favourable associations with the features of the language variety used by influential members of society.

petfluencer animals with their own social media accounts.

phonestheme parts of a word associated with some meaning.

phonetics the science studying the characteristics of human sound-making, especially those sounds used in speech; consists of three branches – articulatory phonetics, acoustic phonetics, and instrumental phonetics.

phonology the study of the sound systems of languages.

phonotactics the specific sequences of sounds occurring in a language.

pidgin a language with no native speakers and a reduced range of structure and use; a trade language developed through contact between speakers who do not share a common language; serves as a lingua franca.

pidginisation language mixing, reduction, and simplification that eventually leads to a pidgin.

polylanguaging users employing any linguistic form that best expresses their aim without caring how well they know the languages.

Praat a computer programme to analyse, synthesise, and manipulate speech and create high-quality pictures; freeware available on https://www.fon.hum.uva.nl/praat/ for Mac, Windows, Linux, Chromebook, Raspberry Pi; developed by Paul Boersma and David Weenink, Phonetic Sciences, University of Amsterdam, the Netherlands.

prefix affix added to the beginning of a word (e.g. *mini*-in *minipanther*).

prestige the high status of language or dialect within a language community; usually the standard language has a higher prestige than a lower-class language; can be overt or covert.

prosody the linguistic use of pitch, loudness, tempo, and rhythm.

purrieties cat-inspired linguistic varieties.

Python a programming language that is open source and can be extended via third-party modules.

quantitative linguistics a branch of linguistics that studies the frequency and distribution of linguistic units using statistical techniques.

R a programming language and environment for statistics and graphics; used to handle data and provide tools for data analysis; is open source and can be extended via packages.

reduplication a word with repeated elements, e.g. *itty-bitty-kitty*.

sampling selecting data or respondents to be studied.

semantics the study of meaning in how lexical words and the relations hips between them are combined to make up the meaning of phrases and how phrases are combined to make up the meaning of clauses.

semiotic mode the medium in which meaning is created (e.g. textual, visual, audio).

semiotics the study of the properties of signs and signalling systems, especially as found in all forms of human communication; the theory of linguistic and non-linguistic signs, such as clothes, facial expression or buildings.

shared story content that is created by several people who produce and reproduce it across multiple posts, reposts, and comments; their contributions are connected to the other texts and assume a common ground with the other people involved in the story-telling.

sign a feature of language or behaviour that conveys meaning; a phenomenon correlated with some state of affairs and taken as a signal for some entity or situation; in linguistics, refers to a stable association of a linguistic form with a particular meaning (e.g. morph, word, phrase, or sentence).

small story a story, often with multiple story contributors and shared in posts and reposts, about short mundane everyday events.

social distance the degree of closeness of the relationship between participants in an interaction (i.e. how well they know each other).

social network the pattern of informal relationships that people are involved in on a regular basis; the web of relationships built up by an individual within a community; sometimes used to explain different linguistic behaviour by different social groups.

social variable social factor such as age, gender, ethnicity, or social background that may account for the use of one speech feature rather than another.

socio-economic status refers to a person's social and economic position in society, often measured by education, occupation, and income.

sociolect the social variety of a language; a social dialect.

sociolinguistic competence knowledge of not only the linguistic code, but also how to use it appropriately (e.g. what to say to whom and how to say it appropriately in different situations).

sociolinguistics the study of language in society; the way it is used and the effects it has on hearers and speakers.

sound symbolism individual sounds are thought to reflect meaning, sounds symbolising the properties of the world in literary context; refers to different types of iconic association between word forms and their referents; the strongest relationship is onomatopoeia, while a weaker form is phonaesthesia, in which parts of a word are associated with some meaning.

speech accommodation speakers modifying their speech towards that of their addressees.

speech community a regionally or socially definable human group, all of whose members share at least a single code/variety and a set of norms and rules for its appropriate use.

stories sharing photos and videos for 24 hours, can be used with text, music, stickers, and GIFs, used on Facebook and Instagram.

style variation in the formality of speech according to the social context, including features of the setting and addressee(s).

substrate and superstrate in language contact situations, a substrate language is an indigenous language and a superstrate language is the language of a more powerful incoming people.

substratum a language that has been displaced by another language but that has influenced the incoming language phonologically, grammatically, or lexically.

suffix affix added to the end of a word (e.g. *-ise* in *pantherise*).

syntax the analysis of words in phrases, phrases in clauses, clauses in sentences, and the grammatical relations between them; the study of word combinations (cf. morphology); the study of sentence structure (including word structure).

translanguaging multilingual users using their languages across all modilities, with code-switching, code-mixing, translation, and transliteration.

vernacular informal language.

vowel one of the two general categories used for the classification of speech sounds – the other being consonants; sounds produced by the airstream flowing smoothly over the upper surface of the tongue; usually described in terms of cardinal vowel system (vowel quadrilateral) and using acoustic or auditory criteria supplemented by details of lip position.

web crawler a code written in a computer language used to gather data from online sources.

Index

4chan, 4, 62, 88, 89, 111

academics with cats, 8, 59, 71, 99,
  120–122, 142, 152, 213, 239
accent, 32, 34, 36, 48, 188, 208
accommodation theory, 286
acronym, 88
affinity space, 6, 64, 114, 117–123
African American Vernacular English,
  196
algorithms, 5, 18, 82, 165, 166, 183, 237
anthropology, 107, 115, 116, 132
anthropomorphism, 91
API, 213
Arabic, 189
ASCII, 159, 160
attitude, 26, 36, 72, 161, 208
  towards purrieties, 282–289
audio, 109–113, 131, 138–144, 164, 165

BBC Voices, 112
big data, 45, 62, 253, 254, 270–272, 274,
  280
bilingualism, 81, 173, 175–184, 188
blogs, 110, 111, 200

cardinal vowel system, 49
cat emoji, 162, 167–171
catspeak purrieties, 7, 101, 185, 197, 209,
  238
chats, 109, 110, 112, 149, 165
CMC, 117, 138–140, 146, 211, 212, 215
  concept, 149, 150, 156
  modes, 141–144, 146, 148, 149, 165,
    166

CMD, 138–140, 144, 179, 187, 211
CMDA, 140, 149
  toolkit, 140–143, 149
co-tellership, 126, 128
code, 141, 143, 173, 174, 178, 180–182,
  254
  choices, 178, 179, 181, 193
code-mixing, 81, 82, 187
code-switching, 140, 173, 178, 182–188,
  196, 210, 285
coding, 201, 284
communicative functions, 163
community
  of culture and subcultures, 114, 115
  of practice, 6, 114, 117, 118
community practice, 114
computer-mediated communication, see
  CMC
computer-mediated discourse, see CMD
computer-mediated discourse analysis,
  see CMDA
consent form, 217
consonants, 34, 48–57, 69
content words, 225
context collapse, 192
creoles, 94
critical discourse analysis, 109, 126
Croatian, 174, 176
crosstab, 253, 255, 259, 261–263
Cute Cat Theory, 108
cuteness theory, 16

Danish, 174, 176
  endearments for cats, 40

data
  analysis, 200–201, 211–212, 224
  collection, 113, 199–201, 203–206,
      211–215, 217
  mining tool, 116
  protection, 113, 199
  sampling, 131, 132, 213, 254
  scraping, 205, 213
database, 92
dataset, 76, 212
dialect, 28, 31, 34–35, 43, 48, 178, 202,
    208
  dictionary, 37–40
  lexicography, 24, 37–38
  maps, 45–46, 113
  research, 113
dialectal differences, 46
dialectology, 24–26, 34–36, 45, 103, 113,
    176, 221–222, 225
dictionary, 34, 37–39, 42–43, 54
digital discourse, 196
digital humanities, 107–109
direct questioning approach, 283
discourse, 138–140, 145, 184
discourse analysis, 126, 131, 138, 140
distributed linearity, 126, 128
docing, 224
Doge, 94
Doggo, 94, 152
domains of language use, 178–182, 254
Dutch, 174, 176, 288
  endearments for cats, 40

EDD, 26, 31, 34, 38
EDD Online, 26
Emojipedia, 167
emoticons, 146, 147, 159–161
English Dialect App, 113
English Dialect Dictionary, *see* EDD
ethics, 113, 199, 217–219
ethnicity, 182, 187
ethology, 16, 17
etymology, 26
exploratory research, 95, 202

Facebook
  as locality, 221, 226–237
  as non-linguistic variable, 256–263
Facepager, scraping tool, 205, 206, 217
faceted classification tool, 141, 143, 149

Farsi, 174, 176
feline accent, 69
fieldwork, 38, 39, 113, 200, 248
fieldworker, 28, 29, 31, 33
Finnish, 190, 288
forums, 110, 213
French, 174, 176, 178, 183, 184, 186, 188,
    190
  endearments for cats, 40
  meowlogism, 71, 79
fun, 292
function words, 225
funniness, 61, 75–77

GDPR, 206, 216, 217
Gephi, 279
German, 7, 81, 125, 173, 174, 176, 178,
    181–184, 190, 193
  endearments for cats, 40
  meowlogism, 72, 288
GIF, 4, 5, 7, 19, 110, 142, 146–149, 164
Github, 206
glossary, 37, 38, 43
Google, 110, 111, 156, 157, 202
Google Translate, 189, 190
grammar, 3
grammatical features, 94
grammatical variation, 29, 48
graphicons, 146, 147, 159, 161, 180, 190
graphics, 110, 141, 142, 144, 146, 149,
    151, 159
Greek, 183

Hambspeak, 7, 43, 46, 47, 102, 103
headword, 27, 29, 37
humour, 72, 74–76, 90, 91, 104, 152,
    156–158, 160, 292

ICHC, I Can Haz Cheezburger, 88, 95,
    97, 100, 103, 104
iconicity, 61, 72–74, 76, 77
identity
  of cat, 89, 174, 185, 194–196, 202, 238,
      281, 285, 286, 288
  change of, 195, 196, 241, 281, 285, 287
  creation of, 173, 184, 194, 201, 202,
      216, 285
ideophones, 73, 76
idiolects, 35, 69, 103, 104

image macros, 88–91, 95, 101, 103, 104, 148, 157
indexical fields, 283
indexicality, 263
informed consent, 217, 219
Instagram
  as locality, 221, 226–237
  as non-linguistic variable, 256–263
Instaloader, Python module, 205, 206, 217
interactive multimodal platforms, 110, 138, 141, 143, 149, 164
International Phonetic Alphabet, *see* IPA
International Phonetics Association, 49
intertextuality, 126, 128, 129
intonation, 57
IPA, 26, 29, 36, 49
Italian, 178, 183, 190, 288
iWeb corpus, 42

Japanese, 73, 161, 170, 174, 183, 190

keyboard-and-screen technologies, 188, 190
keysmash, 190, 192
Korean, 174, 189, 190

language
  change, 78
  choice, 173, 178
  policies, 78
leet speak, 93, 97
legal issues, 113, 216
lexemes, 61, 63, 99
lexical concepts, 238
lexical features, 94
lexical sets, 33, 70
lexical variation, 29–35, 37, 43–44, 48, 104, 176, 221
light community, 118, 123, 124
linguistic ethnography, 200, 202
linguistic landscapes, 62, 78–83
linguistic repertoire, 178, 189, 193
LinkedIn, 157, 209
LiveJournal, 110
LOLcats, 3, 4, 86–97, 101, 103, 104, 114, 156
LOLspeak, 3, 7, 86, 89, 92–104
ludling, 93, 94

macros, *see* image macros
matched-guise technique, 283
meaning, 3
media coactivity, 164
media studies, 107, 108
mediated narrative analysis, 126
medium factors, 141, 149
meme icon, 90
memes, 4, 7, 19, 78, 86–87, 90–91, 101, 111, 142, 146, 148, 149, 151, 156–158
meowlogism frequency, 253, 255
  absolute, 255–257
  relative, 256, 257, 259
meowlogism occurrences, 226–230, 232–234
meowlogism probability, 260–263, 267–270
meowphemes, 63, 70, 104, 122, 211, 223, 234, 255
  in linguistic landscapes, 82–83
  in linguistic studies, 72–77
  as linguistic variables, 254–270
  regional distribution, 225–233
  spelling, 70
  use of, 65–66, 71
metadata, 206
metrolingualism, 187
microcelebrities, 132, 134, 165
Microsoft Excel, 206, 224–226, 257
Microsoft Office Forms, 207
Microsoft Teams, 142, 143
modes, 139, 141–146, 148–150, 165, 166
monolingualism, 175, 178
morphemes, 61, 63, 64, 99
  grammatical, 63
  lexical, 63
morphology, 43, 61, 63, 64, 77, 97, 99, 140
MUDs, multi-user dimensions, 109
multilingual cat accounts, 288
multilingualism, 7, 40, 78, 81, 82, 140, 173, 175, 176, 178, 183, 187, 192, 210, 288
multimodality, 126, 131, 139–141, 145, 146, 148, 152, 179, 211, 238
MySpace, 110

Net Promoter Score, 293
networked audiences, 192

networked multilingualism, 177, 184, 187, 188

observation, 200, 202, 212, 223, 282
OED, 26–28, 31, 34, 38, 156, 160, 161
online discourse, 173
onomatopoeia, 72, 73
orthography, 38, 48, 69, 95, 140, 188
Oxford English Dictionary, *see* OED

participatory culture, 87, 107, 111–113
patterns of usage, 184, 186
perception, 154, 173, 195
   of purrieties, 294, 298, 300
personal photos, *see* vernacular
      photography
phonemes, 72, 73
phonesthemes, 73
phonetic symbols, 49
phonetics
   acoustic, 49, 53
   articulatory, 24, 49
phonology, 33, 94, 95, 113
phonotactic patterns, 76
pidgins, 93, 94
Pinterest, 4
pitch, 55–57
pivot table, 226
play language, 93, 94
polylanguaging, 187
Portuguese
   meowlogism, 288
Praat, 53
practices, 209
   bilingual, 182, 184
   discourse, 201, 203, 216
   linguistic, 92–93, 182, 192, 201, 209–215
   social, 196
pragmatics, 54, 126
prestige
   covert, 289
   overt, 289
privacy protection, 113, 199, 201, 202, 216, 217, 219
pronunciation, 3
prosody, 77
psychology, 16, 74, 75, 109
pupper talk, 21, 94, 152

purrspective, feline perspective, 46, 83, 97, 221, 223, 238, 239, 285
Python, 205

QDA Miner Lite, 201, 206, 224, 225
QDA, qualitative data analysis, 206
QGIS, 30
qualitative methods, 95, 202, 210–212, 216, 224, 284
quantitative methods, 210–212, 216, 253
questionnaire, 207–209, 223

R, 122, 205
rec.pets.cats, 110
Reddit, 4, 21, 90, 151, 152
regional variation, 25, 36, 45, 46, 178, 223
research design, 199
research method, 199
Russian, 7, 174, 176, 178, 183, 193, 288
   endearments for cats, 40

sampling, 132, 199, 201–203, 209, 213, 214
SAWD, 31, 33–35, 40
screen data, 201, 202, 205, 207, 209, 212, 213, 215
SED, 25, 28–31, 34, 35, 37, 40, 113, 281
semantic change, 67
semantic variation, 221
semantics, 54, 76, 131
semiotic modes, 142, 144, 146
semiotic relationship, 89
semiotics, 86–88, 90, 99, 109, 126
SILV, special internet language variety, 93
situation factors, 141, 143, 149
Slack, 147
Slovenian, 40, 174, 176
Snapchat, 110
snek, 94
social identity cues, 216
social network analysis, 116, 241, 253
sociocultural linguistics, 194, 196
sociolect, 35
sociology, 91, 109, 115, 151
sound symbolism, 61, 72, 73
sound system, *see* phonology
Spanish, 174, 176
   meowlogism, 72, 288

spelling, 3, 43, 44, 221
spelling variation, 70
split text tool, 224, 225
Spotify, 131
statistics
  descriptive, 153, 255, 270
  inferential, 153, 270
  methods, 45, 101, 253, 255
  tests, 73
status, 12, 13, 37, 79, 81, 82, 85, 91, 92,
  121, 131–134, 159, 197, 215, 241
stickers, 119, 139, 142, 146, 147, 159,
  162–164
stories, 126, 129, 130, 132, 142, 164, 165
  shared, 126–128, 130, 131
  small, 126, 127, 131, 134, 264
structural markedness, 76, 78
style-shifting, 196, 285, 286
survey, 34, 36, 38, 40, 41, 43, 103, 199,
  208, 209, 215, 217
  dialect, 31–35
  online, 36, 155, 176, 207
  questionnaire, 29, 32, 33
  questions, 40
Survey of Anglo-Welsh Dialects, *see*
  SAWD
Survey of English Dialects, *see* SED
syntax, 86, 87, 95, 97, 99–101,
  140

text speak, 93
TikTok, 4, 110, 149, 206
Tinder, 157
translanguaging, 125, 187
transnational communication, 187
Tumblr, 4
Turkish, 174, 176
  endearments for cats, 40
turn-taking, 165, 166
Tweetolectology project, 30, 37, 113

Twitter
  as locality, 221, 226–237
  as non-linguistic variable, 256–263
  type of cat account, 7, 132–134, 202–270

Unicode, 162, 163, 167, 168
Urban Dictionary, 38, 86, 92
user-based data, 202, 207, 209, 212, 213,
  215, 224, 284
users' perspective, 282

variables
  linguistic, 253–270
  non-linguistic, 202, 215, 254–270
vernacular photography, 91–92, 101, 146,
  147, 151–154, 180
video, 4, 5, 7, 17, 18, 36, 110, 111, 128,
  146–150, 249–252
virtual community, 6, 114, 117, 118, 123,
  237, 240
vocabulary, 3, 37, 43, 94, 95, 102
vowels, 32–34, 49–50, 55–58, 69, 70, 113

Web 2.0, 108–110
web crawlers, 213
Welsh English, 31, 34
WhatsApp, 110
Wikihow, 160
Wikimedia Commons, 163
wikis, 110
word formation processes, 66–71, 78, 99
wordlist, 176, 199, 223–226
WordMapper, 45, 46
WordPress, 4

YouTube
  as locality, 221, 226–237
  as non-linguistic variable, 256–263

Zoom, 142